The Modern Home Guide
to the Signs and Symptoms
of Human Illness

The Modern Home Guide to the Signs and Symptoms of Human Illness

JAMES J. LALLY, M.D.

PARKER PUBLISHING COMPANY, INC.
West Nyack, N.Y.

LIBRARY OF CONGRESS
CATALOG CARD NUMBER: 73-107604

PRINTED IN THE UNITED STATES OF AMERICA

13-594937-8 B&P

To Mark and Martha
this book is warmly
dedicated

HOW THIS BOOK CAN HELP YOU

This book teaches the language of the body and how to understand it, from its small cries of pain to its anguishing distress in warnings of disaster. Here is a translation of the body's everyday signs and symptoms from a vague doubtful ignorance into meaningful, understandable English.

What are the worst diseases of mankind? They are ignorance of the body's cry for help and our false pride in being brave about the body's difficulties. Should a tight feeling of pressure in the chest be silently endured in ostrich fashion so that one may be brave and uncomplaining? The answer is "No!" If we would just look ahead three months to a sudden death, this mistakenly brave and uncomplaining individual will suddenly appear to be a sad victim of his real disease—his ignorance and his foolish ability to "take it." This book will show us how to intelligently examine and discover abnormalities in our body while they are still in their infancy. We can then bring these problems to our physician while the possibilities of cure are greatest.

The self-examination described so thoroughly in this book is directed to all parts of the body, just as all modern cancer organizations now direct self-examination of the breast at regular intervals. The normal state for each body section is described first, and then the possible abnormalities that might be found in this region are completely described in ordinary understandable English. This self-examination can be done at home using only common household articles such as mirrors and flashlights.

After finding something abnormal in the body, the next question is—what is it? The answer is immediately found in a thorough de-

5

scription of all abnormal findings which follows each section of examination. Each abnormality is definitely named and its importance accurately stated. Without any evasion, all the symptoms of the abnormality are listed along with a clear picture of the commonness or rarity of the disease. If a finding is serious, this book tells us; if it is not serious, it tells us that too. Probably most important of all, the book tells when to go to our physician and usually what to expect in the way of treatment.

A table of symptoms guide is an important feature of this book. It presents a list of symptoms pertaining to each body area and connects symptoms such as chest pain or abdominal pain with explanatory descriptions that everyone can understand.

"Does blood in my urine mean work as usual today or should I go to the doctor's office?" "What about this weight loss and that pain in my left side?" "Should I discontinue jogging just because of chest pain?" "Why can't I swallow solid foods anymore and what about that black bowel movement yesterday—what does that add up to?"

Often a person wants a quick answer to his question, "What's causing my heartburn?" Or "Why are my ankles swelling so much toward the end of the day?" The table of symptoms guides the reader directly to the answer in the book and then he may continue reading, if he wishes to find out more about that section of the body. With this fundamental study, a person can gain real understanding of his body's normal and abnormal function.

There is nothing more important to us than our health right now, today and tomorrow, and yet it is sadly true that today we know more about how a moon landing is made than how to examine or care for our own bodies. Sometimes we hear that we must not read about our bodies or be concerned with anything that might go wrong. Some will say this is a job for our physician and no one else. Without any question the doctor should always be the final judge of any significant disease. But today all modern doctors recommend that their patients examine their breasts regularly for possible disease. This is not to bypass the doctor but rather to help him discover possible serious disease as soon as it starts. In the same manner, the entire body should be regularly examined to insure normal good health and to avoid unnecessary disease suffering. As a routine procedure, this examination can best be done personally in the privacy of our home.

This guide will show you the routines the modern doctor uses when he examines a person and it allows you to see and understand how he diagnoses diseases from symptoms, signs and physical findings.

Until now a book such as this for the lay person was not available. It is exciting to read and easy to understand. It can make you a careful examiner and astute observer of your own body function so that you may work hand in hand with your physician to keep in shape and on the job the most important person in the world—yourself.

James J. Lally, M.D.

Acknowledgments

In the completion of this book I gratefully acknowledge the skillful and generous help of Catherine Horvatic, Rosemary Sawyer, Joseph McGee and the Old American Insurance Company.

I am especially indebted to my good friend, Richard Sutton, M.D., for allowing me to reproduce pictures of skin diseases from his book, *Handbook of Diseases of the Skin*—The C. V. Mosby Company, 1949.

I am also indebted to the *New York Times* and to the following companies allied with the medical field for granting me permission to reproduce their art work, drawings, illustrations and graphs:

Abbott Laboratories, North Chicago, Illinois
American Optical Co., Buffalo, New York
Bristol Laboratories, Syracuse, New York
Carter-Wallace, Inc., New York, New York
Eli Lilly & Co., Indianapolis, Indiana
Glenbrook Laboratories, New York, New York
Knoll Pharmaceutical Company, New York, New York
McNeil Laboratories, Inc., Fort Washington, Pennsylvania
Merck, Sharp & Dohme, West Point, Pennsylvania
Parke-Davis, Detroit, Michigan
Pfizer Laboratories, New York, New York
Roche Laboratories, Nutley, New Jersey
Sandoz Pharmaceuticals, Hanover, New Jersey
Schering Laboratories, Union, New Jersey
Sonotone Corporation, Elmsford, New York
Strasenburgh Laboratories, Rochester, New York
Tampax Incorporated, Palmer, Massachusetts
Wallace Pharmaceuticals, Cranbury, New Jersey
Warner-Chilcott Laboratories, Morris Plains, New Jersey
Wyeth Laboratories, Philadelphia, Pennsylvania

CONTENTS

INDEX OF SYMPTOMS

Sensations and conditions in our bodies indicating the presence of disease are called symptoms. We have many symptoms, but the most common one is pain, and it nearly always means some disease or underlying malfunction is present. Symptoms are variable from person to person; in two people with exactly the same backs, one person might complain bitterly of pain and discomfort, while the other person feels little or no back pain at all.

Symptoms are oftentimes confused with diseases. The true symptom is really only part of a disease, but if there are no other component parts to the discomfort, then the symptom becomes the disease. For example, a headache might be a symptom of high blood pressure or brain tumor; but often the headache occurs when no other disease is present—then the headache is a disease instead of just a symptom.

In studying diseases, we consider all kinds of symptoms. Their clear evaluation and understanding are often the best way we have to clearly focus in on a vague and poorly understood underlying disease.

It is simple to learn the meaning of one or more symptoms within the body. After locating the symptom under the body site in which it is noticed, simply turn to the listed page reference for the symptom's explanation and significance.

The Modern Home Guide
to the Signs and Symptoms
of Human Illness

Section

1

NORMAL AND RELATIVE STANDARDS FOR GOOD HEALTH

"You're sure looking good today!" Getting a compliment like this brightens the day and makes us answer, "I feel good."

How do we get greetings like these? The appearance of rugged health has to come, of course, from the visible skin itself, but in a supporting role are the basic functions of body temperature, pulse and respiration. If any of these functions are far out of line, the look of health turns into the look of disease.

Ranges of Normal Body Temperature

Our human body temperature is normal when the oral thermometer registers 98.6 degrees. There is a normal variation through the day, which can be due to the work being done, the time of eating, way of life, or even age itself. A hard-working man, digging a ditch, will run a higher temperature than someone resting in an air-conditioned room.

Temperature is lowest at about 6 A.M., when the thermometer reading is only about 97 degrees. Ordinarily it rises during the day to reach its maximum at about 5 P.M., before falling off again toward nightfall. This daily temperature rise is mainly due to food and muscular exercise, and is called the diurnal rhythm.

Taking the temperature is commonly done with an oral or a rectal thermometer. Rectal temperature, of course, normally runs one degree higher than oral temperature, and older people generally tend to run a little higher than younger people; therefore, a continued elevation of temperature up to one-half a degree, in a person over 60 years of age, would be very common and have very little significance.

Elevated Temperatures

Since an increase in body temperature is a body defense activity against some unwelcome cause, an oral temperature of 99 degrees or more should, if it continues, have an investigation into its possible source. The presence of a temperature-producing or "febrile" disease, such as a cold, a sore throat, or an infected ingrown toenail, may well explain the temperature elevation. But if no obvious reason can be found for a fever that lasts several days, a doctor should be consulted. It is possible that an elevated temperature of several degrees could represent a disease of great concern, even though no other disease symptoms are present.

An example of an unexplained daily fever could be the mild but continued temperature elevation caused by over-activity of the thyroid gland. Only a competent physician could recognize this disease. Any unexplained and continuous fever, therefore, is justification for a trip to the doctor's office.

Lowered Temperature

Whenever oral temperature is considerably below normal, there is also unmistakable and obvious disease present. It is found, for example, in lower-than-normal thyroid activity, adrenal disease, and oftentimes near the end of terminal wasting diseases.

In the absence of any significant disease, however, a slightly lowered temperature have very little importance.

The Pulse

When the heart contracts, it forces blood through the arteries, making them dilate or pulse. Even though all the arteries have the same pulse beat, we usually think it is easiest to feel in the radial artery of the wrist. This artery is near the surface, easily felt by compression, and is the time-honored spot for feeling the pulse.

Only the arteries carrying pumped blood from the heart have a pulse. The more visible veins which carry bood back to the heart usually have no measurable pulse at all.

The pulse tells us quite a bit about the heart itself. It is a mirror of the heart's beating action, and it tells us if the heart is regular, and forceful, or if it is weak and thready, as in shock or near death.

To some degree, the pulse also reflects blood pressure. It tells us something about the arteries themselves—whether they are still elastic and healthy, or if they have become hardened and pipe-like as in arteriosclerosis, commonly called hardening of the arteries.

The doctor always feels for the pulse in the arteries of certain areas when he wants to be sure of circulation, as in the arms, legs, feet, or other sections of the body.

Always the same as the heart beat, the pulse varies considerably with age, activity, sex and general health. In the newborn infant, there is a pulse rate up to 130 or 140 beats per minute, and it may become even faster in crying or during great activity. The average adult male has a normal pulse of 70 to 75 beats per minute while at rest. On the other hand, the female pulse normally beats up to six times more per minute than the male's.

Normal variation of the pulse rate is great, and heavy work or exicitement can bring about a tremendous increase boosting the pulse rate up to 200 or 250 beats per minute. This same pulse may be as low as 50 beats per minute when in deep sleep, or at rest. Of course, some people have a normally faster pulse of about 80; while others have a constitutionally lower pulse, sometimes in the 60's. These variations mean nothing at all.

A meaningful increase in pulse rate comes about during a rise in temperature. For every degree of fever over 98.6, there will be about 10 extra beats per minute. It is common to see a child of four or five years with an acute tonsilitis or severe cold with his pulse rate up to 120 beats per minute.

An extremely rapid heartbeat in anyone could mean significant disease, perhaps even heart disease. Whatever the cause of an unusual pulse, whether it is too fast, too slow, or irregular, it is best to have a good periodic physical check-up by the physician so that no potentially serious disease is overlooked.

Respiration

Even greater than any government administration, the atmosphere about us gives us human beings real cradle-to-the-grave security. Our mechanical connection with this atmosphere, called respiration, effects an exchange of oxygen and carbon dioxide between the living body and the outside air. This exchange, achieved by constant breathing, continually stands between us and the grave. When respiration is interrupted for any reason for a period of five minutes or more, we die of suffocation.

Although we think little about it, each breath we take is humidified, warmed and filtered as it enters the lungs. These important functions are performed mostly by the nose, but there is also an elaborately simple cleansing system inside our lungs for the removal of dust particles and other impurities.

Recent studies have shown how the pollution of the air we breathe with chemical fumes, exhaust gases and cigarette smoke can bring about serious diseases, such as cancer of the lung, disease of the arteries and eye diseases, to name only a few. As more and more people live on the earth, and need more and more air to breathe, it is entirely possible that we will all one day know the meaning of slow suffocation from a poisoned atmosphere.

All government programs dedicated to correction of our air pollution problems must be given high preference since the benefit generated here must be given equally to all. Figure 1 gives us an idea of what air pollution can be in some areas.

The River of Life

To understand breathing, we must understand that the blood stream, our river of life, constantly flows through the lung tissues in enormous quantities. It is here that the blood drinks deeply of the fresh air and oxygen which we have inhaled, and at the same time throws off waste gases such as carbon dioxide which we exhale. The whole purpose of respiration is for our red cells to drink in oxygen and to discard carbon dioxide. The amazing chemical in each red cell that actually carries the oxygen is a substance called hemoglobin, and it actually colors the blood red. Even in this atomic age, no one has been able to manufacture anything approaching hemoglobin.

When the red cells have taken their fill of oxygen from the lungs, they travel through the blood vessel system of the body bringing their eagerly sought parcel of oxygen to the body tissues. Then they pick up the waste gas, carbon dioxide, and return it to the lungs to be exhaled. This completes the respiration cycle.

How often do we breathe in sickness and in health? At rest, the average person breathes in and out about 16 to 24 times a minute. Exertion, excitement or work of any sort increases the breathing rate to bring into the body greater amounts of required oxygen. The fact that we breathe during our sleep tells us our breathing is regulated for us even when we are unconscious. We may voluntarily hold our breath for a time, but we can never suffocate in this way, because as unconsciousness arrives, the brain centers again promote

Figure 1: Once we breathed air; now we breathe smog. What will we breathe in the future?

the regular respiration which will bring back consciousness. This governing mechanism is located within the brain, and if damaged may greatly affect breathing. In many diseases, our respiration can be greatly affected. Some examples concern disease of the lungs, such as pneumonia or tuberculosis. Diseases attended by high fever also increase the respiratory efforts and rate. Because the body calls for more oxygen in these diseases, the remaining lung tissue must expand and contract faster to maintain adequate respiration. Like the heart, the lungs are capable of great effort when it becomes necessary for continuing life.

In the younger years of robust health, the ability of the lungs is much greater than in later years. Consider the enormous ability of the lung tissue for a young man to run a mile in four minutes. Consider also, the huffing and puffing effort of an overweight person of 60 years during the effort of climbing a single flight of stairs. It becomes obvious that the ability of the lungs to oxygenate the body depends to a great extent upon the size, shape and condition of the body to be oxygenated.

There is no pound anywhere on the body that does not lean upon the lungs for support and continuous life-giving oxygen.

Throughout life on this earth, the most important and least appreciated thing we will ever have is an abundance of clean, fresh air to breathe—and a healthy body to appreciate it.

Body Stature and Weight

Each person's body is the end result of its nutritional balance —the complete assessment of all its building-up processes and all its tearing-down processes, constantly operating within the body.

In early life, our nutritional balance is normally tipped heavily in favor of growth, through building-up processes. In middle life the balance remains fairly even, and in later life, the tearing-down processes tip our nutritional balance downward.

The high point in physical achievement as measured by physical ability, strength and endurance is thought to be about 23 years of age. It is from this zenith of physical prowess that athletes are measured. Thus, an athlete with promising ability at the age of 18 or 19 years is theoretically given another 4 or 5 years for further future improvement, whereas boxers and endurance runners are said to be old at the age of 28 or 30.

Outside the athletic world, youth, middle-age and old age are not decided so much by years, but rather by one's personality. Most of us usually think ourselves young no matter what our age, but a few of us are old all our lives.

Tables of average weight for "body build" and height show fairly well what a person should weigh as he goes through life. There are, however, visible variations all around us.

The extremes of nutrition are obesity at one end and emaciation on the other and almost always represent over-eating or some degree of starvation, but they are also associated frequently with disease processes that affect the full body nutrition.

Types of Body Stature

The body frame varies from a long narrow skeleton to a short, broad and stocky build. Generally, we recognize three classes of stature. They are the small or light frame, the medium frame, and the large or heavy frame, as illustrated in Figure 2.

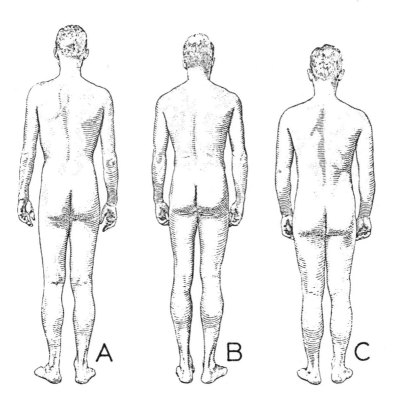

Figure 2: Body types: A) Slender (hyperontomorphic); B) Intermediate; C) Stocky (hypo-ontomorphic).

The small or light frame is the "string bean" type. He is most often the basketball player, the track star, and has the tall, gangly, "Abraham Lincoln" body build. Though some members of the light frame class wish to be heavier, they also enjoy the plelasures of greater height, speed, and longer life.

The medium frame claims somewhat over half of the population, and usually represents the ideal, all-around athlete. Boxing, swimming, baseball, tennis and all sports seem to attract people with an average or medium frame. Coordination, grace, speed and power are probably best coordinated in the medium frame.

The large or heavy-framed person accounts for about one-eighth of the general population of young adults. This type is easily recognized as the football player, the wrestler, the weight-lifter, all of whom engage in sports where power is essential, perhaps at the expense of speed. Although the large-framed person is often thought of as short and stocky, he often grows to above-average height, as we see in heavyweight boxers and professional athletes.

A person usually does not have much to say about what body type he will have. His inherited characteristics most often decide this for him. It is usual for tall parents to have tall children, or heavy parents to have heavy children, and light-framed parents to have children with the same body build. Generally, we acknowledge that the youth of today has grown 2 to 3 inches taller than his peers of two or three generations ago. The reason for this has been attributed to better diet, widespread use of vitamins, better access to sports, sunlight and similar wholesome activities. Perhaps, in a century or two, we may all be giants.

From the three classes of body structure, the life insurance companies compile statistics which formulate our "best weight" for height and age.

A few pounds away from "the normal weights" does not represent disease, but a large and glaring variation from the table may represent internal disease. Generally normal or desirable weights for men and women are scheduled in Figures 3 and 4.

Severe malnutrition, emaciation, or obesity without obvious cause is without any doubt sufficient reason for a trip to the doctor's office for an examination.

The mature adult is usually considerably heavier than the young adult. The reason for this is less active physical exercise in later years, while retaining the healthy appetite of youth. Modern medicine has often shown the inherent dangers in this mature weight

Desirable Weights for Men*

Height in inches (with shoes on)	Small frame	Medium frame	Large frame
62	116–125	124–133	131–142
63	119–128	127–136	133–144
64	122–132	130–140	137–149
65	126–136	134–144	141–153
66	129–139	137–147	145–157
67	133–143	141–151	149–162
68	136–147	145–156	153–166
69	140–151	149–160	157–170
70	144–155	153–164	161–175
71	148–159	157–168	165–180
72	152–164	161–173	169–185
73	157–169	166–178	174–190
74	163–175	171–184	179–196
75	168–180	176–189	184–202

Figure 3

Weight in pounds according to frame, as ordinarily dressed.

Desirable Weights for Women*

Height in inches (with shoes on)	Small frame	Medium frame	Large frame
59	104–111	110–118	117–127
60	105–113	112–120	119–129
61	107–115	114–122	121–131
62	110–118	117–125	124–135
63	113–121	120–128	127–138
64	116–125	124–132	131–142
65	119–128	127–135	133–145
66	123–132	130–140	138–150
67	126–136	134–144	142–154
68	129–139	137–147	145–158
69	133–143	141–151	149–162
70	136–147	145–155	152–166
71	139–150	148–158	155–169

Figure 4

Weight in pounds according to frame, as ordinarily dressed.

gain, and that longer life is nearly always associated with the leaner body.

Does personality associate with body stature? Formerly, this idea was held in high esteem. The popular thought of the day was that thin people formed the cruel and criminal classes, whereas fat people were thought to be jolly and generous.

As Shakespeare said for Caesar—

Caesar: Let me have men about me that are fat;
Sleek-headed men, and such as sleep o'nights:
Yon Cassius has a lean and hungry look;
He thinks too much: such men are dangerous.

Popular opinions come and go, but medicine's decree is firm: the thin man shall outlive his fat brother.

Our bodies are mostly water; less than 6 percent is actually mineral composition, and the chemical value of the body is less than $2.00—a degrading admission for the materialist of today. Figure 5 indicates the composition of our bodies generally.

BODY COMPOSITION	BODY WEIGHT
Water	63.5%
Protein	16.4%
Fat	15.3%
Mineral (Bone)	4.7%
Mineral (Non-bone)	.1%
TOTAL	100%

Figure 5: Basic table of our body composition.

The heavy-framed person is said to constitute about 16 percent of the young adult male population; the medium-statured accounts for a little more than half or 56 percent; the small-framed person makes up about 27 percent. Considerable variation with age is very common.

The Skin

Skin's Function as an Organ

The skin is the cover surface for the body and much more. It is a definite and complete physical organ with a great number of functions upon which the rest of the body depends. Without skin, the body cannot survive. We see this when skin loss over large body areas results from burns or other accidents, for when 50 percent or more of the skin is destroyed, survival itself is almost impossible. So loss of the skin's function as a cover is not nearly as important as loss of the skin's life-essential work for the body.

Most commonly known is the skin's function of cooling. By perspiring, the skin starts an evaporation process which in turn produces cooling, the same refrigerant principle of all our modern day cooling. Also, by blushing, the blood is allowed to course through the skin close to the colder outside air, producing a cooling effect upon the blood by simple contact with the colder environment.

The reverse function of preserving heat for the body is also the skin's function. When we are in contact with extremely cold surroundings, such as cold water or a winter climate, the skin will blanch. This cuts down the amount of bood circulating through the skin next to the cold air, and shuts off contact cooling of the blood. The blood at this time circulates mostly in the inner resources of the body, effectively preserving its heat. This same blanching process also shuts off perspiration, stops evaporation heat loss, and again preserves heat for the whole body.

Heat regulation in this manner is an automatic function carried on completely without our knowledge, and in such a reliable way that body temperature is maintained night and day, either at work or at rest, at nearly constant temperature.

Another skin function is to rid the body of poisonous waste substances. In perspiration, which is constant and at times noticeable, many body wastes are evaporated into the surrounding air. Undetected or insensible perspiration amounts to at least one quart of fluid per day in the average body. If this process is completely stopped, and body wastes are retained by the body, death will occur, as for example when the body is painted completely with substances such as gold or silver gilt which completely close off the skin's perspiration function.

Most people are convinced they perspire excessively, and this psychological thought makes fortunes for manufacturers of a host of "body odor" preparations. The attempt to banish all human odors or create better ones with oils and perfumes is the story of history itself—from Cleopatra and Mark Anthony down to our present concept of advancement on the job because we smell so much better, and are therefore less offensive.

It is well known that the skin absorbs various substances. This formerly was a very popular way of medicating humankind, and is still in wide usage today. Many drugs are absorbed into the body by the simple process of rubbing them well into the skin. These compounds are called unctions, emolients, or rubs, and they can exert considerable drug or chemical effect on the body. For example, the recently discovered drug known as DMSO, extracted from wood shavings, can penetrate the skin almost as rapidly as though injected by a needle. Furthermore, this drug can also carry rapidly through the skin many other drugs mixed in with it. For this reason, use of DMSO has been restricted by the government until its results upon the body become more fully known.

Another absorption function of the skin concerns sunlight. Sun rays penetrating the skin convert ergosterol within the skin into Vitamin D, so necessary for the body's metabolism of calcium.

The states of California and Florida have been quick to capitalize on this fact. Each states that one of the few hazards in their area is the possible development of too much Vitamin D production in an individual from the abundance of sunlight in these areas. This amusing statement has yet to be proven.

Sunlight and ultraviolet light, of course, bring about sun burning and tanning, but they also stimulate the growing of deeper layers of the skin. It becomes evident that the skin of a person who has been subjected even to a moderate amount of sunlight is thicker and has more pigment formation and a greater tone than does the skin constantly sheltered from the sunlight. The reverse is also true; the sheltered skin is thinner and has less tone as well as less pigment in it.

There also arises the lack of Vitamin D in a person constanly sheltered from the beneficial rays of the sun. Since the skin and the sunlight combine to produce Vitaimin D, which, of course, regulates calcium metabolism, it is possible that total lack of sunlight may mean a disturbance of calcium and phosphorus. Sunlight has demonstrated value in rickets and poor bone formation, and it also concerns itself with deposition of normal calcium in the bones and teeth and dental caries. For these reasons, an adequate supply of Vitamin D should be assured to growing children, as well as adults, and when oral vitamin administration fails or is not available, we can still use artificial or ultraviolet radiation. There is a difference of opinion concerning the usefulness of sunlight in may diseases. Proven helpful in some, it has been found to be overrated in others, but the general agreement among physicians is that sunlight has a marvelously beneficial effect upon the skin and the entire body as well.

As in other sections of the body, unfortunately, the skin is affected with many diseases. Some of these diseases, such as wens, are found nowhere else in the body, while other diseases of the skin such as cancer and infection are found in almost every other organ.

Many of these diseases are concerned with age itself. Baby's skin, of course, is most desirable of all with its firm tone, marvelous color, perfect elasticity and able function. However, after 50 or more years of continuous service, the constantly functioning skin has lost many of its natural oils and much of its elasticity. The well-oiled and firm skin of youth eventually becomes the characteristically dry and stretched skin of older age. With it comes lowered resistance and vitality, and diseases which were unknown to it in younger years.

We can do a lot to protect the skin and hold back the affects of age by simple skin care.

Routine cleansing is most important of all. Avoiding too much sunlight of burning degree, and protection against rugged elements such as ranch hands must endure, will cut old age skin problems at least in half. Nowhere else can we do so much so easily for our body than in skin care.

Skin Diseases

Acne

Acne is the number one skin disease. It starts when the skin glands become overfilled with sluggish and irritating sebaceous oils that solidify and become blackheads. Then the irritated and dilated gland becomes an easy prey for bacterial infections (Figure 6).

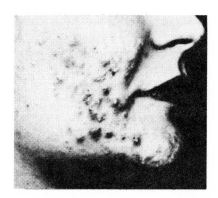

Figure 6: Typical acne in a 17-year-old girl.

The infection begins with a mild soreness which quickly becomes a painful, hardened and elevated sore. The pimple or boil forms a rapidly collecting concentration of pus in its center from bacteria, liquifaction of the skin, and the body's reaction to infection. When several boils join under the skin, they are called carbuncles and usually burst or drain spontaneously. Those which do not head may have to be incised surgically. In the worst stages of acne, extensive disfiguring scar formations result from the inflammatory reaction of the large boils and carbuncles which unfortunately are so common in this disease (Figure 7).

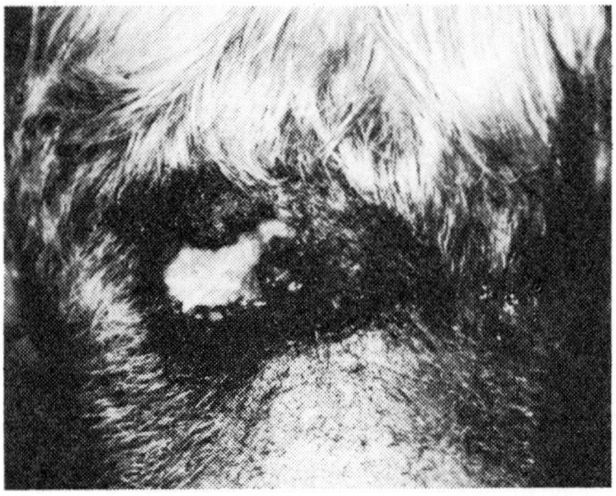

Figure 7: Carbuncle is a difficult and stubborn infection.

Acne is a most unwelcome and widespread disease which seems to be stimulated by the effect of youthful harmones on the young growing skin. It is a far greater annoyance to the male than the female, and is made much worse by ill-advised self-treatment. The face is usually more involved with acne than the rest of the body because other factors besides hormones are at fault in this skin disease. These factors include sunlight, foods and drugs, but probably most important of all is the dirt and grime that is scratched, rubbed, pinched and pressed into the constantly exposed face.

It is common in acne to see the boil and pimple problem about the face and neck directly invited by rubbing collars and the squeezing of blackheads.

The dirty hand is probably the worst enemy of the face in acne problems. Our hands come in contact with every kind of dirt and infected material, from door-knobs, toilet articles, and many other things we touch during the day, and — are covered with bacteria which are then transferred to the face. We often do this unconsciously in resting the chin on the hands, brushing off insects, wiping off perspiration, and, worst of all, squeezing the boils and blackheads.

Skin Care in Acne

Usually, there are several definite causes of acne present and working together, and a definite attack on each cause is necessary for the successful treatment of this skin disease.

Most important of all is external skin care, and many physicians recommend the following routine:

- Clean and wash the involved skin area at least three times a day with warm, soapy water. This is a bare necessity. Secondly, follow washing the face with hot moist towel applications. This will open pores, help melt and wash out blackheads, and stimulate skin circulation.
- Don't make it worse. After washing, rinsing and drying, keep hands off the face. The hands are covered with bacteria and other irritants from every conceivable source—including other people's hands. The acne problem would clear readily if the hands could be kept completely away from the face.
- Diet; don't eat bakery goods, chocolate, ice cream, nuts or cream. Try to avoid fried foods, fats (butter) and other oils.
- Sunlight in light doses will stimulate the skin, kill bacteria and promote healthy skin growth.

When blackheads persist and the boils and carbuncles of acne recur frequently and continuously in spite of true cleanliness and diet routines, underlying diseases such as diabetes, anemia, and thyroid imbalance become definite possibilities. The very difficult acne problem should always be investigated by the physician. He may institute antibiotics, vaccines, x-ray therapy or even surgical measures.

Allergy—Hives—Urticaria—Contact Dermatitis

The word allergy in skin disease is an overpowering word. Allergic skin disease, although sometimes quite simple, can be difficult to diagnose, stubborn to eradicate, and may present a very serious skin disease.

Most allergies are not inherited, but are acquired as we go through life. This means that the skin reacts in an allergic manner only to a substance which the body has previously contacted. The possibilities are enormous. The possible offending substances could be materials such as wool, cotton, or nylon; toilet articles such as toothpaste, powder, shaving creams, the metal in the razor; and, of course, food or inhalants of almost any possible character. Examples of well-known sensitivities are those to strawberries, chocolate, eggs and milk.

Hives or urticarial type reactions are very common in allergies. Hives are elevated, pea-sized nodules accompanied by intense itching that break out just a few minutes after eating, breathing or touching the substance to which the patient is allergic. The small hives may grow into giant hives or so-called urticaria. Here the skin presents an area possibly six or eight inches in diameter with a large, flat, reddened and itching surface as though made up of many small hives. Often the skin that develops hives or urticaria has an easily demonstrable characteristic about it called "skin writing" or dermographism. Writing on such a skin with a blunt object such as a match stick will raise a line or welt to produce the "writing." Figure 8 illustrates the lines or welts described.

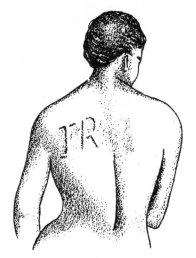

Figure 8

Allergies to strawberries, chocolate, wheat and eggs appear only after these foods have been eaten many times by the sensitized person. Allergic reactions, however, can also be the result of body infections and can even be mentally induced. It is not difficult to understand a mental state bringing about a skin reaction when we see someone blushing. These reactions are possibly best described as the skin attempting to speak for the mind. Hives and other unpleasantly related allergic skin reactions often demand intense study to identify the responsible allergic substance.

Contact dermatitis is a special allergy state of the skin which develops after repeated and prolonged touching of a substance to which the skin has become allergic. Examples of contact dermatitis are allergies to metal watch bands, rings or neckpieces, and to oils found in paints, cleaners and sprays.

Many factors in allergy remain unknown. Often onslaughts of hives thought due to an allergy can persist in come-and-go fashion despite all therapy for a year or more, and then disappear as suddenly as they arrived.

Eczema

Eczema is the name of a watery, weeping skin irritation which accounts for well over half of all skin disease. It is due to contact with an irritating substance outside the body, and is often found finally to be an allergic reaction. The skin is reddened, swollen and itchy, and has the appearance of minute blisters which drain weeping fluids from its wet surface.

Eczema is not an infection. It is a direct reaction to some substance with which the person has had frequent contact. It can appear on any skin area, but most often it is seen on exposed regions such as the hands, arms, face and neck. See Figure 9 for eczeme on fingers.

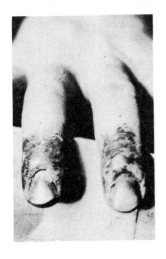

Figure 9: Eczema of the fingers and hand often follows repeated contact with allergies, oils, soaps, paints and chemicals.

The treatment of eczema means a search for the substance responsible for the skin reaction. This is very simple when exposure to poison ivy is known, or when a person works in acids which often affect the skin of fellow workers. It may also develop into a hunt of the most minute and detailed nature. Oils from various products, painted handrails, gloves, animals, foods and dozens of other possible offenders must be suspected. Sometimes it is proved to be a combination of offending substances, and at times the source of the eczema cannot be traced. It may even force the patient to change his environment completely in order to clear his skin difficulties.

The patch test is often used to determine possible offending substances in eczema. Liquids such as nail polish, lipstick or soap are painted on definite identified skin areas. Solid objects such as coins are held to the skin with adhesive tape. When a tested substance is guilty, a redness or eczema of the skin appears in a very short time. If no redness develops, the tester substance was not guilty, and the investigation proceeds elsewhere. Most of the common offending substances in eczema are known to the physician who can test 20 to 30 substances at one time. In this manner, it is possible to discover the cause of the eczema in the shortest possible time. When discovery of the sensitizing substance is elusive or impossible, drugs are available which will temporarily alleviate the symptoms and decrease the patient's discomfort.

It is well to remember that many eczemas are brought about by "curative" drugs and salves. The stopping of all such applications is, of course, imperative. Frequently the applications of emolient creams which have not been used before are of value in protecting the skin from outside contact or irritant.

Most eczema will respond, at least partially, to soaking in a tub of lukewarm water to which cornstarch has been added.

There is no substitute for the physician's routine search for the possible irritant when dealing with stubborn cases of eczema.

Blood Warts—Angioma—Senile Ectasia

About ten pecent of all people over 50 have small ruby-red growths on their skin, especially about the face and chest. These bright red spots can occur in younger years, and even in childhood, but they tend to become larger and more numerous in adult years.

These small blood warts are painless, and made up of tiny, thread-size red blood vessels, grouped in a small mound of the skin surface. If scratched open, they will bleed heavily, but they are not considered to have any cancerous nature. They can be left alone with safety unless in an area of continual irritation, or unless they interfere with cosmetic appearance. They are easily removed with simple excision or cautery by the physician accustomed to removing these benign skin conditions.

Canker Sores—Aphthous Stomatitis

Almost everybody has had a canker sore in the mouth, and knows from personal experience how painful they can be. They are small visible ulcers within the mouth, and they tend to occur on the inside of the lips or cheeks or about the tongue. They are very painful, especially when touched by food or salt. Occasionally they are so painful that a local anesthetic must be used if the patient is to eat at all.

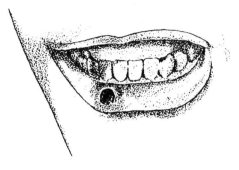

Figure 10: Canker sores of the lips are very sore and irritable.

Canker sores fortunately are not serious, and usually heal without leaving any scar. They are thought by some physicians to be related to the peptic ulcer of the stomach and duodenum.

There are many ways of treating canker sores, but the favorite and time-honored method of healing them is to drink acidophilus milk. This seems to allow healing of the canker sores, but unfortunately they tend to recur frequenty in some people without any provocation.

Eyelid Nodules—Xanthelasma

In senior years, it is very common for painless, yellow nodules to form just under the skin surface about the eyes and eyelids. The

Figure 11: Xanthelasma may signal a high fat content of the blood.

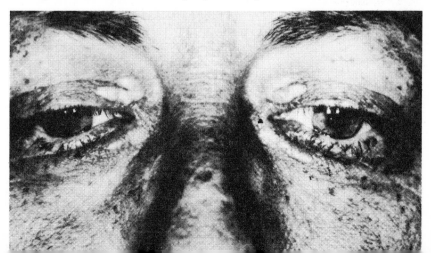

nodules are semi-hard, irregular developments, and are thought to be associated with cholesterol levels within the blood stream. They are not serious themselves, but they occur in mature years of life, and can be a sign of high fat content in the blood. The sometimes signal possible arterial or heart disease. Their appearance should be a warning that all may not be well in the circulatory system, and that it is time for a thorough examination by the physician.

The eyelid nodules of xanthelasma are not painful, and they do not grow into anything malignant. They can easily be removed surgically to improve the cosmetic appearance about the eyes.

Farmer's Beard (Tinea Barbae)

This is a fungus infection of the beard region on the face and neck. It occurs most often in farmers or men who have been working with cattle or other infected animals. There is an associated systemic disease which carries with it a very high fever. Farmer's beard can be completely cured. Although the beard in many cases appears to be stubborn, serious, and even malignant, the difficulty heals with antibiotic treatment whether given by mouth or applied over the involved skin area.

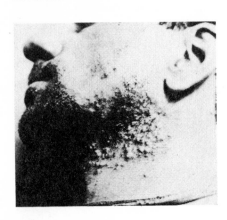

Figure 12: Farmer's beard comes from infected cattle.

Athlete's Foot (Tinea Pedus, Intertrigo, Sweat Rash)

Athlete's foot is a most common infection of the toes and feet. It has earned its name because it is so often found in athletes who frequent showers and locker rooms with wet, unclean floors.

The usual appearance of the skin between the toes is reddened, weeping and itching. The skin may be macerated, and have open painful cracks between the toes. When it extends above the upper surface of the toes and along the feet, there is often a sandpapered appearance of the skin in which small watery blisters seem to appear along with a continual wettened and weeping skin surface. Athlete's foot is a fungus infection which needs heat, moisture, and dead surface skin in order to survive. With constant weeping, improper cleaning, and continual reinfection, athlete's foot can become very serious and discouragingly painful.

The same kind of irritation and fungus infection, when located in the groin region, is known as tinea cruris, jock-strap itch, or Dhobie itch, and sometimes it involves large skin areas.

Reddened, wet and itching skin found under large breasts and in the skin folds of obese abdomens is called intertrigo. The skin is usually macerated, foul-smelling, and frequently dotted with multiple boil-like eruptions.

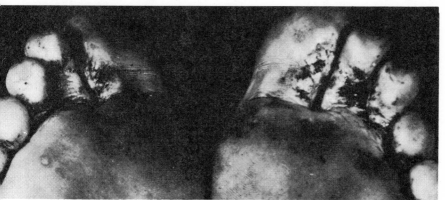

Figure 13: Athlete's foot bothers nearly everyone—not just athletes.

All of these skin conditions exist, not only because of the fungus infection present, but also because of the packed perspiration which macerates the skin and provides an ideal breeding ground for the fungi and any other bacteria which may invade secondarily to set up their own infections.

Simple prevention of these intertrigo-like skin difficulties consists primarily of cleanliness with ordinary soap and water, and exposure to air. It is only when cleanliness is avoided and the air is shut out from the enfolding skin that the fungi can live and the disagreeable skin infection can persist.

Yellow Jaundice

Jaundice is a progressive and rapid development of yellow discoloration in the skin and the whites of the eyes.

In drug-induced jaundice the yellow color of the skin has been duplicated by a drug such as Atabrine in patients being treated for malaria. With the known history of Atabrine medication, the cause of the jaundice is almost always known.

Jaundice in the absence of any drugs is always a significant medical finding, and is usually connected with an absence of brown color in the bowel movement. This is due to a backing up in the blood stream and into the skin of the brownish color which should be in the bowel movement. For this reason, jaundice usually spells out to the doctor a definite story. It may be an indication of hepatitis, a most serious liver disease; it may point to possible gallstone obstruction in the duct work leading from the liver to the intestinal tract; it may, unfortunately, herald the beginning of malignant disease somewhere in the gallbladder or pancreas region.

The diagnosis of the cause of jaundice is perhaps one of the most complicated medical challenges. It may come and go painlessly, and be entirely gone in the short duration of two weeks, or it may grow in intensity to the point where the patient is unrecognizable. At times, the jaundice story is easily understood by the physician, but at other times, it may baffle the most intense efforts of brilliant medical teamwork.

Many laboratory procedures have been devised to indicate the cause of a patient's jaundice, and therefore its meaning and its study may become most involved. Any patient who develops jaundice regardless of any associated pain, temperature or other findings should seek his physician's advice as soon as possible to ward off, if possible, any further serious injury to the body.

Keratosis, Senile

Soft, warty, raised and mole-like growths about the back, hands and face in adult years is known as senile keratosis or seborrheic warts. They are very common aften the age of 50, especially in fair-skinned people. They are soft and painless growth and have no connection with cancer, but they are apparently connected to excessive exposure to sunlight. They are sometimes removed for cosmetic purposes, or if they are in areas subject to considerable irritation. It is rare that any senile keratosis ever becomes malignant. About the worst that can be said for them is that on occasion they will occur in a person of younger years, even someone in the 20's or 30's. A diagnosis of anything senile at this stage is most disturbing to youthful pride.

Lichenplanus

Lichenplanus is an intensely itching skin disease of adult life, attacking both men and women. It usually presents irregular areas of reddish, violet-colored, frecklsized blemishes. Its most common site is on the inside of the arms and wrists and just above the ankles, but it can also be seen on the lips and tongue. The scratching which the disease invites only tends to spread the disease along the new scratched marks. Thus, these areas on the skin tend to grow together to form larger and larger areas, even though each involved freckle-sized area still tends to remain distinct. Then as the disease fades, each site assumes a deeper color much like the tan of a large freckle.

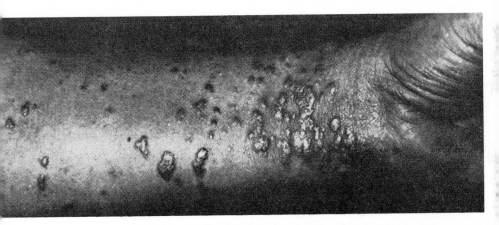

Figure 14: Lichenplanus is very itchy.

When it occurs in the mouth, lichenplanus has a milky appearance that makes it difficult to tell from leukoplakia which may be a pre-cancerous skin disease. A small piece of this inflammed mucous membrane must then be removed for microscopic study to distinguish and identify the disease which is present. On the tongue, lichenplanus has a red, spotted appearance which is characteristic.

The cause of lichenplanus is not known, but since its body distribution is likely to be the same on both sides it is thought to be an involvement of the nervous system. Care of lichenplanus may be very difficult and may go on for a year. Most cases, however, tend to clear in two to four months with only small freckle-like pigmentations remaining.

Lipoma

A lipoma is a soft, smooth growth of fat just under the skin. It looks like a soft bump, and is most often seen on the trunk, neck, arm and armpits. The size of a lipoma varies considerably from pea-sized to orange-sized, and may be single or considerable in number. They can be compressed easily between the fingers and have a feel of sponge rubber.

Lipomas are not cancerous, but because they engender fear of cancer, and because there is frequently some doubt of the true nature of the bump under the skin, they are frequently removed just to be sure. Most often, however, lipomas are recognized by the physician, and the usual reason for their removal is for cosmetic appearance.

Leukoplakia

Leukoplakia is a chronic skin disease of the mucous membrane of the mouth, lips, cheeks and tongue. It is also seen about the vagina in post-menopausal years.

When it involves the lips, cheeks, and tongue, leukoplakia has a whitened fogged appearance and looks as though the person has recently been drinking milk. Oral leukoplakia is usually associated with chronic irritation such as heavy use of alcohol or tobacco, or possibly problems of a dental nature. It is considered to be a pre-cancerous condition, and must be handled adequately by the

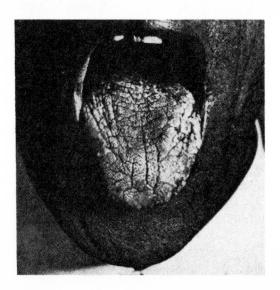

Figure 15: Leukoplakia of the tongue in a heavy smoker.

physician familiar with this disease. The treatment of oral leukoplakia consists of complete removal, usually by cautery, and sometimes by surgical excision.

Leukoplakia about the vagina has a distinctly whitened, dried and abnormally thickened skin appearance. The skin seems to shrink along with contraction of the vaginal entrance itself, and itching is very prominent in the surrounding skin. It invites constant scratching which only increases the soreness about the vagina. Leukoplakia of the genital region seems to be associated with a decrease of female hormones in the body after the menopause, and it will continue its irritating course until properly treated by the physician.

Leukoplakia about the vagina, as about the mouth, is considered a definitely pre-cancerous condition since it frequently turns into cancer itself. The treatment for leukoplakia about the vagina involves the use of female hormones, cortisone-derivative drugs, and other soothing ointments. The best treatment for leukoplakia in this region, however, is complete surgical excision to eradicate the possibility of cancer growth. This simple procedure promises complete cure.

Lupus Erythematosus

"L.E." is usually considered a skin disease involving the face. It

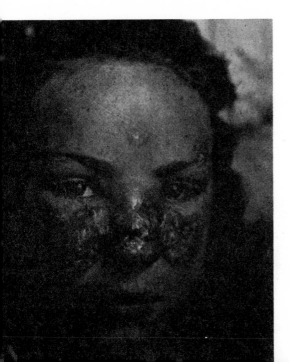

Figure 16: The typical "butterfly" appearance of Lupus Erythematosis in a young woman.

can, however, be a constitutional disease, seriously affecting internal organs, and may even bring about death.

In this skin disease, a bright red, irregularly rounded dry sore appears about the cheeks, and frequently spreads to join over the bridge of the nose. This is the formation of the widely known "butterfly formation." The areas of skin involved are those most exposed to sunlight. Although involvement of the face is characteristic of "L.E.," the difficulty is also found, on occasion, on the lips and the backs of the hands.

L.E. of the systemic disease type involves no skin disease necessarily. Here, typical blood findings, including discovery of the L.E. cells and tests indicative of possible liver disease, make the diagnosis for the physician.

The fundamental cause of L.E. is not known but certain factors are interlocked. For example, it is known that excessive exposure to sunlight frequently brings about the more recognizable picture of this disease in the skin. The care of L.E. requires the prevention of exposure of the skin to direct sunlight, and perhaps the use of skin creams which shield the sun's rays. It is also necessary to have professional treatment by the physician because the seriousness of this disease may, indeed, be grave.

Moles

There are many kinds of moles with great variety in color, shape and elevation from the skin. The ordinary mole begins in youth, but it can start in the middle or even in the later years of life. Usually light brown, and with a slight elevated appearance, the mole is considered harmless and at times even desirable. It was not long ago that a mole on the face was considered a beauty spot, and the mark of glamour demanded a mole in the proper position—even if it had to be painted on to acquire this "natural" beauty.

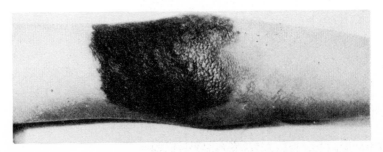

Figure 17: The large hairy mole can occur anywhere on the body.

Most moles, including moles with hairy growths, are not cancerous, but are often large, irregular and ugly. They are frequently removed for cosmetic purposes.

Some moles are considered dangerous; they are the blue or pitch-black moles with a smooth surface which can occur at any age. Because these moles sometimes develop into serious cancers, the physician's attention should be directed to them as soon as possible for their early removal. Again, the ordinary mole in spots of chronic irritation, such as the beltline or shaving area of the face, are also frequently removed, lest continued irritation stimulate a possible cancerous change in them.

Pityriasis Rosea

This adult skin disease is seen most often in spring and fall. We can expect to find it mainly in the trunk of the body, and it looks like a rounded, reddened irritation similar to ringworm. As the reddened, itching skin lesions appear, their rounded appearance develops characteristically into an oval appearance—elongated horizontally.

Each involved skin site tends to be dry, and covered with a fine tissue paper-like scale. There is no scarring from pityriasis rosea unless it comes from too vigorous scratching, and the disease usually goes away within a month.

Further care of pityriasis when itching becomes severe calls for treatment by the physician. He can recommend the use of soothing lotions and light treatment in this disease as they are necessary.

Psoriasis

Psoriasis is about the most common skin disease of mature and later years. It resembles a growth of dull red splotches about the size of a dime, covered with a thin, silvery white scale. Often several of these dime-sized sores will join together and form larger patchy areas which invariably itch furiously and invite constant scratching. If the silvery white scale is scratched loose, a tiny bleeding point will be found underneath.

Psoriasis most often starts on the elbows, knees or scalp, but any region of the body can be involved in both men and women. Figure 18 is an illustration of this disease appearing on front and/or back of body.

Although it is considered primarily a disease of adult years, it is thought by some authorities to have an inherited base.

The care of psoriasis is difficult since its cause is unknown. There

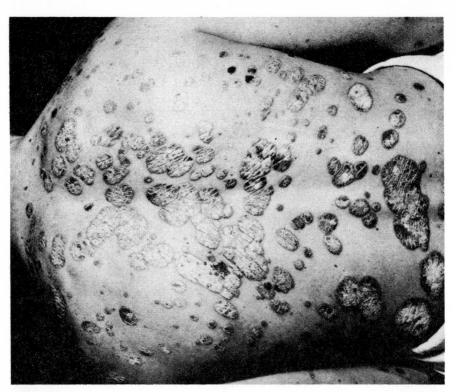

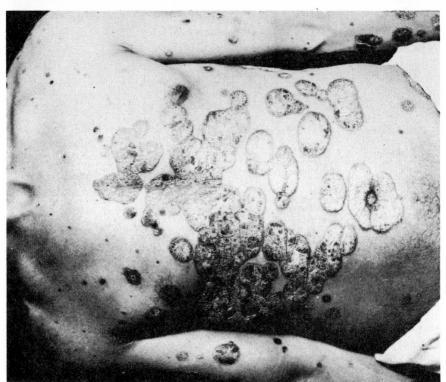

Figure 18: Psoriasis in its most characteristic appearance.

is also no satisfactory cure for psoriasis, but it is characterized by its ability to clear up suddenly without reason. This has led to many worthless ads frequently carried in newspapers claiming cure or care of psoriasis. The wisest course in this disease is to seek the expert care of a skin specialist whose experience has found certain lotions, salves and cleansing preparations to be very helpful. X-ray therapy, diet and internal drugs have also been used with good effect in psoriasis.

Seborrheic Dermatitis

This difficulty, in simple terms, means an over-supply of oils in the skin. It often involves the scalp, but also thrives in the folding body skin sites such as armpits and groins. Besides extensive greasiness of the skin, there is usually found a red crusting accompanied by an intense itching which invites scratching and infection, especially about the hairline.

Seborrheic dermatitis in the infant is called "cradle cap." The disease is, however, worse during adult life when sex hormones flow through the blood stream at the highest level, and hence the disease is often seen at the age of 30 years or later.

Seborrheic dermatitis of later life is difficult to clear up. It demands continual and scrupulous cleaning, frequent shampooing with tar soap, and a diet low in fat. A very popular and frequently advised routine in seborrheic dermatitis is the oatmeal bath. This time-honored care in seborrhea has met with success through the years.

If the seborrhea is stubborn, the physician is the only person who can be of help. He may use antibiotic treatment, endocrine therapy or occasionally x-ray treatment when it is called for.

Most seborrheic dermatitis in later life will respond readily to adequate care, but its recurrences, unfortunately, are commonplace.

Shingles, Fever Blisters, Herpes

Herpes or shingles are virus infections. There are two distinct kinds of these bothersome skin conditions.

The first type is the fever blister or cold sore. These start as small, rounded blistery sores, usually found about the face and near the lips. The blisters then break down into small ulcers which are very uncomfortable and will itch and burn painfully for about a week. One episode of these unwelcome fever blisters usually brings about an immunity, but there are a few people who are bothered with repeated recurrences. These people can be given repeated smallpox vaccinations at monthly intervals even though previous vaccinations were negative. This method seems to strengthen the body's resistence to virus infections.

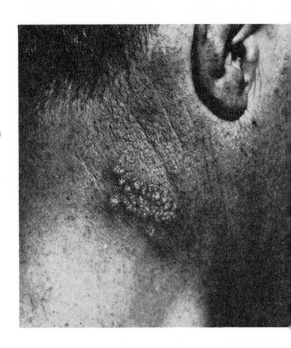

Figure 19: Shingles or fever blisters on the neck.

The second form of Herpes, often called Herpes Zoster or shingles, is a more difficult disease. Here, doctors think a nerve is infected by the virus, causing severe pain along the pathway of the nerve itself. Shingles begin as a burning, itching pain, quickly followed by a skin eruption of small watery blisters on an already reddened and swollen skin. Several waves of skin eruptions may follow, along with the constant itching pain. Shingles will vary a lot. The younger the patient, the less severe is the disease; whereas in the worst cases, the skin eruption can become gangrenous and leave permanent scars. Occasionally, permanent pain results. A typical bout of shingles occurs on the chest wall where the irritation and eruption follow the course of the nerve between the ribs. Such a characteristic eruption makes the diagnosis of shingles obvious. See Figures 19 and 20 for illustrations of forms of shingles.

When shingles involve face nerves, the ulceration and severe burning may involve any area of the face and tragically may even involve the eye itself. In these cases, of course, the ordinary measures for the care of Herpes must be reinforced by treatment of the eye physician, or there is danger of losing vision of the involved eye.

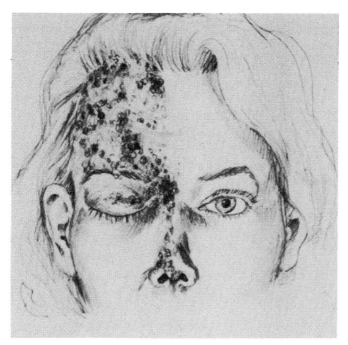

Figure 20: Shingles of the face.

In the care and treatment of severe shingles, as shown in Figure 21, the use of narcotics to relieve the pain is often necessary, since it can reach excruciating levels. Ordinary treatment of the skin in Herpes includes the application of smooth, soothing skin lotions, such as zinc oxide, analgesics and antibiotics.

Fortunately, shingles usually has its own time limit, and generally causes no severe after effects. It is only the most severe cases of shingles that leave any area of scarring or permanent painfulness. Most often, one attack of shingles mercifully vaccinates its victim against future attacks.

Vitiligo

Vitiligo is a skin condition where loss of normal color creates an irregular whitened patch almost anywhere on the body. The appearance is due simply to a lack of pigment in these areas. The vitiligo skin will sunburn readily, but it will not tan like normal surrounding skin.

The color difference between vitiligo and normal skin is very

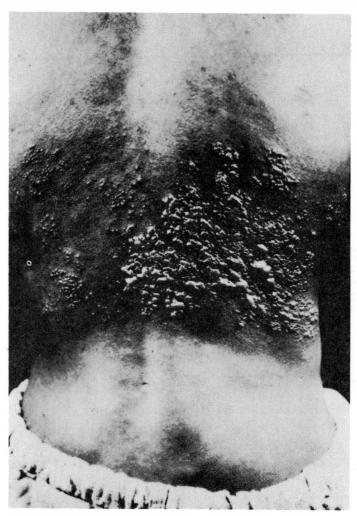

Figure 21: Severe Herpes Zoster has a very painful eruption.

hard to hide, and attempts to cover these patches with pigmented powder and creams is very unsatisfactory. Even tatooing with pigment resembling the normal skin color is not completely success-ful in masking the disease. The reason why the pigment is lost in vitiligo is still unknown, but even though a complete cure is im-possible, this skin condition has no great meaning aside from its very embarrassing cosmetic appearance.

Warts

Warts of variable size, color and location appear as small cauli-

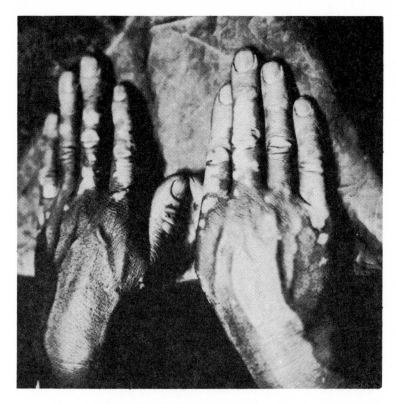

Figure 22: Vitiligo—cause is unknown.

flower-like pods on the skin surface. They are very common in childhood, but can persist even after the age of 50. Warts are thought to be non-cancerous, caused by viruses, and probably mildly cantagious. The folk lore background of warts often makes interesting stories.

Picking up toads, walking through cemeteries at night, and getting dandelion juice on the skin are probably not true causes of warts.

These nuisances can grow almost anywhere on the body, but they grow most often on the fingers, the face and occasionally the sole of the foot where they are named plantar warts. The plantar wart is very painful because it constantly presses against the sole of the foot, like a stone in the shoe.

There are many treatments of ordinary warts. They sometimes disappear by themselves but most often the physician is called to remove them by cautery, chemical or x-ray. The plantar wart demands more treatment than warts in other places. It is constantly irritated on the sole of the foot and develops a deep root with a wide callus formation. It must usually be removed surgically.

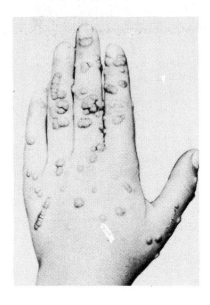

Figure 23: Hand and finger warts.

In the treatment of warts, hypnotism provides an interesting observation. It is well-known that warts often disappear after x-ray therapy. An x-ray machine which is not even turned on is placed over the warty growth with the patient looking on, and for some mysterious reason after this imagined treatment, the warts may disappear. This form of "hypnotism" in the treatment of warts is an example of a mysterious and poorly understood field of medicine. Many other explorations into the field of hypnotism have produced interesting results, and point to a possible new medical tool. Perhaps this may develop into an extensive branch of medicine for the future.

Wens

A wen is a blocked and much enlarged skin gland. The duct of the skin gland becomes blocked by a blackhead-like process, trapping the secretion and stretching the duct into a small balloon-like structure. It is felt under the skin as a smooth, painless enlargement, ranging in size from that of a pea to that of an acorn.

Wens are often found in the scalp, back or scrotum and are definitely not cancerous. However, they can get infected and burst into the surrounding skin to develop a rapidly growing boil-like process which is very painful. See Figure 24 for a scalp wen.

Care and treatment of wens means simple surgical removal. The balloon-like lining of the overstretched gland must be completely removed or it will tend to recur.

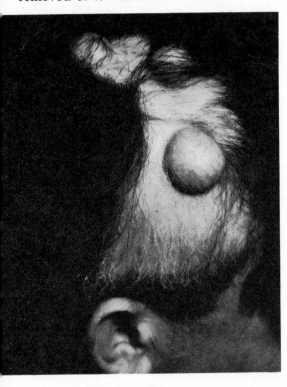

Figure 24: A wen or sebaceous cyst often found on the scalp is never a cancer and will not become one.

Skin Cancer

Cancer of the skin is very common after age 50. It has several forms; it is generally painless; it may grow fast or slow; but usually it never completely heals.

It often begins slowly as a small bead or pearl-looking mound on the skin, which slowly enlarges, then ulcerates at its center, and finally looks like a small moon-like crater. A scab or crust soon covers it and gives the appearance of healing, but sooner or later this crust comes off and exposes once again a raw surface underneath.

Skin cancer usually grows slowly and painlessly. Since it develops most often on the face, hands and other exposed skin surfaces, it is thought to be, at least partly, caused by sunlight. Many other substances, however, are also suspected. For example, cancer about the lips and inside the mouth always arouses suspicion about cigarettes, chewing tobacco, toothpicks, pipes, bad teeth and other suspicious items.

One important form of skin cancer deserves special mention. It is called the melanoma and it develops from the bluish-black mole. This rapidly spreading, fast growing cancer is about the most vicious of the entire cancer growth. Unless it is totally removed in its earliest stages, melanoma spreads widely throughout the body, and eventually causes death. This form of skin cancer fortunately is rare.

All forms of skin cancer have one identifying characteristic—they never completely heal. For this reason most physicians advise that any skin bleeding, discoloration or enlargement which does not heal promptly should be removed. This is especially true after the age of 50 when skin cancer becomes so common. Also, as a preventive measure pigmented moles in the regions of frequent irritations should be removed before they can cause trouble. These regions are the sole of the foot, the palm of the hand, the waistline and the shaving area of the face.

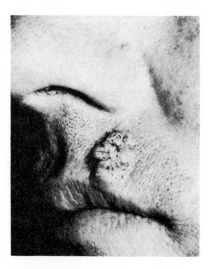

Figure 25: Skin cancer seems to grow on the face more than on other body areas — probably because of response to sunlight.

Fortunately, most skin cancers do not spread rapidly and are not difficult to cure in their early stage. They have one decided advantage over internal cancers—they can readily be seen and therefore treated at an early stage when complete removal and cure are easy.

Cancer of the skin, of course, like any other cancer, must be adequately treated by complete removal or destruction, for any remaining cancerous tissue will continue to grow and spread. It is the sad truth that many skin cancers, even up to the size of several inches or more, are treated for long periods with worthless salves and ointments in the hope that somehow the "sore" will heal. The only effective treatment of skin cancer is the accurate diagnosis and treatment of a skilled physician trained in the use of surgery, x-ray or chemicals necessary to do the complete job.

See Figure 25 for a skin cancer on face.

Section

2

THE HEAD AND NECK

Of all human functions, our act of thinking stands out like a light in the dark. No other function is above it; no other form of life can do it. This great human act of the "think tank" or brain goes on in the head behind strong bony protection, held as far above ground as possible.

As the seat of the soul, the head presents the face with its eyes, ears, nose and mouth. However, until sainthood arrives, even these miraculous faculties are subject to the definite ills of humankind.

Headaches

Headache, the silent crying of an over-burdened mind, is often traceable to a need for refreshment in some disagreeable part of our

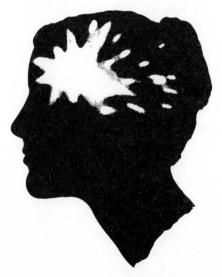

Figure 26: Headache and emotional up-heavals are closely connected. Headache is the most common of all human complaints, and psycho-mental problems occupy over half of all our U.S. hospital beds.

life, for only a few headaches have their origin in genuine physical disease. The popular escape from this malady is the aspirin tablet which is consumed in enormous amounts each year, reflecting the sad fact that over a third of us have headache difficulties.

It is amazing but true that the brain itself is incapable of any feeling, and that it cannot possibly ache, even though severely burned with a red hot iron. It is only the small blood vessels and covering of the brain that possess any sensation or ability to feel pain. The pulling, stretching and dilation of these vessels and brain coverings, in addition to a few painful nerve impulses from outside the brain, constitute all head pain.

Knowing that the brain itself is always painless, we can examine and consider most forms of headache more correctly.

Blood Vessel Headaches

The most common headache is a result of blood vessels in the head dilating and stretching. It is found in people with migraine, high blood pressure, diabetes and hardening of the arteries. The brain arteries involved produce the headache pains when stretched or dilated by reflexes starting in fear, anxiety or resentment. This is not difficult to understand, if we consider for a moment an example familiar to us all. It is the commonplace blush, a visible blood vessel dilitation, caused by reflex mental activity brought about by embarrassment.

Relief from blood vessel headaches usually requires a fresh approach to a disagreeable situation in our lives, or elimination of the situation altogether. This, of course, calls for intelligence in the solving or altering of frustrating problems in our lives. Examples of commonplace frustrations are thwarted ambitions, distaste for work, nagging mates and "keeping up with the Joneses."

Migraine Headache

Migraine is a type of blood vessel headache with several identifying marks to it. It throbs, it is usually on one side of the head and it recurs in similar circumstances—such as every Sunday, when caring for the senile or enduring unwanted company. Known as a sick headache, it is accompanied usually by nausea and vomiting; occasionally by blurring or wavering lines in the vision or difficulty in speech; and on rare occasions, by sensations of coldness or numbness in the upper extremities. Mirgraine is usually seen in intelligent, ambitious people and more often in women than in men. It is frequently seen after 50 years of age, but its beginning is many years earlier. About four out of five people with migraine will have parents, brothers or sisters with this same difficulty, showing its hereditary link. Effective drugs are now available for the prevention and treatment of migraine headache.

High Blood Pressure Headache

The headache of high blood pressure is thought to be due to blood vessel dilation and constriction. It is usually a dull ache in the back of the head in the early part of the day, and most often goes away by noontime.

Most persons with high blood pressure eventually complain of headaches, and sometimes headache is the first sign that the blood pressure is abnormal.

Diabetes Headache

Headache in diabetes is due to brain artery dilation when sugar content in the blood gets too low. This may happen in either of two ways. First, too much insulin has been given to the diabetic patient with resulting abnormal lowering of blood sugar, or secondly, not enough sugar type food has been eaten to balance the insulin already present. This headache, appearing in diabetic people, quickly disappears after eating sugary foods.

Arteriosclerosis (Hardening of the Arteries) Headache

Headaches which begin and keep recurring after 60 are most due to arteriosclerotic damage of the brain blood vessels. This headache is not predictable in location, duration or time of occurrence, but it frequently appears when the head and neck are turned or twisted in certain ways. This is because twisting of the neck also twists blood vessels to the brain which have already become narrowed by hardening of the arteries. A short rest, relief from excitement or removal of exceptional tension most often quickly allows relief from arteriosclerotic headaches.

Tension Headache

Tension headache comprises over one-third of all headaches. In this type of headache, pain does not even come from inside the head but is due to the steady contracture of muscles in the neck and scalp around and outside the skull.

Pain from these unrelaxed muscles, as in pain from blood vessels, has its beginning in mental activity, originating and coming from an unwelcome source. Fear, anxiety or tension brings about a continual contraction of head and scalp muscles, as occurs in the legs of a sprinter, waiting for the starting gun that never goes off. The continuing muscle contraction eventually brings about pain in the neck, over the head, and into the forehead region. Even the scalp itself may become sore to touch.

TENSION HEADACHE

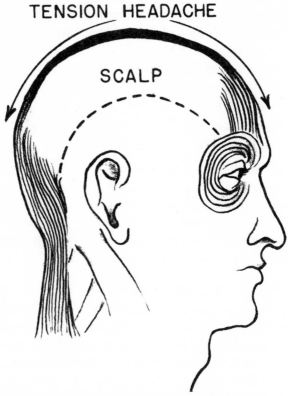

Figure 27: Tension headache is actually due to stretching tension in the scalp, of muscles in front of the head pulling against muscles in back of the head.

Tension headache differs from migraine headache in several ways. It is not severe, does not throb, and creates a soreness of the scalp, neck and forehead. It is not a sick headache, but may last for longer periods of time, perhaps even months. The typical description of a tension headache is "I feel a tight band around my head."

Eye Headache

Contrary to popular belief, improperly focusing eyes possibly in need of glasses for correct refraction do not often cause headaches. It is true that headaches may result from some eye disease, but the widespread belief that many recurring headaches are preventable with glasses in incorrect. In the absence of obvious eye disease, such as redness, soreness, infection or injury, only a few eye diseases such as glaucoma remain as a possible cause of headache. However, because of these rare possibilities, a person with persistent and unexplained headaches should always have the benefit of an eye examination to settle any doubt.

Glaucoma Headache

Glaucoma headache begins about the eyes and spreads into a general type of headache. It is very serious and can be very painful. Glaucoma eye pain is caused by an increase in pressure in the eyeball itself, and is serious not because of pain, but because blindness may follow unless the pressure is relieved. Glaucoma is rare under the age of 35, but it increases greatly after the age of 45. It seems to be an inherited disease and often is found in families where several members are afflicted. People who develop glaucoma also have easily excitable emotions—often a family trait.

As in so many other headaches, glaucoma and its head pain can follow a disagreeable mental experience, such as frustration, fear, or resentment. In this headache, the pain can be excruciating, and the eye itself feels hard to the touch. People who have glaucoma sometimes find out suddenly or by accident that vision in one eye is unexpectedly far below normal and their alarm brings them to the physician's office.

Chronic or long-standing glaucoma presents a similar picture but the pain is not so severe. A dull aching is present over the eye and leads to headache of variable degree.

Sinus Headache

Sinus inflammation is very often thought to be the cause of frequent, recurring headaches, but this is only rarely correct. Less than one headache out of 20 can be traced to sinus difficulty.

Sinus headaches usually begin with a fast developing infection in one or more sinuses, as might be expected following a severe sudden cold. The headache is usually accompanied by a clogged nose and a localized soreness over the sinus involved. The pain of sinus difficulty grows suddenly much worse when the surrounding air pressure is lessened or increased greatly. Thus, rapid ascent or descent in airplanes or tall building elevators may bring about excruciating pain.

Application of heat to the face and aspirin in large quantities have long been the relief of sinus sufferers, but correction of certain nose difficulties by a physician often ends the sinus difficulty permanently.

Headache from Brain Tumor

Headaches caused by brain tumors are extremely rare. More than one-half of all people who go to the doctor have headaches, but fortunately an extremely small number of these people have brain tumors. It is also true, however, that nearly all people with brain tumors, brain abscesses, cysts or brain blood clots will have headaches of definite degree.

The pain of an expanding growth within the skull is due to an increase of pressure which stretches and distorts blood vessels and the brain covering. As previously seen, these are the only structures within the head capable of feeling pain. Brain tumor headache has no distinguishing mark about it. It appears at no regular time of the day. It might be a constant throbbing or a steady ache, and it may have a come-and-go nature. Brain tumor victims often have accompanying changes in the personality, such as irritability and forgetfulness. They also have frequent periods of hallucinations and sudden vomiting. Often these symptoms help in making the diagnosis of the underlying cause, but headaches due to brain tumors are usually endured for a long time before their cause is even suspected. Although the human race does have brain tumors and they are accompainied by headaches of some degree, it is well to know that over half of all brain tumors are not cancerous, and that the surgical removal of these tumors is a commonplace miracle of modern surgery.

Dizziness

Dizziness or vertigo is everyone's difficulty. For some, it means a faint or unsteady feeling. To others, dizziness means a weakness or blurring of vision, but usually it means a sensation of rotating motion. This motion can be in a horizontal plane, in a vertical plane or in an oblique plane, and very often people will complain of nausea and vomiting when their dizziness becomes severe.

Meniere's syndrome is a disease of the balancing mechanism located deep within the ear. It often produces a buzzing, humming or roaring noise and a partial loss of hearing; it is our most common cause of dizziness. The visible part of the ear is only the outer shell designed to collect sound. Deeper within our inner ear is the organ of balance which tells us, even in the darkness, when we are going straight, turning, or perhaps falling. This mechanism looks something like a pretzel which has been hollowed out and filled with water. Like an ordinary glass of water, when the head is tilted the water stays horizontal to the earth's surface but rides higher on one side of the glass than the other (Figure 28). Because of the pressure difference on either side of the glass, a reflex signals us that we are not level. Without such a mechanism as this, it would be impossible for us to stand or walk.

Figure 28: The balancing mechanism in the head is similar to water in a glass. Changes in fluid level are determined within the brain as changes of position.

Circular motion of the fluid in its container also gives us a sensation of turning motion. However, when this fluid container becomes diseased, the sensation becomes widely exaggerated. Then the motion of partial turning to one side creates the sensation of turning completely around two or three times rapidly—the sensation of dizziness. Only when the fluid and the head itself are held almost motionless, can the sensation of dizziness be held down in Meniere's disease.

Sometimes Meniere's syndrome lasts only minutes, but it can last hours, weeks or days; it can be accompanied by a severe nausea and vomiting, and can force the sufferer to lie in bed completely motionless if he wishes to prevent a return of his dizziness and nausea.

Hardening of the arteries, or arteriosclerosis of the blood vessels in the brain causes about one-third of all dizziness. In this disease, blood intended for the brain and certain special nerves is decreased because the brain arteries have too much arteriosclerotic "rust" in them. When there is a temporary under-supply of blood to the brain, dizziness is noticed.

Physiologic dizziness can occur when we stand up suddenly after we've been sitting or lying down. This kind of dizziness is unknown in youth, but becomes more common with age. It is explained like this: When we lie down in a relaxed position, our blood pressure is at a relatively low level. Now, if we suddenly arise as if to answer the telephone, the blood in our bodies tends to run downhill like water in a pan. Unless our internal reflexes are as fast as they are in youth, this action may mean a slight reduction of blood for the brain, resulting in temporary dizziness. There is rarely any experience of nausea or vomiting with this condition, and it usually clears up as soon as the body's reflex mechanism has "caught up" to equalize the blood pressure throughout the body.

Most of us have experienced at least a few small episodes of dizziness. But after the age of 50, it suggests the possibility of diabetes, thyroid disease or diseases of the blood vessel system. If this problem recurs often, we should seek out our physician for his examination and diagnosis to see if any treatment is necessary.

Examination of the Scalp

Stand under a bright light before a close-up mirror and observe the hair and scalp closely.

1. Note that the hair is lightest where the scalp is thinnest, on the top, in the temple and just back of the highest part of the skull. The normal scalp has about 1,000 hairs per square inch. Baldness begins when vanity arrives—somewhere from 1,000 hairs per square inch down to no hairs at all.

2. Gently scratch the scalp between the hair shafts. A loosening of snowy skin scale from the scalp, plowed up by the fingernails, without any doubt means dandruff. If a crusty scale adherent to the scalp is raised, and it seems to leave a sore skin surface underneath, it may mean seborrheic dematitis.

3. Fix the palm of the hand on top of the scalp, and move it in all directions. It should move freely and be entirely painless. Any painful swelling of the scalp, especially toward the rear, may mean boils, carbuncles or wens.

4. Look for any inch-sized circles in the scalp where the hair shafts appear to be broken off, and the periphery of the circle has very tiny pimples cropping out. This is usually the appearance of ringworm.

Ringworm of the Scalp

Circular areas on the scalp with an appearance of broken off hair shafts, and with small rings of tiny pimples, usually speaks of ringworm. This difficulty is found in the scalp which is habitually unclean. Its name is misleading, since it has no connection with worms but is essentially a fungus disease. These diseased scalp areas glow in the dark under ultra-violet light; they will disappear with repeated cleansing and tar shampoos and, happily, will disappear completely and permanently with the onset of adolescence.

Common Baldness

More than 96 percent of all baldness is found in men. Hardly a disease, baldness nourishes a million-dollar-a-year business for checking, preventing or curing this malady.

Two interesting facts about baldness are known: 1. A strong inherited tendency influences hair growth, and most men can predict their hair life from their father's and grandfather's hair. 2. Male sex hormones are important in baldness because they stimulate scalp oil secretion, usually associated with loss of hair. We see also that the time of greatest hair loss occurs when the male sex hormones flow in the blood stream at the highest level, and if castration should occur before maturity, baldness would be rare. A bald man, therefore, can be comforted with the thought that the loss of his hair is proof of his virility.

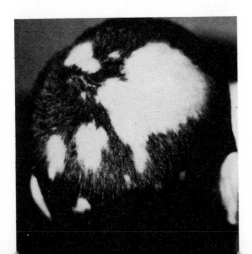

Figure 29: Alopecia Areata nearly always clears up. Hair will regrow no matter what "treatment" is used.

Baldness as a Disease

Only about 4 percent of baldness results from disease. Scalp disease and high temperature from bodily disease are most frequently the cause of this baldness. Most of these disease types of baldness are only temporary and therefore curable.

The best-known and most often cured baldness is the patchy, moth-eaten type called alopecia-areata. This baldness difficulty always clears up regardless of the treatment.

Dandruff

Dandruff is a flaking off of dead skin. It is not serious and appears to some degree in everyone. But further difficulties arise when it accumulates and forms crusts that irritate the scalp and cause it to itch. Then the combination of an over-supply of oil, dandruff and crusted lesions about the hair line is called seborrhea. Prevention of seborrhea demands an effective routine scalp cleaning for removing excess oil and crust accumulation, plus a diet regulation best prescribed by the physician or skin doctor.

Boils and Carbuncles

These infections readily begin on the neck and occasionally the scalp. The neck is an ideal region for bacteria to start an infection because collars and clothing so often rub this skin area and allow bacteria to enter under the skin surface and start boils. If bacteria from boils tunnel in several directions under the skin and start an

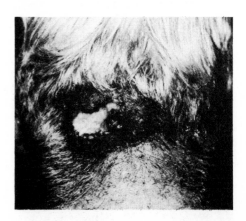

Figure 30: Carbuncle is a difficult and stubborn infection.

accumulation of numerous small boils, a carbuncle is formed. This is very difficult to cure whether in the neck or scalp.

Covering the infection with a clean bandage gives some protection against further infection, but opening and draining a boil is usually necessary for complete recovery. Mother Nature herself often performs this operation by a heading and bursting process, but when pus accumulation is too deep, an incision and drainage may be necessary. Carbuncles, much more than boils, require a thorough incision and drainage operation of the many infected tunnels in the surrounding skin. Only a doctor should attempt to incise and drain this serious infection.

The Eye

Eyesight is our most treasured physical possession. If we had to choose between loss of sight and loss of any other sense, ability or body function, we would always choose to keep our sight. Just about every human activity concerns the eye somehow, and without sight all of our ventures would lose much of their meaning.

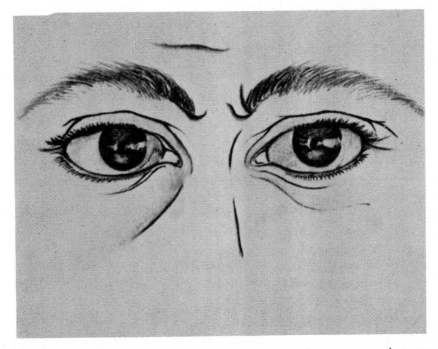

Figure 31: Nothing on earth has more value to us than our eyes, but we abuse them often. Care of eyes is very important; they can develop many severe diseases.

Like a camera, the eye is taking pictures constantly, but the eye does not keep rolling film; its picture is always changing, and storage of its pictures is kept in the brain, cataloged under the name of memories, either vivid or faint.

Examination of the Eyes

Examine the eye in a mirror with the aid of a strong light. When testing eyesight ability, prop up the eye chart at eye level, and stand back a measured 20 feet.

1. Closely examine the inner and outer surfaces of the eyelid, the eyeball itself, and the clear surface of the cornea. Lift the eyelid to look for any particle, hair, or other substance embedded in the eye surface. This is a foreign body.
2. Carefully examine the clear cornea of the eye. There should be no redness, large blood vessels, or milky growth present over this clear area. Presence of these findings may mean eye inflammation or pterygium.
3. Note the pupils; both are of equal size; they both become smaller in bright light and larger in dim light. Failure of this pupil action or any unequalness of size may mean infection or disease within the eye or brain.
4. Fix the vision on a distant light such as a street lamp during the evening. The appearance of rings, visible around the light like a halo, along with a blurring of the light itself may indicate glaucoma.
5. With the vision fixed on a light object, quickly close and open the eyelids several times. If blurring or distortion is constant in any one particular portion of the eye field, it may indicate astigmatism.
6. At a distance of 20 feet from the eye chart, accurately measured, determine the lowest line you can read correctly for each eye. Do this both with glasses on and off. The 20 - 20 line is considered perfect distance vision. Determine the smallest readable print on the hand chart of varying size print. Print size Number 1, although perfect, is almost too good to be true.

Interprets vision according to universal standards. The $\dfrac{20}{20}$ line is regarded "pefect."

Based on a visual angle
of one minute.

1     $\dfrac{200\ \text{FT.}}{61\ \text{M}}$ F P $\dfrac{20}{200}$

2     $\dfrac{100\ \text{FT.}}{30.5\ \text{M}}$ P E $\dfrac{20}{100}$

A O Instrument Company, Buffalo, N.Y.

3 70 FT. / 21.3 M

4 50 FT. / 15.2 M

5 40 FT. / 12.2 M

6 30 FT. / 9.14 M

Z O T

D E P L

F C P

P Z C E

20/70 20/50 20/40 20/30

7   25 FT. / 7.62M   F E L O P Z D   20/25

8   20 FT. / 6.10M   D E F P O T E C   20/20

9   15 FT. / 4.57M   L E F O D P C T   20/15

10   13 FT. / 3.96M   F D P L T C E O   20/13

11   10 FT. / 3.05M   P E Z O L C F T D   20/10

Figure 32 (cont.)

Acuity Rating	Visual Efficiency

14/14 **100%**

Certain weather forecasters have used an official scale in which winds are defined in terms of their rates of speed. When the velocity is less than one mile an hour, the term "calm" is used. A "light" wind travels at the rate of one to seven miles an hour. Eight to twelve mile an hour winds are called "gentle." "Moderate" winds travel at the rate of thirteen to eighteen miles an hour. "Fresh" winds have a higher velocity of nineteen to twenty-four miles per hour.

14/21 **91.5%**

Winds traveling twenty-five to thirty-eight miles an hour are termed "strong." When a speed of thirty-nine to fifty-four miles an hour is reached, the term "gale" is used. "Whole gale" describes winds having velocities of fifty-five to seventy-five miles per hour. When wind velocity exceeds seventy-five miles an hour, the term "hurricane" is used.

14/24.5 **87.5%**

Two items of information are required for making weather forecasts—the direction and rate of change of atmospheric pressure, and the direction of the wind. Atmospheric pressure is measured on the barometer. A high and steady barometer indicates fair weather and little temperature change.

14/28 **83.6%**

A rapidly falling barometer always indicates increasing wind. In association with a low reading, a rapid fall indicates approaching storms. When the wind is east to north, northeast gales with heavy rain or snow are to be expected. In winter, a cold wave usually follows.

14/35 **76.5%**

If the barometer is high and is falling slowly, different forecasts are made according to the direction of the wind. When the wind is south to southeast, rain is expected within twelve to eighteen hours.

14/42 **69.9%**

When the wind is east to northeast, with a high barometer falling slowly, light winds and fair weather are expected in summer, but in winter this means rain in twenty-four hours.

14/56 **58.5%**

Winds near low pressure areas shift in a counterclockwise direction; near high pressure areas they shift in a clockwise direction.

14/84 **40.9%**

Clearing weather accompanies changes from low to high pressure.

A O Instrument Company, Buffalo, N.Y.

Figure 33: Near vision ability is determined by the close reading chart, according to standard variation in the size of print.

Eye Difficulties

When the eyes develop a genuine problem of cross-eye or wall-eye (so-called squint), the eye doctor must be consulted. These

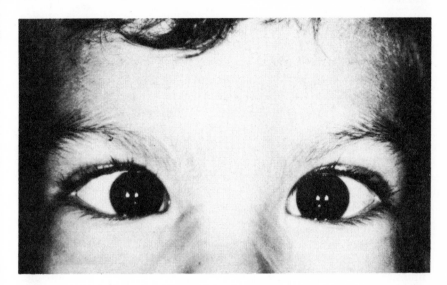

Figure 34: Cross-eyes can be slight or severe. It is a fault of the eye muscles.

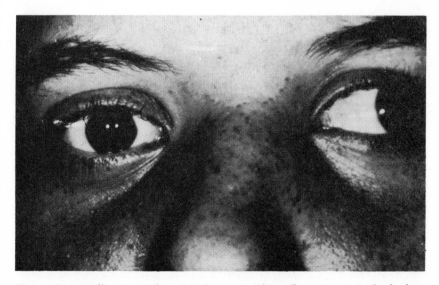

Figure 35: Walleyes can be straight or wander off—an eye muscle fault.

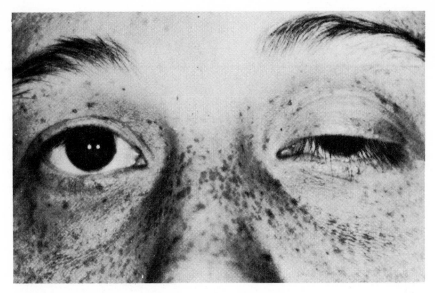

Figure 36: Ptosis or sleepy eye is a difficulty of the nerve. Without the nerve,
the eyelid muscle can't open the eyelid.

difficulties may be caused by faulty development of the muscles
which turn the eyeball, nerve difficulties and infection, or other
disease within the head.

These difficulties are easy to notice, and are easy for the eye
physician to diagnose. His expert direction is essential for the
correction of these eye defects. At times glasses are enough to
correct cross-eyes, and at other times surgery is necessary. This
surgery involves the shortening or lengthening of muscles which
turn the eyeballs, thus allowing them to correct the faulty direction
of the eyeball. Such surgery is extremely successful, but the eye
doctor alone must decide which treatment should be followed.

Foreign Bodies of the Eye

Very few people live long on this earth before getting something
in the eye. These particles are called foreign bodies, and they usually
cause sharp pain with an excessive flow of tears as nature attempts
to float the particle out of the eye. Most dust particles from winds
and storms are effectively handled by the eye without any more
treatment than a few winks and blinks. Any foreign bodies that do
not wash out with tears will invite rubbing, a most natural reaction.
Is is best, however, to confine any such rubbing action to gentle
stroking of the closed eyelid towards the nose. If the foreign body

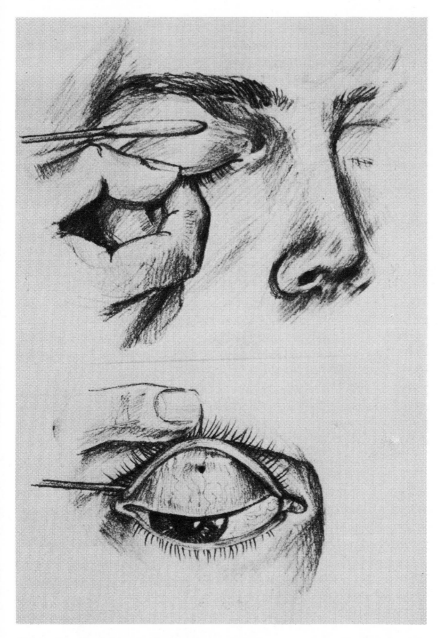

Figure 37: Something in the eye is an everyday occurrence. Turning the eye-lid is easy, if the patient will hold still. Wipe off the foreign body with wet tissue paper.

particle still remains in the eye, a nurse or doctor should examine the eye for possible injury. Occasionally a foreign body becomes lodged in the cornea or white of the eye, and unfortunately at times penetrates the eyeball itself.

When "something in the eye" does not wash out freely, consider no other course but the doctor's recommendation. The best of intentions in rubbing the eye can, unfortunately, turn insignificant eye injuries into serious ones.

Inflammation in the Eyes

Sties, pinkeye, and other eye inflammations usually caused by bacterial infection are very common, quite painful, and often considered to be contagious. The eye is visibly reddened, contains pus and throws out a constant flood of tears. Bright light worsens the pain and burning, and the reddened, thickened lids often stick together with crust formation during sleep. The ever-present

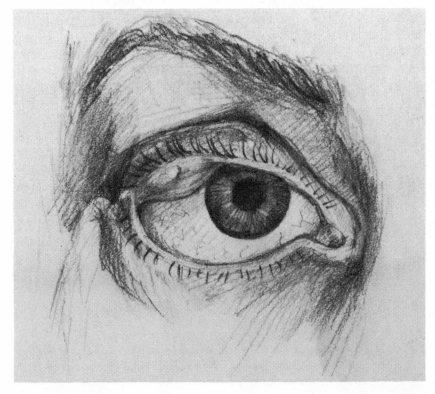

Figure 38: A sty is everybody's problem. Unless the right antibiotic is used, more sties may follow.

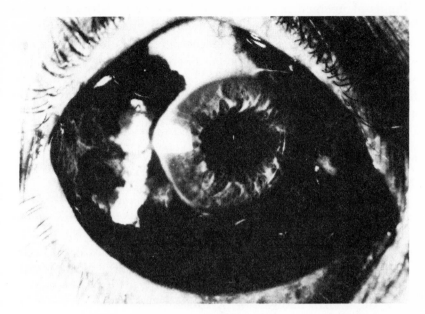

Figure 39: Redeye, a hemorrhagic sclera, looks like a horrible injury. It usually follows an injury but normally clears up completely.

tear is probably the best eyewash and germ killer in the entire world for these situations, but determined self-treatment still commonly causes most of our eye damage.

The best rule to follow in eye infections is to do nothing but close the eye and possibly apply mild heat until the physican can see it. Modern drugs, antibiotics, and methods of treating eye inflammations have changed considerably, and these should be considered preferable to any kind of home treatment.

Inflammation elsewhere in the body, including possible tumor growths, may reflect themselves in eye conditions.

Figure 40: Cancer of the eyelid is a serious situation. It must be removed completely to keep the eye protected.

Pupils of unequal size may indicate neurological disease within the brain, requiring extensive professional study and treatment. Pupils which do not constrict in the presence of bright light or expand in the darkness may be considered a possible indication of systemic disease of the entire body. Syphilis, an infectious systemic disease, has long been known to affect the eye pupils in this manner.

Any eye findings such as these should drive the individual to his physician for an examination.

Cataract

Cataract is a loss of transparency in the lens of the eye. It usually grows progressively greater from the rim inward toward the center. Most cataracts occur in the over-50 group, and seem to be caused by systemic diseases such as diabetes and difficulties of the parathyroid gland, among others. They are also caused by difficulties within the eyeball itself such as chronic uveitis (inflammation of one of the eyeball linings), or by excessive heat and infra-red rays such as are experienced by glass blowers and open hearth steel workers (Figure 41). When cataract occurs without any disease within the eye, or without, in the later years of life, it is called senile cataract.

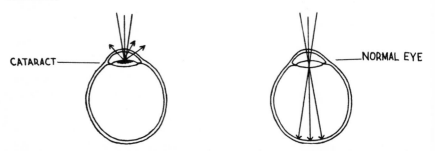

CATARACT   NORMAL EYE

Figure 41: Cataract is a disease of the eye lens—growing from clear glass-like transparency to an opaque, milky appearance in which some light rays are prevented from entering the eye. Caused by diabetes, infection and other difficulties, it can be removed and sight restored if proper glasses are used.

Removing the lens from the eyeball is the only satisfactory therapy for severe cataracts. Drugs and other treatment have been found worthless in restoring vision or preventing blindness but the surgical treatment of cataract is very successful with well over 95 percent recovering good eyesight. Only a physician can accurately diagnose a cataract and perform the necessary surgery.

Glaucoma

Glaucoma, the thief in the night, is a disease of increased pressure within the eyeball. It afflicts nearly two people of 100 over the age of 40 years, and is responsible for one out of every eight cases of blindness.

Pain is not always a prominent factor in glaucoma, but a dull ache in the eyes is almost always present. Reasons to suspect glaucoma are: (1) progressively poor vision in one or both eyes, (2) blurring vision with halo rings, visible around bright lights, and (3) so-called "gun barrel" vision in which the field of vision is narrowed to a small "target" with difficulty in seeing toward the sides.

The eye doctor has drugs, surgical procedures, and other measures effective for the treatment of glaucoma.

Astigmatism

Astigmatism is a mechanical fault of the eye. It is an unequal curvature in the eyeball which we ordinarily think is perfectly round. When the unequal curvature is in the cornea through which light rays come, our vision is distorted and causes eye strain. Because nothing in this world is perfect, no eyeball is perfectly round, and therefore everyone has some atigmatism. It is usually easily relieved with suitable glasses.

Exophthalmos

This uncommon eye condition makes the eyeball appear enlarged and staring; often it is the result of disease. The wide-eyed appearance of exophthalmos is caused by a pushing outward of the eyeball itself by a swollen or congested area behind the eye. Sometimes it is caused by over-activity of the thyroid glands, but it can also be caused by high blood pressure or kidney disease, or (rarely) can be a simple inherited family characteristic. Men have it more than women, and most often develop it in middle age. Even after effective treatment has been given, it is usual for exophthalmos to remain permanently to some degree.

Senile Ectropion

In the later years of life, when the skin has lost some of its elasticity and firmness, the facial skin may sag. The lower eyelids often are affected, and may sag so that they no longer touch the eyeball and the inner surface of the eyelid becomes visible to others.

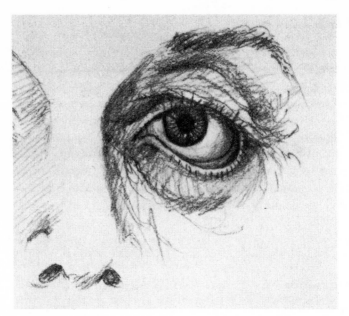

Figure 42: In the years past middle age, sagging, drooping eyelids, called
senile ectropion, are due to a loss of skin tone of later life and
occur mostly in thin-skinned persons of the outdoor type, such as
farmers. This difficulty can be cured by plastic surgery.

This difficulty, called ectropion, does not reflect any systemic disease other than aging of the skin and its loss of tone. Ectropion frequently brings about irritation of the eyeball which has lost some of its protective eyelid covering. The constant tearing that follows is so annoying that a minor surgical operation is often recommended. This treatment means the removal of a portion of the sagging lower eyelid, and stretching out the remainder to a normal appearance. When this procedure is done by a surgeon skilled in plastic surgery, the results are very gratifying.

Pterygium

A pterygium is an accumulation of scar tissue over the eyeball resulting from exposure to dust, wind, sun, and general outdoor life. This scar tissue on the eyeball is a pie-shaped wedge of milky tissue, extending outward from the nasal border of the eye. It is nature's attempt to heal areas of constant irritation so frequently found in the eye of people who live the great outdoor life. Unfortunately, the pterygium may grow to cover the pupil and cause partial blindness.

The treatment of the pterygium scar is its complete removal by surgical means. It is not a fatal disease, but may lead to permanently impaired vision or blindness if it is allowed to go untreated. The prevention of a pterygium calls for care of the eyes during outdoor activities with goggles, sun glasses, et cetera.

Figure 43: Growth of eyelid-type tissue over the eyeball, usually from the nasal side, is called pterygium. Affected by long years of outdoor life, wind and dust, the growth may grow completely over the pupil to blur vision or even cause blindness. It is very slow growing, never cancerous, and easily cured with surgery.

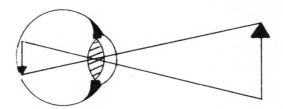

Figure 44A: The normal eye focuses exactly on the retina, the back wall of the eye. The lens thickens itself for close vision and thins itself for distant vision. In early years, the lens has great adaptive power.

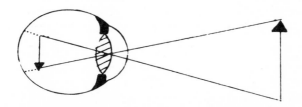

Figure 44B: The near-sighted, or myopic, eye has an elongated shape and entering light rays focus into an image before reaching the back wall, the retina. When these same rays finally do reach the back of the eye, they are no longer in focus and blurry vision results. Near-sightedness is easily corrected with glasses. It tends to improve with age.

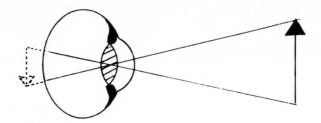

Figure 44C: The far-sighted, or presbyopic or hyperopic, eye is slightly flattened and entering light rays can focus into an image only
beyond the back wall itself. Since rays hit the retina before
focusing, blurry vision mars close-up sighting. Far-sightedness
is also easily corrected with glasses, but it tends to grow worse
with age.

Types of Sight

Near-Sightedness, Myopia

The near-sighted eye, as its name suggests, sees well up close,
but poorly at a distance. It is due to an elongated eyeball, which
focuses its image before it reaches the retina on the backwall of the
eye. This eye looks like a protruding, staring, or beady eye. It is
not the desired vision for aviators, surveyors, or people who must
see at a distance, but certainly is great in later years when grand-
mother can thread her needle without even wearing glasses. Near-
sightedness is easily corrected with glasses.

Far-Sightedness, Presbyopia

The far-sighted eye which sees best at a distance and poorly up
close is a somewhat flattened eye. Here, the light rays entering the
eye reach the retina before they have had time to focus. The
image would focus theoretically at a distance behind the eyeball
itself. Far-sightedness may not bother flyers or star gazers, but it is
difficult to read small print or see well up close. Far-sightedness is
the eye state at birth when we can't see up close, and also in older
age when we need glasses to read. It is also easily corrected with
glasses.

Color-Blindness

Some of us have perfect vision except when it comes to seeing
color. About one out of 56 people can't tell red from green, and
about one in 50 confuse brown and green. Blue and green often

look alike to some people; and pink and yellow look the same to others. A few people see everything in black and white alone.

The difficulty in color-blindness lies in the retina where a deficiency exists between the rods and cones, where color is sensed. It is found more in men than in women, and most often its discovery comes as a surprise in some sort of test.

Railroads, airlines, and branches of the military cannot accept color-blind personnel, for no cure is available at present.

Reading Problems

Reading problems begin in childhood. Correct reading is easy reading that opens the universe to us. If we shy away from reading because it is difficult, we lose the tremendous benefits of good reading habits and often create lifetime burdens for ourselves.

READING CAN BE EASY WHEN THE

EYES FOCUS ON THE SAME WORDS

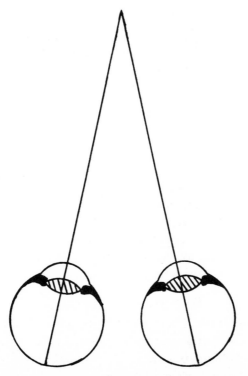

Figure 45: Reading can be easy when the eyes focus on the same words.

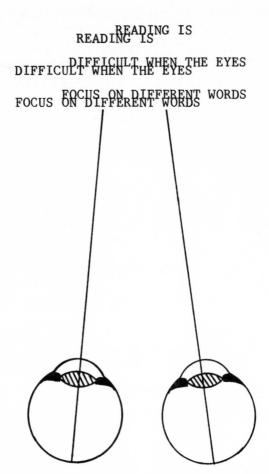

Figure 46: Reading is difficult when the eyes focus on different words.

The "whys" of reading problems should always be investigated. Often a physical problem of the eye exists which can possibly be corrected. Among others, the problems of dyslexia and monocular vision should be recognized and remedied. Remedial reading exercises which are available today are worth years in anyone's future.

Glasses

Too many of us feel that our first pair of glasses means we are growing old. It is true the eye often needs some extra help as it leaves youth behind, but then many people need glasses in their younger years and even in childhood.

The use of glasses to avoid eye strain and regain accurate vision amounts almost to rebirth. In other eras, a man of 40 years was old and given a back seat because he couldn't see to do his job. Now, at age 60 and 70, he is still going strong because his glasses give him sharp vision at an age of real knowledge. Today, if our glasses were taken away, our industry would stop overnight.

It is important to have a thoroughly reliable eye doctor fit our glasses; we must never pick out a pair to suit us from trial and error glasses in the stores.

Eye Exercises

The eye muscles, like any muscles, can become weak and faulty. Exercising them can help in some eye problems, but of course, not in all.

The eye doctor has access to sets of glass prisms which he often directs people to use to strengthen their eye muscles, as in tracking problems. He alone can tell when the eye exercises will be of any real value to a person.

The Ear

When we think of the ear, we think of hearing ability or deafness, and this is correct. But the ear also has the function of providing balance without which we could not even stand erect.

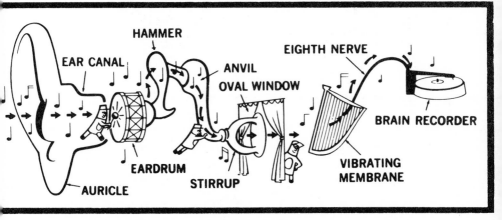

Figure 47: Hearing translates a vibration in the air into music, a story or communication between human brains.

The value of hearing is hard to understand; it is best known to those who have lost their hearing and are now buried in a tomb of silence. To gain some insight into the problem of deafness, we might stopper our ears with swimmer's ear plugs and attempt to go through our usual day. We would find it almost impossible.

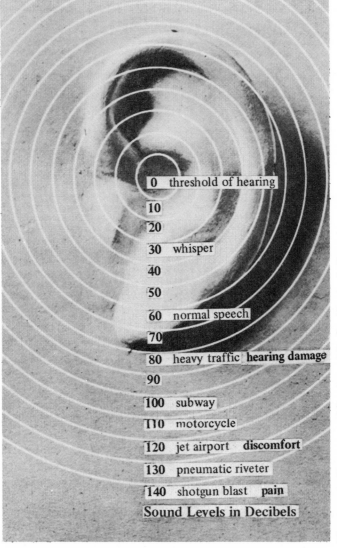

Figure 48. A whisper registers 30 decibels, a shot-gun blast 140 decibels. Noise over 80 decibels will impair hearing in time.

Ear problems, especially hearing loss, form one of the three biggest problems of senior years. Our education, speech, music and even reading are dependent upon our hearing; the bells, signals and sounds of everyday life are so taken for granted we rarely give them a thought—until our hearing begins to fade.

The wonderful world of sound is more likely to remain with us throughout our lives if we care for our hearing and have our ears periodically examined.

Examination of the Ear

With a good light and two mirrors, examine closely the ear skin and its shell. Look for any obvious skin sores, redness, irritation or cracking on the ear surface. Look for any obvious blocking of the ear canal and test the ear's hearing ability as suggested below:

1. Examine the external ear for any soreness, bleeding or discharge from the ear canal. These findings can mean skin infections, skin cancer or infection from the inner ear.
2. Gently pull the ear upward and backward and use a double mirror to sight into the ear canal. If the ear canal is blocked, it probably means impacted wax, or if it is painful, possibly an infection exists in the ear canal.
3. Tap the hard mastoid bone directly behind the ear with the finger tips and note any soreness or tenderness which might indicate infection in the middle ear.
4. Achieve complete silence by holding a pillow to both sides of the head. Note any ringing or buzzing noise which usually means otosclerosis.
5. Note any continuing dizziness after rapidly turning the head side to side 20 time and then facing directly forward. Continuing dizziness or unsteadiness could indicate labyrinthitis, an irritation of the balance mechanism in the far inner ear.
6. Test your hearing ability by holding a ticking watch 6 to 12 inches away from the ear; check the results against the other ear. Inability to hear the watch ticking can mean drum or nerve deafness.
7. Wrap the handle of an ordinary table knife in a cloth and grasp it firmly between the teeth. Twang the blade to start it vibrating, and note your ability to hear the vibration. When vibration cannot be heard, nerve deafness is a definite possibility.

Difficulties of the Ear

Difficulties of the ear involve the functions of hearing and balance along with external ear problems.

Deformity of the External Ear

The shape of the ear is variable and of very little importance in actual hearing ability. It may be huge or oddly formed and can be a source of embarrassment, but rarely does the shape of the ear interfere with real hearing.

An example of external ear deformity is cauliflower ear, named because it faintly resembles the surface of a cauliflower. It is the result of bleeding and clot formation under the skin and results in permanent deformity. Loss of hearing is slight and plastic surgery can achieve very good cosmetic results. These results are seldom appreciated, however, since cauliflower ear is usually found in prize fighters, wrestlers and rugged individuals to whom cosmetic appearance has very little meaning.

Infection of the External Ear

Most external ear infections are fungus infections or exzema. (See skin diseases.) This kind of external ear difficulty is prevented largely through cleanliness and avoiding the overruse of frequently advertised medicines and healing agents. Routine gentle cleaning of the ears inside and out is recommended, providing nothing smaller than the elbow is put into the ear canal. Any ear or skin disease which does not respond in two or three weeks to simple cleansing could be serious and should be seen by your physician.

Skin Cancer

Skin cancers on the ear are infamous for their confusing appearance. The skin cover of the ear is a favorite site for skin cancer because of the ear's exposed position which openly invites irritation from sunlight, chemicals, windburn and other agents. Unfortunately, skin cancers about the ear are slow growing and most often are confused with simple chronic infections or "something that just won't go away."

Any external skin sore on the ear over two weeks old could be a cancer, and should be seen by the physician. (See Skin Diseases.)

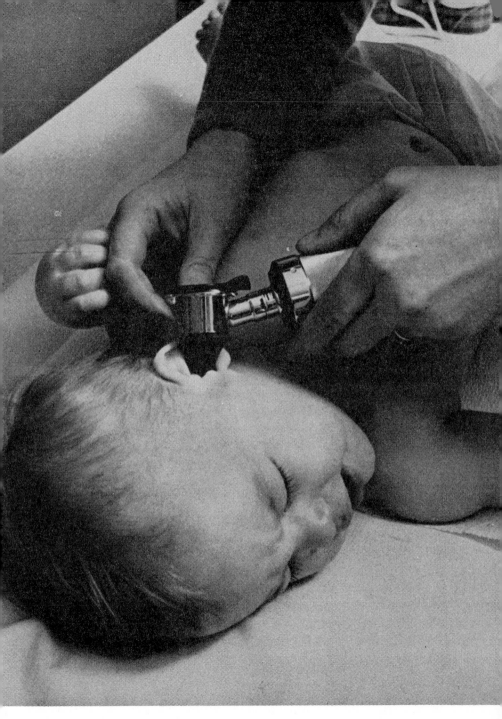

Figure 49: The physician's expert examination is necessary for accurate treatment of middle ear infections.

Infection of the Inner Ear

Infections of the inner or middle ear, the hearing part of the ear, are called "otitis media" and usually begin in childhood; they often persist, however, into later life. Middle ear infections are accompained by the intense pain in the ear and high temperature. A perforation of the ear drum, with the constantly draining ear, commonly follows.

It is important in infections of the inner ear, even more than in other areas of the body, to maintain general health at a high level in order to successfully combat this lingering type of infection. The aid of the experienced physician is absolutely necessary for the successful treatment of infection in the middle ear.

Otosclerosis (Buzzing in the Ear)

Otosclerosis is a continuing disease of the ear's hearing mechanism which reduces fine hearing and produces a buzzing, ringing sound in the ear. The problem concerns the three small bones within the ear, named the hammer, the anvil and the stirrup. These bones normally tremble or rattle against one another to transmit sound, but in otosclerosis they stick to one another and pass a continual message. The result is a constant buzzing, ringing or even roaring noise which seems loudest when it is most quiet, as in bed at night. Otosclerosis does not interfere completely with hearing and it is least noticed out in noisy public places. It is very common in the upper age bracket and is most difficult to cure, but a good ear doctor can be of considerable help in this disease.

Deafness Due to Ear Canal Blockade

Occlusion of the external ear canal often is the sole cause of reduced hearing, and removal of the block may produce sudden and definite improvement. Wax is most often the offender, but the occlusion may be due to a boil-like infection in the ear canal or a formation caused by accumulative dust particles. Irrigation of the ear with warm water is sometimes sufficient to clean out the ear canal and improve the hearing. It is important to repeat that nothing smaller than the elbow should ever be put into the ear. This means that match sticks, hair pins or tooth picks should never be used for cleaning the ear canal. When the warm wash rag over the tip of the little finger does not adequately clean the external ear canal, it becomes a job for the doctor to do.

Deafness Due to Eardrum Difficulties

Perforation or destruction of the eardrum can result in decreased hearing but not a complete loss of hearing. Perforations of the drum are common and most often result from old middle ear infections. The eardrum with a hole in it will continue to function fairly well until the eardrum is almost all gone, and then clear, distinct hearing is lost. Loss of the entire eardrum, however, does not cause total deafness since sound can still be conducted through the bones of the ear and the skull.

Nerve Deafness

A person is not really deaf until the hearing nerve is lost. This is particularly important as age advances, since there is distinct loss of hearing (especially for higher tones) with each decade of life. Like the eye, the ear has a gradual decline in hearing power with age.

A simple test of nerve deafness is to hold a buzzing object, such as a tuning fork or kitchen knife, tightly against the skull or between the teeth. When the fork or knife is plucked and caused to vibrate, hearing a buzzing means that the nerve is intact. If it is not heard, improving the hearing may be very difficult or impossible since this usually indicates that the nerve itself is not working. A hearing aid may be of some help for partial nerve deafness but not for total nerve deafness.

Inner Ear Infection, Labyrinthitis, Dizziness

After we pass through the external ear, beyond the drum into the middle ear, we arrive at the deep or inner ear. This is a fluid-filled compartment within the bone which contains the balancing mechanism and the actual nerve hearing apparatus. This compartment, termed the labyrinth, may become irritated or infected to produce a labyrinthitis. It is here that dizziness ordinarily is produced. (See Meniere's Disease.)

Deafness Due to Noise

It is true that ears exposed to loud sounds will experience, at least temporarily, deafness. For example, when a hunter discharges a shotgun, the ear suffers a temporary loss of hearing. But the deafness does not progress after the noise has ceased. However, people who must suffer a prolonged exposure to noise of an ex-

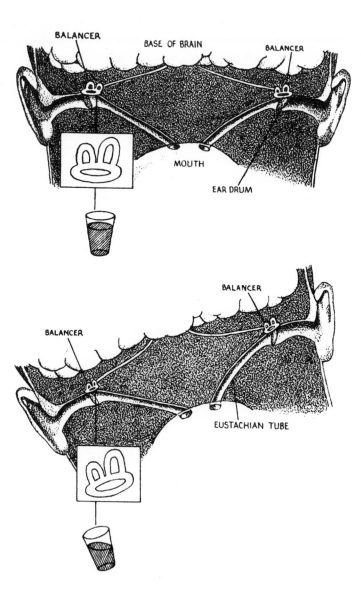

Figure 50:   Inside-ear machinery gives us our sense of balance. Like a glass of water, it contains fluid which remains stationary when we turn or tilt. The position of the fluid allows recognition of body position even in darkness. When faulty, this mechanism may be a source of annoying dizziness and a spinning sensation.

WHAT THE DEAF HEAR

Normal hearing:

*TH*E *F*IR*S*T *S*OUND*S*
LO*S*T ARE *TH*E
*F*RIC AT IVE CON*S*ONANT*S*

Moderate loss:

E IR T OUND
LO T ARE E
RIC AT IVE CON ONANT

Severe loss:

E IR OUN
LO ARE E
RI A IVE ON ONAN

Therapeutic Notes, a publication of Parke, Davis & Company

Figure 51: What the deaf hear.

ceptionally loud character will lose part of their hearing ability permanently. This environment would include the avid hunter, the air-hammer operator, the jet airplane handler, the motorcycle rider, the subway operator and many others who endure a high degree of unwelcome noise.

People with hearing loss can hear a conversation of normal loudness, but only with impaired clarity. The first sounds they lose are the friction produced sounds—*sh, ch, th, f* and *s*. As hearing loss continues, the sharper sounds of *p, k, t, b* and *d* also become difficult to hear.

The Nose

The nose, as the center of the face, can have either human grace or cosmetic despair to it. Its shapes and sizes are many but its functions far outweigh its appearance. In animals such as the dog, the sense of smell may detect the presence of enemies or the direction of the next meal, but man depends upon his nose very little. His sense of smell however, still gives man great protection against possible poisoned foods or gases. On other occasions, such as in spring, it is also his source of enjoyment.

As the nose prepares all our inhaled air for the lung, it is also subjected to many ills. Intense cold, dust, fumes and airborne allergens all are jobs for the nose to handle. It is surprising how well the nose can carry on its difficult job.

Examination of the Nose

The nose should be examined along its external contour, as well as within the nostrils themselves, with the aid of a strong pen light or flashlight. Self-examination can be achieved with the aid of close-up mirror observation.

1. Examine the skin of the nose for any unhealing sores, warty growths, soreness, redness, recent enlargement or bleeding areas. These findings may indicate skin cancer, rhinophyma or other benign growths.
2. Examine the profile and the centering of the nose on the face. Both nostrils should be equal in size with the nasal septum in the center. Major differences indicate the very commonly found external nasal deformity called deviated septum.
3. Determine the patency of each nostril by rapid inhaling and exhaling while obstructing the other nostril in turn. An obstructed nostril can mean an internal nasal deformity, allergic rhinitis, sinus disease, nasal polyps or simple upper respiratory infection.
4. Tap along the bony ridge of the eyebrow, cheek bone and bridge of the nose with the knuckle. Tenderness in these regions, especially when associated with continuous discharge from either nostril, usually denotes sinus trouble.

Diseases of the Nose

Skin Cancer and Other Growths

Skin cancer and other growths often begin on the skin of the nose, especially where the nostril flares into the cheek. In its forward and prominent position, the skin over the nose takes the worst beating of all from sunlight, wind and weather. For this reason, many skin growths including cancer, warts and blood-filled tumors are found in the nasal skin of the weather-beaten faces of farmers, hunters and outdoors men. (See Skin Diseases.)

External Nasal Deformities

Irregularities of the nose are very common. It is rare to find both sides of anyone's nose exactly alike. The inside of the nostril varies slightly in size and shape, but is of little or no importance as long as the airway is patent through the nose.

The septum of the nose is often off to one side somewhat, possibly as a natural occurrence or as a result of trauma, but aside from beauty, a deviated septum is of no significance as long as it does not interfere with proper breathing.

Deformities in the profile of the nose claim most people's attention because of their cosmetic appearance. The nose profile can be reshaped considerably and easily with plastic surgery; however, it is the rare patient who is completely satisfied after cosmetic surgery to the nose (Figure 52).

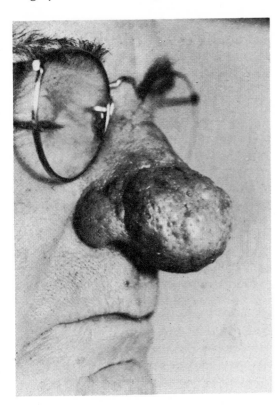

Figure 52: Rhinophyma is a cherry-nosed growth, not caused by alcohol. Its cause is unknown, but it is not a cancerous growth.

Allergy (Rhinitis)

Allergic rhinitis, or hay fever, has for its unmistakable mark a wet, dripping nose annually during the allergy season. There is usually considerable irritation of the nose along with swelling and soreness, and tears often spill over onto the cheeks because they cannot drain properly into the blocked-up nose.

In seasonal rhinitis, airborne pollen from trees, grasses and weeds is our most frequent offender. However, a few unfortunate people are plagued with a nasal allergy year round. The allergic factors in the continuing types of allergy are more likely to be animal danders, house dust, feathers or mattress stuffing and unidentified paint fumes. Those people who have constant allergies must make every effort to avoid these offending substances. Their greatest hopes will lie in an exact investigation and testing by an allergist, a doctor who specializes in the investigation and treatment of allergic diseases.

Sinus Trouble

Our sinuses are really our eyebrows, cheek bones and nose bones. They are air filled spaces and are exactly like small rooms opening directly off the main nose chamber. They are easily infected, do not drain easily, and are prone to carry infectious material for long periods.

The poor sinuses have been blamed for nearly all our body diseases from poor eyesight to headaches, arthritis and even anemia. While the sinuses are no doubt over-blamed, it is also true that a large proportion of people who live in humid climates have some difficulty with their sinuses. A lot of sinus difficulty is thought to follow nasal deformity, allergy or low body resistance.

Bony Nasal Deformity

A broken nasal bone oftentimes heals improperly and partially blocks air passage through it. This sometimes blocks the sinus opening into the nose; it may block the tear duct from the eyes resulting in tears spilling under the cheeks; and it may produce obstruction to fee and easy air flow through the nasal passages into the lungs.

A broken nose should be repaired before it has a chance to heal in an improper position. Nevertheless, at a later date, if undue difficulties arise from the bony nasal structure, the nose can be re-broken and reset for a proper structuring of the bony framework.

Common Cold

Swollen, baggy and inflamed mucous membranes in the nose tend to block the sinus openings, irritate the sinus linings and stimulate them to produce infectious material which cannot drain out easily.

It is difficult to separate allergic nasal problems from the ordinary

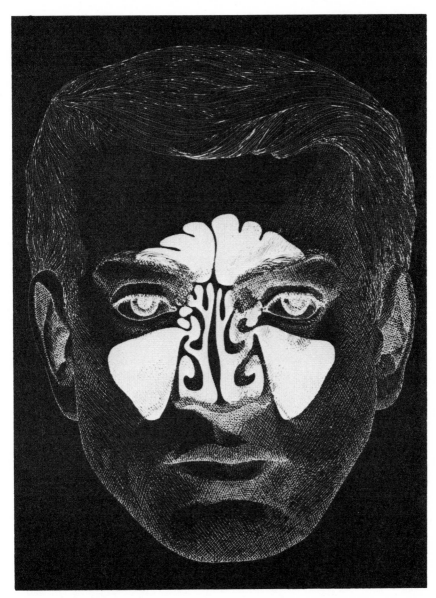

Warner-Chilcott Laboratories, Morris Plains, New Jersey

Figure 53: Allergy in the nasal area affects a wide area throughout all the sinuses as well.

common cold. Both present a similar picture, and one may lead to the other condition.

In allergy, it is important to remove from the nose any polyps or enlarged and swollen mucosal folds, which can block the nasal passageway and magnify the alergic disease background.

Low Body Resistance

Improper diet and nutrition can produce very low resistance to infection. This applies particularly to areas prone to infection, like the sinus areas.

Because chronic sinus infection is often a focus of infection for many other ailments, it is well to consult a physician that he may prescribe proper treatment for possible sinus problems. Heat application is a popular and safe home remedy, but all other forms of treatment should be under the direction and guidance of a physician if one is to gain relief from sinus problems.

It has been estimated in the Great Lakes areas that nearly three-quarters of the people have some form of sinus problems. Since not all of these people have physical defects in the nose to blame for the sinus problem, it is usually thought that most sinus disease comes to us through no fault of our own, save our living in the wrong atmosphere.

The Face

The face is you. All the rest of your body exists for it, and without it the personality as we knew it is gone. We can lose any part of the body, but with our face intact, we still remain the same person.

As the outlet of the soul, the face expresses love and anger, hatred, fear and despair. Out of its depth flow joy or sorrow and the look of friend or foe.

From it also shines the appearance of health or the marks of disease (Figure 54).

Examination of the Face

Examine the face and its features before a close-up mirror, using a secondary mirror for side viewing.

1. Examine the texture of the facial skin. Note any recent growth, one-sided enlargement, bleeding points, long un-healed sores, or any painful swollen areas anywhere on the face. These abnormalities indicate skin growth possibili-

Figure 54: The face mirrors one's general physical condition.

ties. They can also reveal underlying disease of the salivary glands, bones, teeth and muscles.

2. Observe any involuntary twitching movement of the face, eyes or mouth. Note any difference in motion between sides of the face during facial movement: raise the eyebrows, squint the eyes, bare the teeth widely as in smiling, pucker the lips in a whistling motion. Unusual findings like twitching or loss of motion may indicate tics or facial paralysis.

3. By placing two mirrors at right angles, mirror the face so that the left side of the face is a mirror of the right. The difference between the two sides of the face may show the normal facial deformity and asymmetry, or it can uncover recent one-sided growths.

Diseases of the Face

SKIN CANCER AND OTHER GROWTHS

The skin of the face is the site for most skin cancers because it is the body area most exposed to sunlight, wind and weather of all sorts. It is now very definite that prolonged and intense weather, especially sunlight, is a certain cause of skin cancer. A skin cancer may begin as a small pearly growth that continues unhealed, crusted or bleeding and probably oozing most of the time. Other growths of the skin are also very common on the face. They are warts, blemishes, moles and ruby-red blood warts. (See Skin Diseases.)

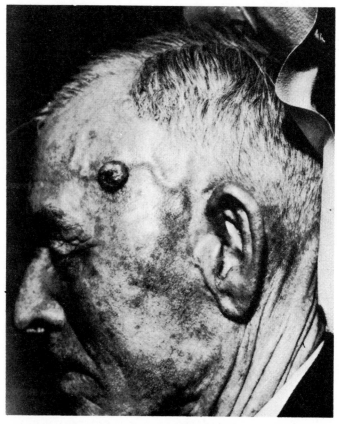

Figure 55: Skin cancer finds the face suited to its growth. This is possibly due to exposure to sunlight and external weather conditions.

FACE GROWTHS

In the face, large or small growths can appear just beneath the skin. On the side of the head just in front of the ear is the region of the parotid salivary gland which gives rise to frequent enlargements.

MUMPS

Mumps is a systemic disease, usually seen in childhood but sometimes in adults, which causes the most frequent enlargement of the parotid gland.

In the adult, mumps has the reputation of being a more serious disease. This is true because of the great possibility of involvement of the testicle, which unfortunate complication may produce problems of sterility for young men. It is common for the doctor in adult examinations to find one testicle smaller than normal. He knows without asking that this patient has had mumps in childhood. When both testicles are seriously involved, it is true that the patient may be rendered sterile for life.

PAROTID GLAND GROWTHS

A growth in the region just anterior to the ear, especially if it is rather small and one-sided, may be of cancerous nature, and should be strongly suspected until proven otherwise by the physician.

Figure 56: Mumps-like enlargements of parotid salivary gland occur below and in front of the ears in later life, possibly due to infection or tumor growth. Tumors of the parotid gland are slow growing, painless and questionbly cancerous; they can be dealt with surgically.

The treatment of facial growths of the parotid gland, as in other glands about the body, is essentially a surgical operation in which the removal of the growth is usually curative.

In cases where facial enlargement about the parotid gland is only one instance of many enlargements all over the body, other disease is undoubtedly present and other treatment is necessary, depending upon the physician's judgment.

TICS, UNINTENDED FACIAL MOVEMENT

Tics are unusual nervous musclar twitches in the face, caused by spasms of local facial muscles. Some twitches can be stopped at will, but others are entirely uncontrollable. Tics are not serious when they represent temporary excessive nervousness, but if they are persistent they may represent serious underlying disease. Most commonly, tics are seen about the eyes, nose and throat. Occasionally, they are connected with allergic states.

Tic Douloureux is a well-known type of tic usually seen in the later years of life. It is very painful, strikes without warning, and usually affects only one side of the face. It produces a savage lancing pain in the temple, jaw, or teeth, and is oftentimes brought about by the slight stimulation of shaving or exposure to cold. Sometimes it occurs without any stimulation at all. The pain usually does not last long, but it may recur with agonizing frequency.

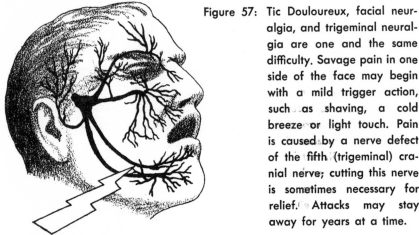

Figure 57: Tic Douloureux, facial neuralgia, and trigeminal neuralgia are one and the same difficulty. Savage pain in one side of the face may begin with a mild trigger action, such as shaving, a cold breeze or light touch. Pain is caused by a nerve defect of the fifth (trigeminal) cranial nerve; cutting this nerve is sometimes necessary for relief. Attacks may stay away for years at a time.

Tic Douloureux involves the nerve of sensation to the entire face, teeth, nose and eyes. The exact cause of this painful problem is unknown, but medical and surgical measures in the hands of the physician are definitely available for adequate relief.

FACIAL PALSY

Paralysis of portions of the face is very common. Palsies of only one side of the face frequently are the result of exposure to the cold or extreme emotional disturbances. They may accompany a recent stroke, especially in the older age group, but here, of course, they are also accompanied by paralysis of other portions of the body such as the arm or leg.

Another type of facial palsy is called ptosis of the eyelid, an eyelid which opens only partially. When confined to one side, it may associate with more serious underlying disease. An example is Horner's Syndrome, a most complex difficulty involving not only the eyelid, but other complex body structures within the chest as well. Only a skilled physician can recognize and prescribe treatment for this difficulty.

INGROWN HAIRS

At times, there are hairs which grow underneath the skin rather than out over it. This difficulty arises from shaving beards with

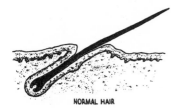

NORMAL HAIR

HAIR SHAVED SHORT

INGROWN HAIR

Figure 58: Trouble with ingrown hairs begins with the shaving process. The very short remaining hair grows into the overhanging skin to begin an infection. Most often it seen in men whose beard hair grows on a slant.

INGROWN HAIR (INFECTED)

whiskers that do not stand up straight, but rather grow sideways in all directions. The sharp, stubby and slanted hair plows into the skin next to it, and as it elongates its sharp point burrows further and further into the skin.

The treatment of ingrown hairs requires the undermining and elevation of each involved hair, followed by patient cleanliness to prevent infection. When we learn that only the very closely shaven hair can become an ingrown hair, we learn to change our shaving habits so that the very close shave is eliminated.

Some find electric razors are good in preventing ingrown hair, while others have found that blade razors work best for them.

FACIAL DEFORMITY AND IRREGULARITY

No two sides of anybody's face compare exactly alike. The eyes differ, the ears differ, the sides of the face, nose and mouth are not equal; and facial expressions also differ on each side of the face. A characteristic facial expression such as smiling is done more with one side of the face than the other, and so are most other facial expressions.

In our examination above, the mirror image of each side of the face is reproduced for observation. It becomes readily apparent that one side of the face is more handsome than the other. Mythological history would have us believe that one side of the face represents man's soul, while the other side represents his will. Exactly which side is which is hard to determine.

The Lips

The lip is the visible junction of the inside and outside of the body. At its borders, the skin abruptly changes to mucous membrane or inner skin which lines our entire digestive track and most of our breathing passages.

In human beings, the lips have many functions such as talking, drinking, eating, smiling and producing other expressions.

Since they are outside and yet covered with an inside lining tissue of lesser strength and resistance, the lips are very often the site of important disease difficulties discussed below.

Examination of the Lips

The lips are examined in adults with a close-up mirror with the aid of a good light. Remove artificial dentures for better inspection of the lips' inner surface.

1. Closely examine the adult lips externally and internally. Note any areas of bluish discoloration or a whitish leathery formation, especially on the inner surface of the lips. These findings in the adult may represent birthmark discoloration or leukoplakia.
2. Note any definite cracking in the skin in the corners of the mouth where the lips join. Cracking here may mean the Vitamin B deficiency, ariboflavinosis.
3. Look closely along the lip's surface for any cracking, bleeding points, ulcers or long unhealed sores. Usually in the lower lip these findings may indicate fissure or cancer.
4. Observe the contour and motion of the lip. Note any paralysis, drooling saliva, or weakness in the lip movement. Compress the lips, smile widely, bare the teeth and pucker the lips as in whistling position. Inability to perform these lip actions may represent facial paralysis, a light stroke or possibly part of a complex nerve disease within the body.

Diseases of the Lips

ANGIOMA OF THE LIP

A birthmark's discoloration of the lip is quite common as it is on other areas of the face. This difficulty is not dangerous, but it can be deforming and embarrassing. Its removal is a fairly simple plastic surgery practice if undertaken at the right time of life by a competent surgeon experienced in this field.

TRAUMA

The lips, in plain sight, are the center of much activity during life, and have usually suffered bruising, biting, chafing and often a cut or two. Aside from scar formation and possible mild deformity which results, trauma to the lips heals quickly and is seldom serious. Severe lacerations of the lips obviously require surgical repair.

CRACKED AND FISSURED LIPS

Cracking of the lips, with deep fissure formation, often comes from over-exposure to sunlight and cold. It can be very painful and smile-preventing. Fissures are seldom serious and heal quickly when protected with pomade or skin cream.

Cracking in the corners of the mouth of adult people often

indicates ariboflavinosis, a Vitamin B deficiency. If the lip cracking accompanies malnutrition or disease resulting from an inadequate diet, healing of the cracked corners of the mouth usually responds to an adequate diet containing sufficient Vitamin B.

Figure 59: Harelip is a tragedy if not surgically corrected. It is possibly slight as shown here, but can extend completely through the nose.

LEUKOPLAKIA

A milky-colored, slightly thickened coating on the wet inner lining of the lip is the appearance of laukoplakia, considered to be a precancerous condition. It can occur in any area of the mouth and is often associated with the use of tobacco in any form.

Leukoplakia condition always calls for removal by surgery or cautery and for ceasing the use of tobacco. Mouth cleanliness and routine oral hygiene become imperative.

CANCER OF THE LIPS

Any sore, crack, ulcer or other lip disease that persists for over a month could be a lip cancer. This serious problem comes from chronic irritation of common items such as nails, hooks or pipes in the mouth, and to excessive exposure to sunlight. Cancer of the lip has one characteristic feature about it—it never heals completely. Lip cancer, like cancer everywhere, is usually small in its beginning, but is often allowed to reach considerable size before medical aid is sought. Good judgement is overridden often by the hopeful thought that somehow the lip sore will go away by itself.

Happily, malignancies of the lip can be adequately treated. X-ray therapy and surgical procedures combined enjoy a high rate of cure. Only the long-standing, neglected malignancy of the lip grows and spreads beyond the point of possible cure.

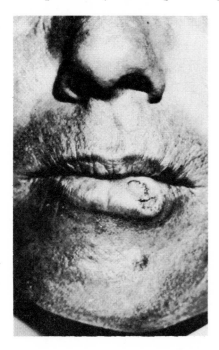

Figure 60: Cancer of the lip is a common disease and a serious one. The lip is exposed to sunlight, tobacco, and many other irritations.

LIP PARALYSIS

Inability to move the lips through certain normal functions, such as puckering, compressing the lips or smiling, or even loss of sensation about the lips, usually means some or all of the muscles controlling the lips are paralyzed. These situations may occur in facial paralysis, in strokes, and in several other complex bodily nerve diseases. These difficulties should quickly be brought to the attention of the physician for early diagnosis and correct treatment.

The Teeth

Modern dentistry and modern America have advanced together. The first dentist came to America in 1776 when the United States was being born. At that time, George Washington's artificial dentures were carved from elk's teeth, and the large part of dentistry was "yanking out the bad ones."

From a beginning concerned entirely with pulling out painful or diseased teeth, dentistry is now concerned primarily with preventive measures which adhere to the adage: "An ounce of prevention is worth a pound of cure."

Examination of the Teeth and Gums

Adult teeth are examined before a well-lighted mirror, possibly with the use of a small, round pocket mirror inserted under the teeth.

1. Examine the teeth for discoloration. Black indented lines in teeth crevices are often indications of decay. A yellow discoloration in worn-down edges of the teeth is the appearance of the inner dentine of the tooth. Gross discoloration of the adult teeth is usually due to tobacco or other external stain.
2. Feel the teeth with tongue and fingers for sharp, jagged edges. The teeth should be smooth and rounded everywhere, and sharp, jagged edges may mean broken teeth or decayed portions of the tooth structure.
3. Determine the firmness of the tooth in its setting. Grasp each tooth and attempt to move it gently in its socket. Very loose teeth, possibly in reddened or retracted gums, may mean pyorrhea.
4. Examine the gums for swelling or soreness about the remaining teeth. Gently press a finger against the gum both inside and outside; look for any blood and pus discharge to indicate pyorrhea. An accompanying tenderness and swelling may represent abscess formation.
5. Run the tip of the finger along the gum surfaces for any soreness, ulceration or external swelling sores, possibly indicating abscess, cancer or other growths.

Diseases of the Teeth and Gums

CARIES AND TOOTH DECAY

Caries and tooth decay are essentially diseases of our younger years and drop significantly in later life.

Decay of the tooth is brought about by acids from sugars and other carbohydrates which remain lodged against the tooth enamel

Fluoridation of our drinking water will do much to resist tooth decay which is practically unknown in many valleys of Switzerland where the water is naturally fluoridated.

The best measures to prevent tooth decay are (1) reducing the frequency of eating candy and other carbohydrates; (2) brushing the teeth well after every meal; (3) use of fluoridated drinking water or tooth paste; (4) regular routine dental inspection to remove and prevent extension of caries in the teeth, along with the dentist's instruction on oral hygiene.

In later years, tooth life is in direct proportion to the care they receive.

ABSCESSED (INFECTED) TEETH

Abscessed (infected) teeth with an accumulation of pus in and about the roots, develop from cracked or decayed teeth. Sometimes the abscess is small but it can reach the size of a walnut with terrific pain, high fever and a greatly swollen jaw and neck.

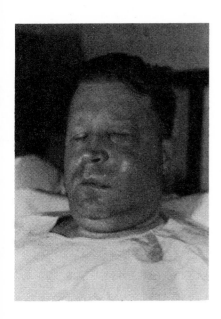

Figure 61: Abscessed teeth create serious infections with terrific pain.

Because of the serious consequences to the rest of the body, and because of the great pain, abscessed teeth must be treated as early as possible. The x-ray can easily locate the abscess and can even pick out small abscesses before they are otherwise discovered.

CRACKED TEETH

A tooth broken from trauma has an exposed dentine or pulp, and perhaps even a nerve. This open invitation to decay can be very painful or not even noticeable, depending on the location of the crack. Unfortunately, jagged, sharp edges of the teeth are often points of chronic irritation for the gum, cheeks and tongue are a strongly suspected cause of cancer within the mouth.

PYORRHEA

Pyorrhea is responsible for the greatest loss of teeth during the adult years. The tooth itself may not be involved, but its surrounding gum is infected and discharges pus as it recedes upward along the tooth. It is very difficult to check and seeks to destroy the tooth socket in the bone.

Pyorrhea is due to a slackening of routine dental care in our later years because we wrongly conclude that the teeth will be lost anyway no matter what care we give them. After the teeth are lost, the gums overcome the infection and the pyorrhea is ended.

CANCER AND SIMILAR GROWTHS OF THE GUMS

Cancer involving the gums has usually extended from a cancer growing in the floor of the mouth or the sides of the tongue. Gum cancer looks like an ulcerating, irregular canker sore and it bleeds easily. Most mouth cancers are though to be due to chronic irritation from broken, jagged teeth, fisherman's hooks or carpenter's nails held in the mouth, and chronic heavy smoking. Several other diseases strongly suspected to invite cancer in the mouth are leukoplakia, syphilis and pernicious anemia.

Non-cancerous growths of the gums are difficult to distinguish from cancer, especially if they will not heal. Accurate diagnosis then requires an expert medical investigation and microscopic identification.

The treatment of cancer anywhere in the mouth is usually a matter of surgery or x-ray treatment. Because these treatments are so markedly successful in early stages but so sadly unsuccessful in later stages, a continued soreness anywhere on the gums or any other region in the mouth should be brought with haste to your doctor's attention.

Care of the Teeth

In adulthood, care of the teeth has two musts about it—a daily routine of cleaning of the teeth and a periodic inspection by a qualified dentist.

Unfortunately many adults still have the opinion that the adult teeth will be lost regardless of the care given them. It is apparent that after the age of 30, this wrong impression creates a "give-up" attitude about our teeth which are then neglected and given no care whatsoever.

Before the age of 25, decay of the teeth is very common because the body has great demands on calcium, phosphorous and other minerals for bone development in competition with the teeth.

After age 25, dental caries and tooth decay dramatically decrease, but even with this good news the adult teeth must strugglle for life in the mouth of a person who gives them little care. Because of this, pyorrhea, infection of the gums, becomes very common. It is true that the life of our teeth is exactly proportional to the care that we give them in adult life.

False Teeth

After the loss of permanent teeth, the wearing of dentures and plates is dictated more by customs of society than by absolute necessity. Few things make an adult look more ridiculous than the absence of one or more front teeth when he smiles.

Adjustment to the wearing of artificial teeth may be diffcult, but patience and the care and guidance of a good dentist will overcome this difficulty.

The Tongue

"Let me see your tongue" has long been heard from health examiners, grandmothers and doctors alike. It has long been known the tongue reflects greatly our state of health or disease.

In function, the tongue enters into chewing, swallowing, tasting and talking; it also has definite diseases to contend with.

Examination of the Tongue

1. In a natural light, examine the tongue for any unusual discoloration. Press the extended tongue between the thumb and forefinger (wrapped in handkerchief), and pull the tongue gently forward and downward for complete exposure. Note any irregular "map-like" gray coating, yellowish-brown discoloration, bluish discoloration or extreme fiery redness.

2. Examine the tongue for any white, leathery and possibly stiffened areas. Such whitened regions are often leukoplakia.

3. Observe closely in the forcibly extended tongue any sore, ulcer, bleeding or unusual growths visible or touchable. Particularly examine the sides, under-surface and back of the tongue as far as possible. The finding of any definite sore or lesion of the tongue as described may mean cancer.

4. Observe the tongue's ability to move in all directions, to all regions of the mouth. Paralysis in any direction is an important finding of the tongue.

Diseases of the Tongue

The tongue, like the rest of the inner surface of the mouth, may have diseases in common with the inner mouth cavity. However, its refinements in touching and tasting bring it in contact with all substances entering the mouth and expose it to more irritations than the rest of the oral cavity.

TONGUE-TIE AND STUTTERING

Tongue-tie and stuttering are not the same diseases.

Actually, tongue-tie is a tieing of the tongue to the floor of the mouth by a thickened, shortened frenum. We see it in the mirror by raising the tongue up high. The simple surgical procedure of cutting the short frenum ends the tongue-tie.

Stuttering is not a difficulty of the tongue, but of the nervous system behind it. Often a tide of temporary anxiety brings on stuttering, which most doctors think is connected with too much stress somewhere in the background.

Overcoming difficult stuttering problems takes patience and possibly professional help. One successful therapy has been the development of singing ability. Singing will override a stutter—and sometimes, quite by accident, develop an accomplished singer.

DISCOLORATION

Gray Tongue Discoloration, a coat on the tongue with a map-like appearance, is called "geographic tongue" and is of little significance. This condition is known to persist for years without any serious disease being present. Most of the time, it disappears quickly without any treatment and often represents a temporary gastric upset.

Brownish-yellow Tongue Discoloration has two possible meanings. The first is the over-use of tobacco which stains the tongue with nicotine and tars to produce a brownish stain on its surface. The stain will disappear shortly after the use of tobacco is stopped.

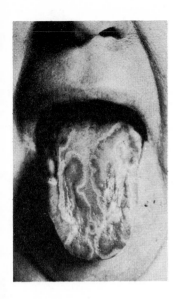

Figure 62: Geographic
tongue does not
mean serious
disease.

The second possible meaning of a brownish-yellow tongue is pernicious anemia. When the possibility of tobacco staining is not present, and the patient is 50 years of age or over, the lemon-yellow tongue may have serious meaning and should be seen by the physician.

Bluish Discoloration on the tongue is usually a type of birthmark. It is painless, does not bleed and is not sore. It is slightly elevated and occasionally covered with small amounts of hair. These birthmarks have nuisance value but little actual danger and, of course, they exist from birth.

Fiery-red Discoloration of the tongue usually means glossitis, an irritated tongue. It can be quite painful but appears to have no single definite cause. It can be due to actual burns from hot foods or caused by commonplace mouth infections, and frequently it accompanies vitamin deficiences, particulary Vitamin B_{12}. When Vitamin B_{12} is given to the patient, the glossitis frequently disappears. The condition is thought by some physicians to be a precancerous condition, and therefore it is worthy of careful observation.

LEUKOPLAKIA

Leukoplakia looks like a whitish discoloration or a soft wet crusting on the tongue surface and on the inner surface of the cheek. It is the result of chronic irritation such as over-use of tobacco, but is also thought at times to be related to syphilis or other systemic diseases.

Leukoplakia definitely is a pre-cancerous condition and must be treated by the physician. The treatment of leukoplakia is its removal with cautery or surgery by the physician.

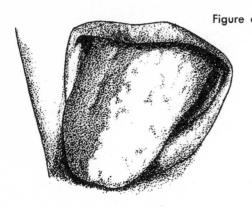

Figure 63: Leukoplakia on the tongue is a white, leathery, sometimes sore formation resulting from chronic irritation. Often caused by smoking, it is considered potentially cancerous and should not be ignored.

CANCER OF THE TONGUE

Any ulcer or sore on the tongue could be the beginning of cancer in the adult. Tongue cancer makes up three percent of all bodily cancer and is found much more often in the male than the female. It is definitely a disease of later years and is often associated with jagged and broken teeth or other disease irritations such as leukoplakia, glossitis or syphilis. In recent years its association with heavy smoking has been growing higher and higher.

Any sore on the tongue present for over two weeks demands a physician's attention.

PARALYSIS OF THE TONGUE

The tongue normally has great agility to move in any direction including straight out. When it loses its ability to move, especially to one side, difficulties such as strokes are quickly suspected. Paralysis of the tongue, whether in whole or part, almost always represents difficulty with nerves which bring motion ability to the tongue muscle, and the physician's examination alone can uncover the basic difficulties.

ENLARGED TONGUE

An enormously enlarged tongue (macroglossia) sometimes is found in unusual diseases, along with accompanying enlargement of other soft tissue areas of the body, such as the lips, nose and facial features (Figure 64). Diagnosis and treatment for a greatly enlarged tongue become considerably involved even for the physician.

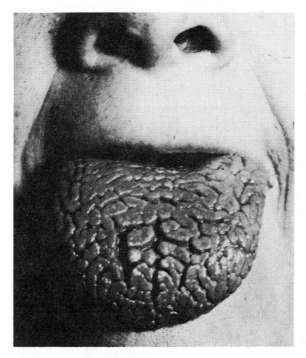

Figure 64: This enlarged tongue was part of an involved disease of the entire system.

The Pharynx

The pharynx is the chamber behind the mouth. It extends upward behind the nose and down behind the tongue as far as our vocal cords, the larynx. We use this pharynx to breathe through, speak through and swallow through, and it bothers us mostly with its tonsils, adenoids and sore throats.

Examination of the Pharynx

We can see the back wall of the pharynx in a mirror by opening the mouth wide and pulling on the tongue with the fingers wrapped in a handkerchief. It is difficult to see up behind the nose or down behind the tongue.

1. Look at the sides of the pharynx where the tongue appears to originate, and see the irregular, flesh-colored tonsils on each side. In adults, they can be atrophied to pea-size but when infected, the tonsils appear enlarged, reddened, and flecked with visible pus pockets.
2. With a flashlight, examine the back wall of the pharynx while pulling on the tongue. An all-over redness with noticeable soreness usually means pharyngitis, as in colds, sore throats, tonsilitis et cetera.
3. Examine the wall of the pharynx on all sides and the back of the tongue if possible for any one particular sore, ulcer or bleeding point. This may mean abscess formation or tumor growth in the adult.

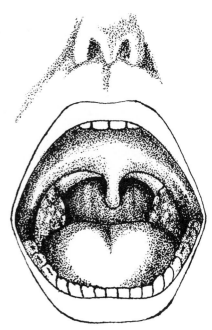

Figure 65: The pharynx is the region of the tonsils, back part of the nose and swallowing area. It is probably the most examined of all body regions, and reflects many diseases.

Diseases of the Pharynx-Larynx Region

PHARYNGITIS

A general redness like that of raw hamburger, covered with many small blood vessels, is the appearance of the irritated pharynx—called pharyngitis. It frequently accompanies upper respiratory infection, bronchitis, sinus disease, virus infection and various types of sore throat. If hoarseness is also present, it means that the vocal cords, which cannot be seen easily, are also irritated along with the rest of the pharynx and larynx. Treatment of pharyngitis by itself frequently consists of gargling with plain water or salt water solution. But since ,pharyngitis usually accompanies other diseases, such as tonsilitis, a cold or an allergy, the treatment for these associated diseases may have to come first.

The treatment for most pharyngeal or upper respiratory "infections" includes salt water gargling, warm drinks, ordinary aspirin and bed rest. After this, the doctor may elect the use of antibiotics such as Penicillin, Sulfa drugs or other antibiotics.

Continued, chronic pharyngitis is very common in large crowded cities with day-to-day breathing of heavy fumes, dust and just plain big city dirt.

These problems annually drive many people from large towns into suburban areas or smaller towns where the air is clear.

TONSILITIS

Infection of the tonsils is frequent in childhood and in adults as well. Also, tonsils which might look innocent may harbor and distribute bacterial organisms responsible for other diseases such as arthritis, kidney disease and sore throats, among others.

The treatment of tonsils and adenoids (the pharyngeal tonsils) is surgical removal, which is usually done in early years. Only occasionally will the difficulty recur.

Removal of tonsils in later years is slightly more difficult than in childhood, but it is often followed by relief from arthritic pains and a host of other diseases which have been kept alive by long infected tonsils.

CANCER OF THE PHARYNX

Malignant growth, usually cancer, occurs in the pharynx, the base of the tongue and the vocal cords. Unfortunately, this area cannot be seen without the aid of special mirrors and lighting arrangements.

The features which arouse suspicion of malignancy in the pharynx are hoarseness, pain and bleeding which occur together to a varying degree. Anyone aged 50 who is caughing blood and has a soreness in his throat certainly should see his physician. Hoarseness is a very common difficulty at all ages, and is no cause for alarm following brief periods of sore throat, upper respiratory disease or following football games. However, a persistent hoarseness of several weeks or more in a person of middle-age or later should prompt suspicion of serious vocal cord disease including cancer.

There are other growths in this region such as polyps, cysts and plain irritations, all of which are easily treated by the physician, but the possibility of cancerous disease in the pharynx region demands early attention, diagnosis and treatment.

HALITOSIS (BAD BREATH)

This difficulty concerns everyone and can be very offensive and embarrassing, and though it is exaggerated by widely publicized advertising, halitosis is still a very real problem today. Prevention of an offensive breath is mostly a matter of effective oral hygiene including cleaning the teeth and mouth after every meal, and at the very least rinsing the mouth well. Presistent cases of halitosis, however, warrant the physician's help in determining the cause. His investigation may uncover disease within the mouth, nose, or sinus area, or even in the lung and bronchial tubes.

COUGHING

The ordinary cough is due to irritation of the larynx or vocal cords by colds, infections or irritations in the pharynx. It is frequently described as a tickling or rasping soreness and is dry and hacking; it often responds to gargles and rest.

When large amounts of sputum are produced with coughing, the most probable site of difficulty is in the lungs or bronchial tubes. Figure 66 illustrates one "cure" for coughing.

ALLERGY

Allergy of the nose and throat covers many ills. Continuous or repeated colds, sore throats, sinus troubles, coughing and other pharyngeal problems which do not respond to usual medical treatments often are actual allergic problems. Probably the question of exactly when and where allergy begins and ends will never be entirely settled, but there is much we can do about this problem today.

Often the history of an allergic disease identifies it. The sufferer's story of seasonal recurrence can be very characteristic. So is his story of repeated troubles with a certain food, a certain geographic area, certain animals or certain fumes, oils and chemicals.

The ordinary allergic history is a long story in which the suf-

Strasenburgh Laboratories, Rochester, N. Y.

Figure 66: Constantly coughing at people could lead to a direct type of cure.

ferer has learned the hard way—by trial and error. He has learned from experience to stay away from possible allergens such as strawberries, chocolate, cleaning fluids, heavy wooded areas, or perhaps, horses. He has also learned that he is not alone during certain periods like hay fever season. If he is a wise man, he will already have engaged a physician experienced in allergic diseases to guide him through his problems.

Allergic diseases begin shortly after birth in a few, but for most of us, these problems arrive later on—after enough time has elapsed to allow us repeated exposure to some allergenic substance. We know that almost 25 percent of people have some large or small allergic problem which usually grows increasingly noticeable year after year.

If one has an allergic problem he should consult a good allergist for genuine experienced help.

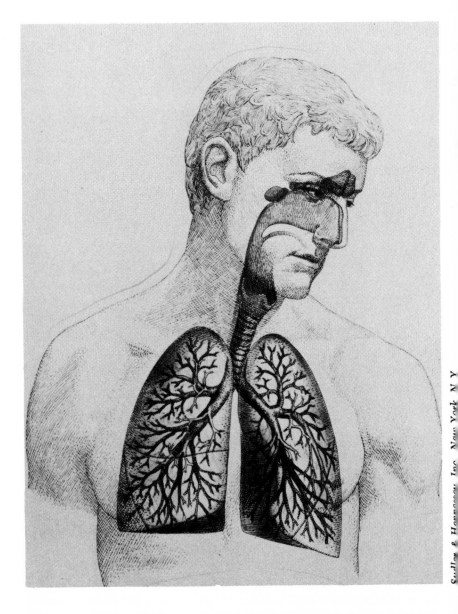

Figure 67: Allergy problems of the respiratory tree—like asthma and hay fever—are our best known allergic diseases.

The Neck

The neck does much more than merely support the head for the body; it carries into the system every drop that we drink, every bite that we swallow and every breath that we inhale. It also carries the large blood vessels to the head and brain; it carries the entire spinal cord to the body; it is the location of our all-important thyroid gland.

In many ways, the neck is more than just another body area; it is a thing of beauty in women and a location of serious disease in the long history of mankind.

Examination of the Neck

The neck is best examined in a well-lighted position with the adult standing before a double mirror for self-examination.

1. Note the flexibility of the neck. Bend the head slowly forward and backward, from side to side, and rotate to the right or left. Stiffness or soreness brought out by these actions may indicate arthritis, irritation in the neck muscles and ligaments, or an infection in the neck.
2. Feel for enlarged neck glands. Bend the head back and feel along the sides of the neck muscles, stretching from the breastbone to the mastoid bone just behind the ear. Englarged glands in this region can be rolled under the finger tips and often are painful to touch.
3. Feel in the region of the thyroid gland. With the thumb and forefinger, press gently on the sides of the windpipe just above the collarbone. Swallow and feel the normally smooth thyroid gland rise and fall along the windpipe.

Diseases of the Neck

SORE STIFF NECK

Stiffness in the neck is caused by irritation in the muscles, bones, and ligaments that make up the spine and the neck region. A sudden soreness or stiffness is often due to the strain of unusual neck-bending activities, such as gardening work or income tax preparation, and usually a day or two of rest will bring about relief. Stiffness or pain of the neck of a recurrent nature is most often caused by continuing difficulties resulting from sprains, fractures or arthritis. These continuing difficulties also bring up the possibility of infection elsewhere in the body, such as the teeth or tonsils.

The treatment of neck stiffness and soreness of a long-standing or recurrent nature depends upon its cause. X-rays may reveal local difficulties in the vertebrae, or examination of the entire body may reveal a distant infection causing arthritis in the neck. The only treatment a person should attempt for himself in these matters is regulation of elimination, diet, proper rest and avoidance of exceptional exercise in the neck region. Attempts to "work out" a long-standing neck difficulty usually only make the problem worse. Continuing soreness or pain in the neck should be investigated by the physician for possible underlying disease.

ENLARGED GLANDS IN THE NECK

Enlarged neck glands usually follow an infection in the mouth, possibly of the teeth, tongue or pharynx. These enlarged glands can be felt just below the ear, under the angle of the jaw. They extend downward along the neck muscles and are often tender to touch. If they are infected, these glands are usually painful without being touched at all.

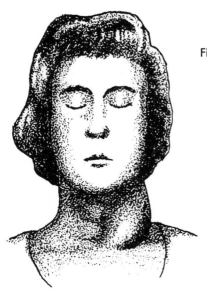

Figure 68: Neck growths and enlargements, present since childhood, often are the result of abnormal development. Fost-growing enlargement at any age is most likely due to infectious processes, but may mean cancerous disease. Goiter moves up and down with the swallowing act and is most often close to the midline.

Enlarged neck glands are also associated with tumor growth in the oral cavity of the lip, tongue, gum, jaw or tonsil. These glands in the neck also accompany systemic lymphoid diseases such as Hodgkin's Disease and leukemia. Any neck enlargement lasting more than a week may represent serious disease and the physician should be consulted without delay.

THYROGLOSSAL DUCT CYST

Occasionally, young adults may discover a smooth rounded enlargement in the midline of the neck down an inch or two from the chin itself. This is the classic location of thyroglossal duct disease which is a minor defect of incomplete embryonic growth. This smooth growth may come and go, but in its worse stages will rupture and constantly drain. It is due to the presence of a small channel directly into the pharynx at the internal end of the tongue.

Treatment of thyroglossal duct disease is complete surgical removal.

THE THYROID GLAND AND ITS DISEASE

The thyroid gland is our fire and ambition gland, and its diseases therefore affect us in our drive, our willingness to work, our "on the ball" attitude, and generally determine whether we become fireballs or rocking chair cases.

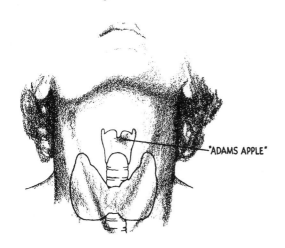

"ADAMS APPLE"

Figure 69: The thyroid gland is butterfly-shaped and wrapped around the front of the windpipe. Hard to feel in its normal state, it rides up and down with the windpipe in the act of swallowing.

Also any enlargement of the thyroid gland is significant because this gland embraces the windpipe and is firmly attached to it. If this enlargement is great enough, it may compress our windpipe and create difficulty in breathing and sometimes in swallowing.

COLLOID GOITRE

This smooth balloon-like enlargement was often found in young women who were otherwise in perfect health. This was the goitre which resulted from insufficient iodine in the diet, and which was so sharply reduced by adding iodine to table salt. When seen today, colloid goitre is treated with iodine therapy for a temporary period, and is usually followed by a rapid reduction in the size of the thyroid gland.

OVERACTIVE THYROID (HYPERTHYROIDISM)

Thyroid overactivity often causes extreme nervousness and weight loss. The gland is not necessarily enlarged, but it often does have a bumpy, nodular or grapelike surface which can be felt with the fingers during the act of swallowing. An overactive thyroid is very likely to create cardiac disease, loss of weight, tremor of the fingers, excessive perspiration and extreme nervousness.

Overactivity of the thyroid is treated either by medication, surgery or x-ray. It is only after an adequate examination that the course of best treatment can be known.

In the past, an overactive thyroid was simply removed by surgery. Soon came the development of so-called anti-thyroid drugs which seemed to put a brake on the overactive thyroid, and still later medical research introduced radioactive types of thyroid drug therapy.

In this treatment, patients with an overactive thyroid are given to drink a measured amount of radioactive iodine. This is simply iodine which has been exposed to the atomic emission from government controlled atomic piles, and when it is ingested into the body, the radioactive iodine lowers the function of the overactive thyroid to a desired level. These treatments today are undergoing refinement and improvement constantly.

UNDERACTIVE THYROID (HYPOTHYROIDISM)

A thyroid gland with too feeble a function is soon registered throughout the body as weight gain without over-eating, long sleep accompanied by constant fatigue and often a dry skin with dull unmanageable hair.

Since the thyroid is our get-up-and-go gland, we feel that all drive is lost when its function is low. Treatment of an underactive thyroid is simple. It is thyroid hormone taken orally under the guidance of the physician, who thus can raise the thyroid influence in the body to the desired level.

CANCER OF THE THYROID GLAND

Thyroid cancer is not a common disease and it is difficult to discover. This disease is suspected whenever a solitary lump is felt in the thyroid gland during the act of swallowing. Such a finding demands the examination and diagnosis of a doctor skilled in this field as treatment of cancer anywhere in the body should never be postponed.

Treatment of cancer of the thyroid often is treated by a surgical operation but sometimes also by radioactive drug therapy. Only the physician can judge the extent and nature of the disease, and thus accurately prescribe the right treatment.

Section

3

THE CHEST

The chest is a cage of ribs, vertebrae and breastbone connected with muscles, ligaments and covered with skin. Externally, the chest includes the collarbone, the breastbone, the ribs and upper spine, the muscles to the arm and the breast. Internally, the chest houses and protects the heart, lungs and esophagus.

Examination of the External Chest

The adult stands unclothed to the waist before a full-length mirror to make the following observations:

1. The adult breastbone has a bony ridge two inches from its top, named the sternal angle, but it is otherwise flat from top to bottom. In the center, where the ribs join, a small tender bone called the ziphoid process is easily felt. It is often somewhat off to one side.
2. Breathing should produce painless and equal rib motion on both sides. Limited or painful motion on one side could mean internal lung diseases such as pleurisy, bronchiectasis, pneumonia, lung abscess or tuberculosis.
3. With the fingertips, press firmly against the ribs along the sides of the breastbone; painful spots in this region on firm pressure or possibly even with deep breathing, may indicate Tietze's Syndrome, a form of arthritis.
4. In right-handed people the right shoulder is lower than the left, but a vast difference in shoulder level may mean curvature of the spine or deformity of the shoulder.

Examination of the Female Breast

1. Stand before the mirror in your usual erect position with all clothing removed above the waist (Figure 70). Note any difference of the breast in size, shape or position and closely inspect the nipple itself for possible inversion.

2. Raise both arms straight overhead and lean slightly forward in front of the mirror (Figure 71). Note any denting or bulging irregularity of the skin surface. Look especially for skin areas of "peau d'orange", a finely dimpled orangelike skin.

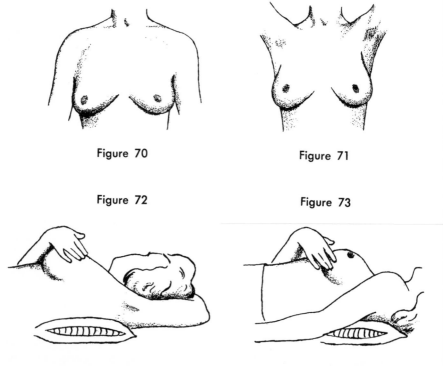

Figure 70   Figure 71

Figure 72   Figure 73

3. In a lying-down position, elevate the left shoulder blade on a pillow and rest the left arm under your head (Figure 72). With the right hand, feel the left breast along radial (wagon wheel spoke) lines. Next, feel the inner half of the breast and then the outer half. Note any solitary enlargements, lumps or masses.

4. Now place the left arm at your side, and with the right hand again feel the left breast along its radial lines (Figure 73).

Feel first the outer and then the inner half of the breast. The normal rubbery soft breast tissue may have an all-over granular feeling, but lumps, nodules or soreness are definitely abnormal findings.

Abnormalities of the Chest Wall and Breast

Emphysema (Barrel Chest)

This chest is constantly enlarged, actually looking like a barrel. The real disease, however, is deeper within the thinned-out lung tissue, and the chest wall overexpands in an attempt to better use the remaining tissue.

Lateral Curvature of the Spine (Scoliosis)

Curvature of the spine is common at all ages, but seen mostly in later years, and is the result of a birth defect, childhood rickets, mild poliomyelitis or leg difficulties.

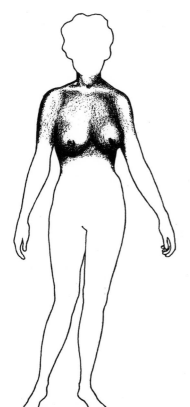

Figure 74: The breast has just one function but many diseases. Most of its difficulties occur in the female, but both sexes share in breast diseases.

Work habits can produce a mild degree of curvature of the spine, but most curvatures are not even suspected until the deformity is accidentally found in an examination. Unless they are severe, lateral curvatures seldom cause any difficulty. (See Deformities of the Spine).

Breast Abnormalities

Typical female breast development begins at about age 11, and has attained nearadult development by about the age of 14.

Breast difficulties and abnormalities in adults give rise to one consuming fear—cancer. The sobering news is that 15,000 deaths occur yearly in the United States alone from breast cancer. It is well to know, however, that most breat difficulties are not cancers.

Extra Breast (Polymastia)

This is not a disease; it is more a curiosity than anything else. Usually, only the nipple is present and located just below the normal breast in a line towards the umbilicus. An extra breast is thought to be possibly a throw-back in genetics to the lower vertebrate animals in which six to eight teats were present to nourish the newborn litter.

Extra breasts are not indicative of cancer or any other disease; they are usually removed for cosmetic reasons only.

Enlargement (Hypertrhopy)

The greatly enlarged breast may present considerable inconvenience for some, or it may be a highly desired goal for others. It has no great significance in disease for the present or future.

Nipple Retraction

A retracted nipple which has existed since breast development be-

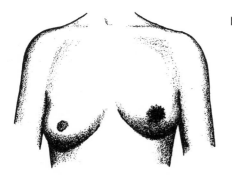

Figure 75: Nipple retraction of many years usually has no significance, but a recently retracted nipple may mean serious disease.

gan has little significance. However, when the nipple retraction has been a recent development, it may have great significance for malignant disease of the breast. It is the first sign of trouble in about three percent of all breast cancers, and demands a physician's examination immediately.

Skin Disease about the Nipple

A reddened or itching irritation of the skin immediately about the nipple may have genuine disease significance. When the irritation has an obvious cause, such as in nursing or following trauma after an auto accident, the course of treatment also becomes obvious.

When a breast skin irritation is without apparent cause, and lasts longer than two weeks, it is possibly the "Paget's Disease" present in one percent of all breast cancers. It should be examined by the physician immediately.

Discharge from the Nipple

The breast's normal function is discharge of milk during nursing.

There are periods when the adult breast produces a discharge not associated with nursing, from hormonal over-stimulation of the breast, but they require a physician's examination to be distinguished from other more significant disease.

A nipple discharge has definite disease significance in the later or post-menopausal years. Studies have shown that a nipple discharge, not blood stained, is associated with about three percent of all breast cancers. When a nipple discharge in this age group is blood stained, the cancer possibilities in the breast rise to nearly 50 percent. The physician's examination of all breast discharges is imperative for accurate diagnosis and correct treatment.

Dimpled Skin

Skin of the breast with a dimpled orange skin appearance has great significance in breast disease. This somewhat hardened skin has the name peau d'orange (look of an orange), and it signifies increased pressure under the skin. If it follows trauma, such as an automobile accident, it has very little meaning, but when it occurs in the over-50 age group, without any explainable reason, it assumes great importance. It is the first sign of trouble in about one percent of breast cancer, and it makes necessary the physician's examination.

Lump in the Breast

A lump, mass or nodule is all important finding in breast disease.

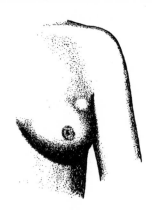

Figure 76: A breast lump is always significant. While only one out
of ten lumps is actually serious, only a physician can
advise a proper course of
action.

It is most often discovered accidentally during routine bathing or
dressing, and more recently through routine self-examination as
recommended by so many health societies. Unfortunately, the discovery of a lump in the breast usually creates panic in a woman
who then makes a fearful half-despairing visit to her physician for
an examination. It is well to know that although 10 percent of all
breast lumps are of cancerous nature, the remaining 90 percent are
not. It should be apparent, however, that all breast lumps should be
examined by a physician without delay.

Pain in the Breast

Pain is not importantly related to cancerous disease of the breast.
Cancer in the breast is notoriously silent and painless until far
advanced, and only two percent of all cancers are painful. However,
in the post-menopausal age, pain combined with a breast lump,
nipple discharge or skin changes demands the physician's examination for correct diagnosis.

Cystic Disease of the Breast

This is the most common of all breast difficulties. It is caused by
the ebb and flow of the hormonal tide, a normal feature of every
menstrual period.

Preceding each menstrual period, the compartments of the breast
enlarge and the entire breast swells. When the tide flows out, a

few of these compartments become blocked and do not reduce in size as they should. After this process is repeated three or four months, the compartments of the breast which have not reduced in size as the neighboring compartments have, begin to stand out and can be palpated with the fingers as painful and tender lumps in the breast.

Multiple lumps always speak of a noncancerous condition.

In the treatment of cystic disease we must first remove the possibility of cancer. This is achieved with a breast biopsy, a minor surgical procedure removing a small portion of breast tissue for microscopic study.

The physician often uses hormonal therapy for relief of the pain and tenderness of cystic disease of the breast.

Cancer of the Breast

Cancer of the female breast is very common and accounts for almost one out of every five human cancers. Only rarely does it occur in the male breast.

Breast cancer is rare before the age of 35 years, but then it rises to a peak incidence at 54 years. Because it occurs more often in women who have had no children, pregnancy appears to have a protective influence. This contrasts sharply with the other common cancer in women—cancer of the cervix—which is definitely more common in women who have borne children.

Most medical authorities agree that trauma from the outside is not a factor in this disease. As though to prove this we find cancer of the breast less frequently among laboring and farming women than in women with lighter pursuits in life.

About the best thing that can attend cancer of the breast is an early discovery. Toward this goal, we direct our efforts in periodical physical examinations and regular self-examination.

The technique and possible findings of self-examination of the female breast are detailed in previous pages.

Examination of the Internal Chest

The internal chest must be examined without the aid of sight or touch, except when the x-ray can be used. Therefore the heart, lungs and esophagus are examined by determining how well they are functioning, and from their function we judge their condition. See Figure 77 for details of normal chest structure.

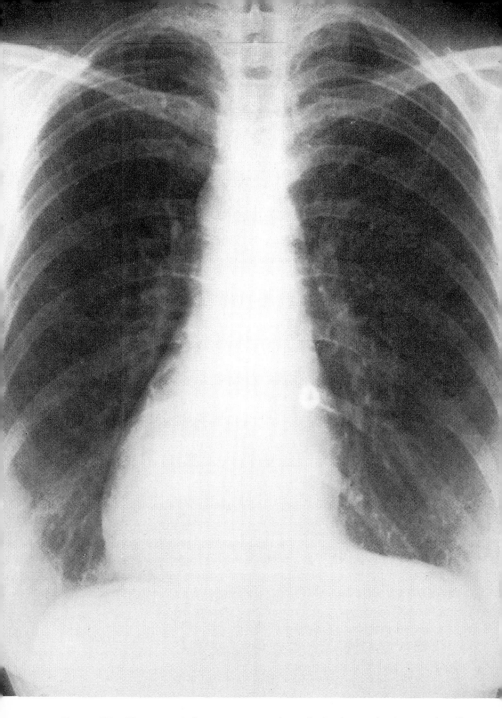

Figure 77: The normal chest x-ray sees through the lungs. It pictures the ribs, the heart, the clavicle or "collarbone" and the diaphragm at the bottom of the chest itself. The normal lung markings are faintly seen toward the center of the chest and are the root or hilus of the lung.

The Esophagus

The function of the esophagus (swallowing tube) is to carry swallowed nourishment from the throat into the stomach. Nearly all esophagus difficulties interfere with this swallowing act.

1. Swallow on ordinary glass of water. This is normally done easily, but pain or vomiting is usually due to an obstruction. In children beyond the infancy stage, such an obstruction can occur from the ingestion of dangerous chemicals such as lye or other caustics sometimes found about the home. In the adult, painful swallowing means a stricture of the esophagus (usually caused by swallowing lye in childhood), a diverticulum, or a cancer in the esophagus.

2. Swallow some soft foot, like cereal or mashed potato. This is an advance over swallowing water, but these soft foods are normally carried down the esophagus without sensation. The appearance of pain on swallowing may indicate an obstruction of the esophagus which is not complete.

3. Swallow a piece of solid food, such as meat or soft rolled bread. Normally, solid food can be felt passing down the esophagus painlessly. Pain with this swallowing act may indicate esophagitis (heartburn), or beginning tumor growth.

DISEASES OF THE ESOPHAGUS

Heartburn (Esophagitis)

Heartburn is a sharp, burning chest pain beginning slowly an hour or so after eating, and growing constantly to feel like a knot inside the chest. It is caused by stomach acids backing up into the esophagus to create a painful irritation which is often thought to be a heart attack. This is where the name heartburn comes from.

Severe as heartburn pain is, miraculously quick relief can be obtained by drinking milk, soda or even plain water. Relief is obtained because the swallowed food or liquid washes the stomach acids out of the esophagus and relieves the irritation.

After many years without treatment, severe heartburn may eventually stricture and obstruct the esophagus.

Heartburn is very simple, both in cause and in temporary treatment, but its complication of stricture formation creates an extremely complex medical-surgical problem requiring exceptionally skilled treatment for necessary relief.

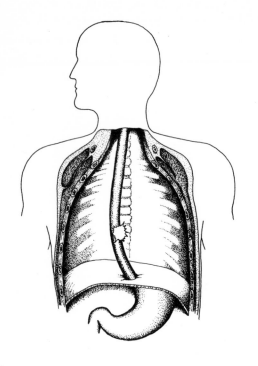

Figure 78: Heartburn is caused by stomach acids backing up into the esophagus. The resulting pain is felt in the chest and may become severe. It is often thought to be a heart attack.

Diverticulum of the Esophagus

A diverticulum is a ballooned-out weak spot on the esophagus, usually in the neck level, that causes swallowing difficulty when food lodges in it. This difficulty does not completely and permanently obstruct the swallowing tube, but rather gives partial obstruction on and off for a long time. An x-ray examination is required to identify a diverticulum but further treatment is often not necessary.

Stricture of the Esophagus

Stricture of the esophagus is simply an abnormal narrowing of the swallowing tube, partly obstructing its channel. Most strictures are the result of a scar which contracts as all scars do. Probably the greatest number of scar strictures in the esophagus form after accidental swallowing of caustic liquids which burn or erode the lining wall and leave a scar behind.

An esophageal sticture is treated by dilating it or stretching it open, and the physician has specially made instruments for this purpose. Surgery is used only for the stricture of severe degrees.

Cancer of the Esophagus

Cancer of the esophagus occurs mostly in men of middle age and older. It grows slowly and gradually obstructs the esophagus to make swallowing progressively more painful and difficult.

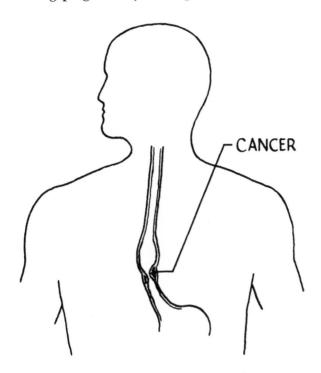

CANCER

Figure 79: Stricture blocking the esophagus or swallowing tube is usually due to cancer when it begins after the age of 50, but accidental swallowing of lime or other corrosive liquids also may cause stricture. Surgical correction of the stricture is necessary to allow food to pass.

At first the difficulty is slight, but as the growth enlarges, the swallowing chanel grows narrower and it becomes more painful to swallow solid foods. To avoid pain, the diet is changed to soft or liquid, but with further obstruction of the swallowing tube by the tumor growth, even liquids eventually produce pain in swallowing. Finally, because food intake is so diminished, weight loss begins and extreme weakness rapidly follows.

Treatment of cancer in the esophagus demands relief of the swallowing obstruction and removal of the cancerous growth. This can be achieved by surgical means and sometimes by cobalt x-ray therapy. This treatment requires exceptional skill and should always be placed in the hands of a physician experienced in this field.

The Lungs

Our lungs exist for just one purpose—bringing the blood into close contact with air. In the lungs, the blood absorbs oxygen from the inhaled air and throws off CO_2 in the exhaled air. We must have constant lung function at the moment of birth and through all of life. If man is removed from his "sea of air," he cannot live. See Figure 80 for details of the lungs.

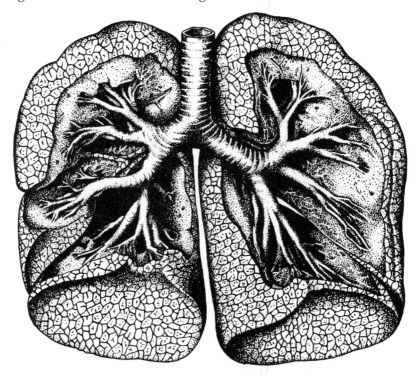

Figure 80: Like tree roots, the airway from the throat branches into the spongy lung tissue. Millions of tiny air balloons on its branches are thus connected to the outside; lung expansion sucks in fresh air and contraction forces out exhaust air. The cycle is completed about 20 times per minute for effective respiration. An adult's deepest breath generally has a volume exceeding one gallon of air.

Examination of the Lungs

1. Attempt to continue inhaling and exhaling normally while counting the breaths per minute. Normal breathing varies between 16 to 20 breaths per minute and should be absolutely painless. Rapid breathing, considerably in excess of this rate, may indicate a bodily fever or lung disease. Painful breathing, especially if sharp, is usually the pain of pleurisy.

2. Place the palms on each side of the bare chest and breathe deeply several times. No vibrating or rasping sensations should be felt; no wheezing or gurgling sound should be heard. Detection of such abnormalities may indicate asthma or bronchitis.

3. After breathing deeply several times, exhale completely and then cough until some sputum is obtained. Normal sputum contains no bloody flecks under any circumstances. The presence of blood may mean tuberculosis, lung abscess, bronchiectasis or cancer of the lung.

4. Measure your breath volume by exhaling the deepest possible breath completely into a toy balloon. Clamp the balloon and push it down into an already filled pail of water. When the water has ceased to overflow, withdraw the balloon and measure accurately the water necessary to refill the pail. This volume should equal at least one gallon —the same as the smallest normal breathing capacity of the lung. A total breath volume markedly under one gallon may indicate heart disease, emphysema or other lung-destroying diseases.

Diseases of the Lungs

BRONCHITIS

Bronchitis is an inflammation of the bronchial tubes. It frequently follows a cold and produces a cough, a sensation of tightness in the chest and a mild fever. Bronchitis can occur by itself, as when heavy dust or noxious vapors are inhaled, but it usually occurs with other difficulties such as a cold, influenza, grippe or allergic states.

BRONCHIECTASIS

Bronchiectasis is a chronic lung disease which affects nearly three percent of all adults. In this disease, the bronchial tubes become stretched and ballooned out. It is most often caused by measles or whooping cough infection of early childhood, which tends to weaken the bronchial tubes. Then as age increases and repeated episodes of bronchitis occur, bronchiectasis begins. Most people with slight bronchiectasis have little trouble and usually do not know they have the disease, but people who have severe bronchiectasis often will cough up in a day a full cup or more of thick, yellow sputum, which at times is blood-streaked.

This disease becomes most disabling and is occasionally confused with lung cancer. The successful treatment of bronchiectasis requires the careful guidance of a physician skilled in lung diseases.

PLEURISY

Pleurisy is not itself a disease, but rather is a chest pain caused by the lung and chest wall rubbing against each other. In ordinary breathing, the smooth glistening lung surface glides painlessly over the inner chest wall, as the eyelid glides over the eye. But if either the lung itself or the chestwall becomes irritated, this gliding action becomes a painful rubbing action, made worse with deep breathing and relieved only with very shallow breathing.

Many pains are called pleurisy, but unless the pain can be made worse with deep breathing and relieved with shallow breathing, the pain is probably not true pleurisy pain.

Pleurisy is most often caused by colds, bronchitis or pneumonia, but it can indicate the presence of more serious disease such as lung abscess, tuberculosis or cancer of the lung. Besides having an annual check-up and chest x-ray, frequent or severe pleurisy calls for the physician's investigation and diagnosis.

EMPHYSEMA

Emphysema is a thinning out of the lung tissue itself, and is rare below the age of 40. Over the years, repeated lung infections, allergies and industrial atmosphere can destroy large amounts of lung tissue. Then when not enough lung tissue remains to carry on easy breathing, more rapid breathing is required. It is similar to being on mountain tops where breathing is difficult because the air is rarified, and more rapid breathing is necessary to make up for the lesser amount of air present to be breathed. See in Figure 82 how emphysema causes a barrel chest appearance.

Emphysema is accompainied by a chronic cough described as a dry hack, which does not produce sputum as in other lung diseases.

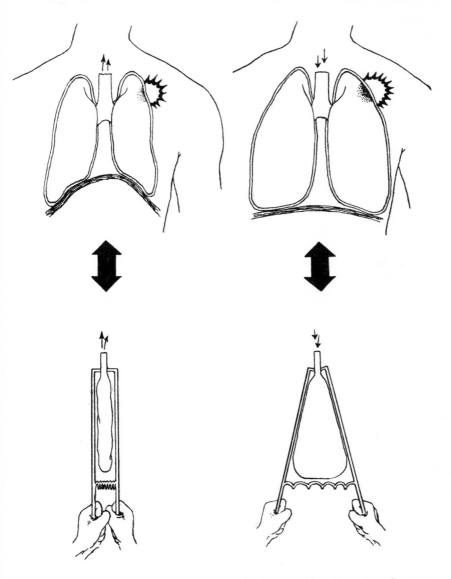

Figure 81: Pain of pleurisy is caused by the lung "rubbing" against the outer chest wall. In normal breathing, the lung glides in the chest, like a swimmer in water. Brushing against a rough surface (broken ribs) produces knife-like pain. To and fro motion of the lung is produced by the bellows-like motion of the outer chest wall. Holding the breath stops the pain; shallow breathing produces only slight pain; deep breathing causes terrific pain. But breathing in any way would not effect pain from the heart.

Cure of emphysema is not entirely possible, but the physician can advise measures which make breathing easier. They are cessation of smoking, avoidance of dusty areas, and even recommending a move for the patient to a climate with clearer air.

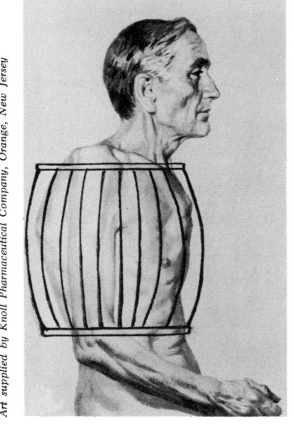

Art supplied by Knoll Pharmaceutical Company, Orange, New Jersey

Figure 82: Emphysema means a thinned out lung. This lung expands in an effort to contact more air and to absorb more oxygen. The result is the barrel chest so characteristic of emphysema.

LUNG ABSCESS

Lung abscess is a boil-like pocket of pus in the lungs. It is accompained by pleurisy pain, fever and chills, loss of weight and the general appearance of very severe disease. It is also accompanied by a very productive cough which brings up great quantities of pus and often a bloody sputum as well. Any of these symptoms should be enough to send a person running to his physician.

Lung abscess is a very serious infection of the lung following pneumonia or other lung infections. It can also follow the inhalation of solid particles, such as fragments of infected tonsil, foods which "went down the wrong way," or objects held in the mouth such as nails, nuts, et cetera.

The treatment of lung abscess requires the use of x-ray for its localization, and often surgery for its complete removal.

TUBERCULOSIS

Tuberculosis is amazingly widespread, but most people who have had this disease are not aware of it. In our large cities, where tuberculosis infections are most common, about 40 percent of the 21-year-old population has already had tuberculosis and 95 percent of adults over 50 years of age have had the disease.

Fortunately, very few people develop this disease to a noticeable state, and for most of us only a few scars, seen by x-ray, remain as evidence of a bygone, unnoticed disease. Today, it is most often discovered in routine examinations of the chest—another reason for thorough and regular examinations—especially if we have been in contact with anyone known to have tuberculosis.

The more severe case of tuberculosis is accompanied by fatigue, loss of weight and characteristic mild fever. When a cough commences, possibly along with a pleurisy pain and the production of a sputum containing flecks of blood, solid evidence of serious lung disease is present. A chest x-ray at this time reveals tuberculosis.

Formerly this dreaded disease meant long periods of bed rest, even for years. Today, drugs like Isoniazide and Nicotinamide have been effective in a rapid cure in most T.B. cases. Because of this happy advance in medicine, most tuberculosis sanitariums in the United States have been closed or turned over to other uses.

ASTHMA

Athma (the devil's disease) is due to a temporary spasm and closing down of the smaller air passages in the deep lung tissues where effective breathing ordinarily takes place.

Asthma can be recognized by these findings:

1. Labored, wheezing breathing.
2. Spasms of coughing between gasps for air.
3. Choking following the wheezing, and uninterrupted coughing, often until the skin turns blue—a sign of lack of air.

Of the millions of cases of asthma, studies indicate that nearly 50 percent are due to allergic problems, such as dust, feathers and pollen, while in others the asthma is brought on by colds, emotional excitement, or periods of great effort—and sometimes for no identifiable reason.

Many people learn to live with their disease and often find great relief in inhalers and drugs, but the greatest relief from the problem can be expected from a thorough medical evaluation. This includes a complete physical examination, including sensitivity tests to food and items of contact in the patient's daily life, such as dusts, fumes and possibly pollens. A nose and throat examination, plus a chest x-ray and complete blood counts, are musts for the asthmatic patient. Considerable relief can be expected under the guidance of a physician schooled in asthmatic disease.

CANCER OF THE LUNG

Cancer of the lung was a rare disease in the early years of this century, but since 1920 it has grown faster than any other kind of cancer and is today the most common cause of all cancer deaths in men. It occurs much more often in men than in women, and its alarming growth is the headache of modern medical research. The cause of lung cancer remains unknown. Possible causes which have been studied include nickel, soot, tars, asbestos, automobile exhaust fumes and radioactive materials. The greatest evidence, however, points to tobacco's guilt, and studies show that the chance of death from lung cancer in men who have smoked for 20 years is nearly 10 times greater than in men who have never smoked.

Cancer in the lung begins without warning. Most often, there is simple fatigue and the loss of a few pounds. A cough develops which may be dry at first, but soon becomes productive of sputum which may be blood-tinged. Soon pleurisy pain in the chest, horseness, increasing weight loss and loss of appetite indicate the presence of serious disease.

The diagnosis of lung cancer is usually made with a chest x-ray. This is confirmed with a bronchoscopic examination (examination through the bronchial tubes). After the diagnosis is certain, surgery for removal of the diseased lung or heavy x-ray therapy over the lung are the modern established treatments of this disease. Because these treatments are only effective in lung cancer which has been detected very early, it is worthwhile for all of us, especially heavy smokers, to have a yearly chest x-ray. See Figure 83 for an x-ray of an advanced lung cancer.

PNEUMONIA

This is an infection and inflammation of the lung itself. Its two

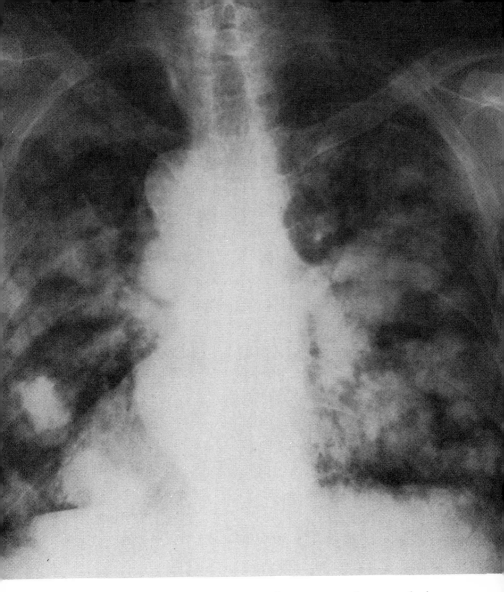

Figure 83: Cancer of the lung in far advanced stages, seen by x-ray, looks almost like snowballs within the chest. This cancer as pictured is called metastatic—a cancer which has come from somewhere else in the body.

usual forms are the common virus pneumonia and the more serious bacterial pneumonia. Figure 84 shows the effect of pneumonia on a lung.

Virus pneumonia is a mild lung infection, and just about everyone contracting it recovers. It is often considered a deep-seated cold, accompanied by a dry, hacking cough, a moderate temperature and

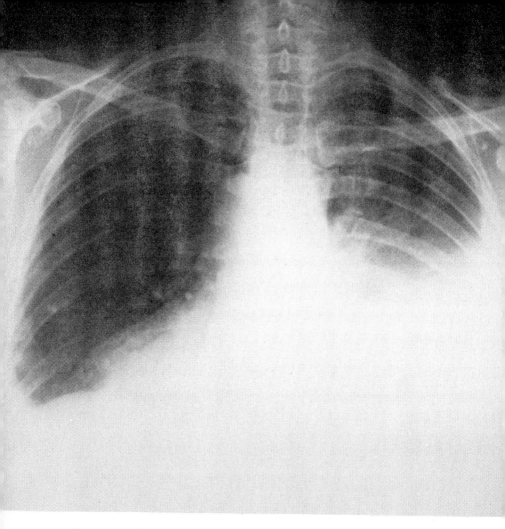

Figure 84: The infected or diseased lung on one side becomes much different from the normal lung on the other side. This left lung had a pneumonia process in it, followed by a weeping of fluid which collected and formed the typical picture of "effusion."

great fatigue. Many physicians treat virus pneumonia with rest, diet, aspirin compounds and occasionally antibiotics. Without chest x-ray, its diagnosis is difficult to make and is sometimes entirely overlooked. Fortunately, nearly all virus pneumonia patients eventually recover without complications.

In the more serious bacterial pneumonia, the lung tissue itself becomes solid with bacteria, pus, blood and thick mucous. The symptoms indicate severe disease with high fever, severe pleurisy pains in the chest, and considerable coughing with the production of a bloody or rust-colored sputum.

The treatment of bacterial pneumonia requires an x-ray diagnosis, considerable supportive treatment such as adequate fluids and rest, and usually powerful antibiotics.

Although effective treatment is now available, pneumonia should never be taken lightly as it still causes significant and permanent body damage and still brings about many deaths each year.

The Heart

The heart is the master muscle of the body, as shown in Figure 85. It must begin beating before our birth, and continue until the last moment of our life; when anything goes wrong with the heart, our entire life is endangered.

As a pump, the heart pushes blood under pressure into the arteries which are the pipes carrying blood to every corner of the body. This function of pumping must be maintained at any cost if life is to continue.

Today, we read of heart transplant operations in which one person's heart is grafted into another person. This fantistic achievement feeds fire to the wild imagination, but in living practice it is a rare, very dangerous and most complicated operation attended by many difficulties. There is grave question in the minds of most doctors that this operation will ever become widespread.

We think of our hearts as constanly working, and that is true; but every muscle must have a rest period, and this is also true. Unlike other muscles in the body, the rest period of the heart can be obtained only in between beats; hence, it is the organ in the body with the shortest rest period of all—a fraction of a second at a time.

We can overwork our hearts in several ways. Too violent exercise, too prolonged exercise, an overweight body, constantly supplying it with tobacco smoke rather than oxygen from the air, and forcing it to engage in violent emotional upheavels. Anything which tends to disturb the balanced work and regularity of the heartbeat will produce trouble if it is kept up long enough. If we would live a normal life span, we must learn to keep our hearts out of trouble.

How to Make an Examination of Your Heart

1. Sit motionless and determine if the heart's action is noticeable. Normally it cannot be felt, but sensation within the chest such as "flip-flopping," palpitation, or exceptionally rapid beating sensations often have their origin in the heart. These sensations may be caused by extra-systole (extra heartbeat), or heartbeat irregularity.

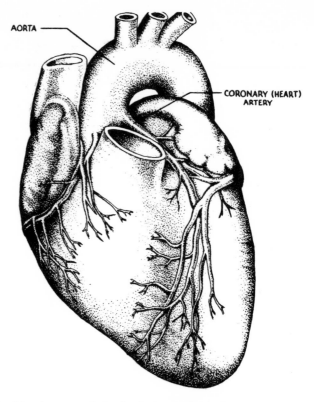

AORTA

CORONARY (HEART)
ARTERY

Figure 85: The blood pump of the body is nearly in the center of the chest and is larger than imagined. Weighing less than a pound, it lies on its side, looking little like the typical "valentine" heart. It pumps 10 tons of blood daily and beats over a million times every 10 days. The heart works hard enough each day to lift you 1000 feet straight up in the air; it is expected nowadays to keep working for 70 years "plus." The heart must receive enough of the blood it pumps or it "cries out" with pain. The heart or coronary arteries return to the heart from the aorta, the main blood vessel from the heart. Chest pain, shortness of breath and palpitation (feeling the heart bounce) are signals of heart trouble. Diseases of the heart annually account for half the deaths in the U.S.

2. Press your right hand palm just below the left breast, and then lean forward against a solid wall. The normal heartbeat can be felt in this manner. Heartbeat sensation of a sawing nature (thrill) is definitely abnormal, and may represent mechanical difficulties which produce murmurs.

3. Count your pulse rate (same as heart rate) at the wrist, while watching the second hand of a watch. Normally, the pulse rate is between 60 to 80 beats per minute. A pulse rate above 100, especially during rest, may represent tachycardia (rapid heart), or a fever and infection somewhere in the body. A beat unlike the steady beat of marching feet is a heartbeat irregularity.

4. Press one finger firmly against the leg just above the ankle for a moment or two. Now quickly withdraw the finger and see if a deep dent is left in the leg itself. A dent deeper than a quarter of an inch, which persists for a minute or more, may indicate inadequate circulation due to partial heart failure.

5. Inhale and exhale rapidly several times and finally hold a deep breath. If the breath can easily be held for a full minute, serious heart disease is not likely to be present.

Diseases of the Heart

All heart difficulties are not necessarily serious. We recognize them in terms of noticeable heart action, breathing difficulty, chest pain or swelling of the ankles.

HEART MURMUR

Heart valves which open and close imperfectly often give rise to a sound similar to the whistling of wind rushing through a partially closed doorway. When our heart valves open widely and the blood flows freely through them, there is no sound made, but when heart valves are deformed and do not close completely, onrushing blood often creates a "murmur."

Figure 86: The heart valve normally closes perfectly, but a diseased valve cannot close correctly. An imperfectly closing valve is the cause of heart murmur, heard during heart beat. The tricuspid valve has three lips, the bicuspid two lips.

There are different types of murmurs in the heart; some of them have significance while others are of no importance. If a heart murmur is known to exist, explanation and expert guidance by a physician experienced in heart diseases become extremely advisable. His examination and testing with the electrocardiogram "E.K.G.," along with other tests, have an incomparable value if we are interested in keeping our hearts (and ourselves) alive for the foreseeable future.

HEARTBEAT IRREGULARITY

The regular heartbeat is similar to the steady rhythm of marching feet in a parade. Anthing disturbing this steady beat is called an irregularity. Irregularities are very common; some are important and some are not.

SINUS ARRHYTHMIA (BREATHING IRREGULARITY)

This most common heartbeat irregularity is insignificant. The rate of the heartbeat increases as we breathe in and decreases as we breathe out. It is hard to call this a disease, any more than we can call breathing a disease.

EXTRASYSTOLE (EXTRA FAST HEARTBEAT)

This is a single heartbeat out of step, and it feels like a flip-flopping with the chest. In this irregularity, one heart beat arrives ahead of step and is followed by a slight pause, awaiting the next beat back in regular rhythm. The heart then goes on beating regularly until another extrasystole appears in the heartbeat order. This irregularity is shown in Figure 87.

EXTRASYSTOLI
(OCCASIONAL FAST BEAT)

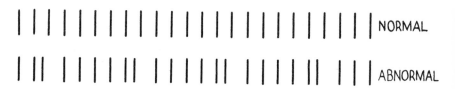

Figure 87: Extrasystoli is irregularity of the heart beat. It is due to an occasional beat stepping in ahead of schedule, creating an apparent pause before the next regular beat. A common irregularity, it is not necessarily serious.

An extrasystole frequently follows heavy eating, excessive smoking or other excitement, and is often noticed when lying down in bed. Heavy tension and over-indulgence in tobacco are suspected as the possible chief causes of extrasystole irregularity.

The flip-flopping within the chest, sometimes called palpitation, often causes great alarm in people who think they have heart disease. The ordinary occasional extrasystole is not serious; however, the experienced physician's opinion and his examination of the heart will usually relieve our worries and discover any possible underlying difficulties.

TACHYCARDIA (FAST HEART)

In this frequent condition, the heartbeat rate speeds up two or three times its normal rate. It is often found in people who have no serious heart disease, but who have these terrifying attacks. The sensations of tachycardia are those of pressure within the chest, difficulty in getting breath, and occasionally nausea.

Relief of tachycardia is often obtained by drawing in and bearing down on a deep breath for a minute. Another method of obtaining relief is firm massage of the side of the neck about the level of the thyroid cartilage (Adam's apple). Occasionally successful is the drinking of ice cold fluids.

Though tachycardia is usually not serious itself, there may possibly be some important underlying factor involved, and for frequent attacks the physician should be consulted to see if any precautions are in order.

FIBRILLATION OF THE HEART

This means a loss of all regularity in the heartbeat, which then sounds like the falling of raindrops with no rhythm at all. A sample irregularity of the heartbeat is shown in Figure 88.

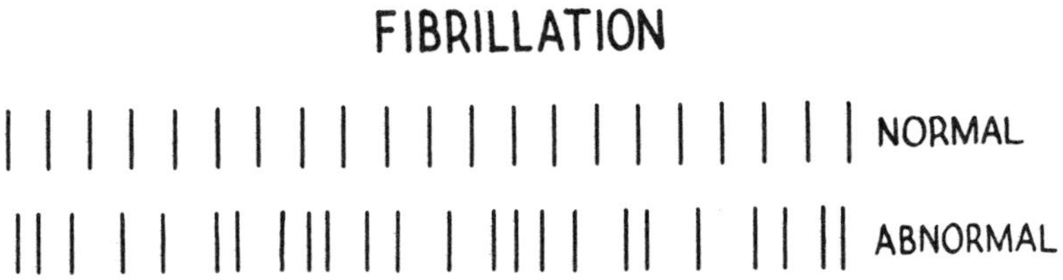

Figure 88: Fibrillation is heart-beat irregularity with no semblance of "bouncing ball" rhythm. Irregular as rain on the roof, it may go on for years, with questionable significance.

Fibrillation can be temporary or permanent, and is most often related to other disease, either within the heart, as in rheumatic heart disease, or completely outside of the heart, as in thyroid disease. Fibrillation has been known to go on for years in some people with no apparent ill effects, but certain dangers are constantly present in a heart with this condition.

The regaining of a regular heartbeat in fibrillation is possible, and if no other disease is found, useful drugs now available may stop the irregularity and be of great help to the heart muscle as well.

HEART BLOCK

This heart irregularity goes on regularly like marching feet, but one beat is noticeably missed at regular intervals. The missed beat may occur after every 24 regular beats or possibly after every six beats, or even after every four beats. The more frequent the missed beat, the more serious is the outlook for the heart block. This is a disease of senior years, and the heart doctor's examination and guidance can be of great value here.

ANGINA PECTORIS

Angina pectoris is a heart pain of come and go nature, varying from a mild pressure sensation in the chest to an agonizing pain in the chest, the left arm and neck. It is brought on by forcing the heart to work harder than it can, as in heavy effort, excitement, digesting heavy meals and adjusting to cold weather. It is noticeably relieved by rest. Angina usually builds up in a patient over a period of years, and the amount of extertion that will cause chest pain to appear is usually known to the patient. Thus, he can predict that walking up a certain two-block hill will almost routinely bring about his chest pain and require a four-minute rest for relief. Experience teaches him his physical limits. Figure 89 shows areas where anginal pain is usually experienced.

Angina pain is a cry form the heart muscles for more blood. The normal heart arteries can carry an excess of blood to the hard-working heart muscle, but the heart arteries in angina are considerably closed by a narrowing spasm or a hardening arteriosclerotic disease. Heavy emotion, high tension, and aged arteries are all suspected of magnifying the pain of angina pectoris, so it is wise to eliminate any such episodes in the angina patient's life and to spare the heart any sudden periods of great work. In angina pectoris, the head must rule the heart.

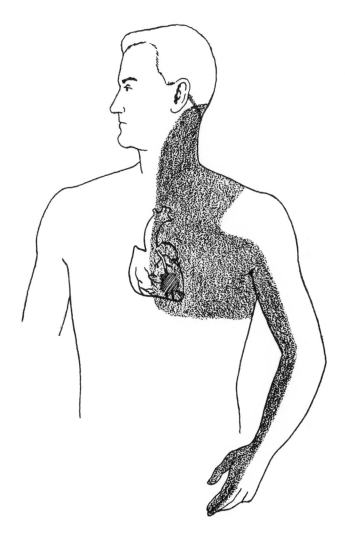

Figure 89: Heart or anginal pain (in shaded region) is variable, generally left-sided, also in the left arm. Pain distribution is due to nerve arrangements to and from the heart region. Pain in the left arm is, therefore, usually more significant than pain in the right arm.

Here again, treatment involves the physician's examination and opinion. He frequently prescribes drugs which are effective in enlarging the heart arteries, relieving their narrowing spasms, and organizing the patient's activity around his heart's abilities.

HEART FAILURE (CONGESTIVE FAILURE, DROPSY)

The normal heart pumps more than enough blood for all body functions, but the diseased heart may not be quite able to pump the minimum amount of blood. Then the heart is said to be failing. It fails by slow degrees and is marked by increasing shortness of breath, pressure in the chest, and a frequent flip-flopping or palpitating senation of the heart. Water logging of the body may be noticeable as heart failure begins, and the body water begins to gravitate down into the lower legs. In this state, the legs are of normal size in the morning but they become considerably swollen by evening after the patient has been upright most of the day.

Heart failure is sometimes a result of childhood rheumatic fever, or in later years, of artiosclerosis of the heart arteries themselves.

The physician can markedly strengthen this weakened heart with digitalis-like drugs, which are effective in eliminating excess fluids from the body and allow the heart to have a stronger function.

HEART ATTACK (CORONARY OCCLUSION)

A heart attack means a sudden block in a heart (coronary) artery which stops the blood flow in that artery to a portion of the heart muscle, which is then quickly damaged. If this damage is slight, it may even go unnoticed, but if there is greater damage to the heart muscle, we are likely to experience severe chest pain. There are many degrees in the severity of heart attacks.

The pain in the chest during a heart attack can be excruciating, causing nausea, weakness, pallor and perspiration as in extreme exhaustion, and the patient may collapse. When severe chest pain strikes, a heart attack is nearly always suspected, but we cannot be sure until an electrocardiogram has been taken since other diseases may cause a similar picture. Possible candidates for heart attacks include those who have never known any discomfort or disease. However, most vulnerable of all to a heart attack is the person with already existing heart disease, in whom extra precautions are necessary to spare the heart muscle as much as possible.

Recent studies have pictured the typical individual who will have a heart attack. He is middle-aged, has very little physical activity, and is flabby and slightly overweight. He smokes a lot, and likes his meals with large amounts of fats, oils and sugars. He also has a little high blood pressure, is short-winded, and has a family history of diseases such as diabetes and gout. Surprisingly, and unfortunately, one out of every four adult American males fits this picture.

The person who dies a few minutes after his heart attack cannot benefit from any known treatment today, but for those who live through the early attack, the physician with truly marvelous life saving drugs can greatly magnify the chances of survival.

High Blood Pressure (Hypertension)

High blood pressure is a disease of the heart and arterial blood system all over the body, occuring at any age including childhood. But it is usually considered a disease of adult life and is found in childhood only on rare occasions when severe kidney or adrenal disease is present.

About 25 percent of 25- to 60-year-old adults have an abnormally elevated blood pressure. Women outnumber men with this disease more than two to one, and it is a fact that more people die directly or indirectly because of high blood pressure than from all types of cancers combined.

Studies have shown that death due to high blood presure is brought about by diseases of the heart itself in 60 percent, a rupture of the brain blood vessels (stroke) in about 30 percent, and an ultimate destruction of the kidney with resulting uremia in about 10 percent of blood pressure deaths.

The beginning of high blood pressure is usually discovered between the ages of 30 to 50 years, in amazed people who immediately presume the worst. We have been taught to think that high blood pressure is due to kidney disease, adrenal gland disease, thyroid disease, heart disease or some other disease. Actually, over 80 percent of all high blood pressure patients do not have any other associated disease, and so this blood pressure is usually called essential (alone) hypertension.

An understanding of blood pressure is basically simple. It is the pressure generated by the heart muscle to drive blood through our blood vessels. This pressure varies considerably with work, rest or sleep, and we determine what normal blood pressure should be from the average of many thousands of people.

The cause of high blood pressure is simply too much resistance to the blood flow in the small arteries throughout the body. It is similar to driving one's car with the brakes on, where too much power must be generated to drive forward.

Of more interest, however, is the effect of high blood pressure

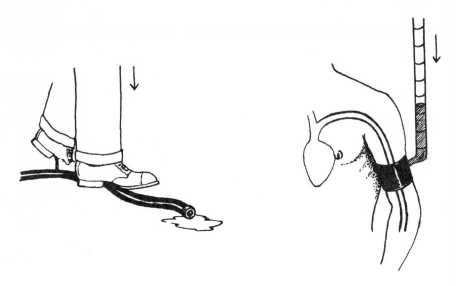

Figure 90: Blood pressure in an artery is similar to water pressure in a hose. It is measured by the amount of weight necessary to stop the flow by squeezing the artery shut—exactly like stepping on a hose to shut off the water.

upon our daily lives. Experience has taught us that this disease frequently robs us of our strength and results in easy fatigue, poor endurance and a lack of healthy reserve. A few of the symptoms of high blood pressure are headache, dizziness, shortness of breath and palpitation, but always in the background of the high blood pressure patient, the spectre of stroke and heart failure hovers menacingly.

One of the favorite (although unproven) causes of high blood pressure according to a few would-be authorities is excess excitement, worry and tension. There is no conclusive evidence that these everyday emotional experiences actually bring about real high blood pressure disease, although they can have a momentary effect in raising blood pressure. "You worry too much," and "You're too tense," give the well-meaning physician something to harp about, but this advice on how to live one's life does very little for the high blood pressure of his patient. The only person today with no worries or tensions is already in the cemetery.

Treatment for High Blood Pressure

The treatment of high blood pressure today revolves about body weight, diet restriction, drug therapy and the elimination, if possible, of any other body disease which could be causing the blood pressure elevation. Thus, a complete physical examination must always precede the sensible treatment of the high blood pressure patient.

Diet restriction in high blood pressure treatment usually removes salt from the table, a restriction which allows elevated blood pressure to fall. Other weight-reducing factors of the diet are also important, but none is so striking as removal of salt from the diet in this disease. Besides ordinary table salt, bacon, ham, salted peanuts, potato chips, olives and other foods stored, preserved or prepared in salt are included in this restriction.

Drug therapy has undergone many changes in the treatment of high blood pressure. Sedation in the treatment of high blood pressure is in dispute today since the idea of putting a person partially to sleep for the relief of one disease only invites the probability of bodily harm from other disease or accident.

Another group of drugs in the treatment of high blood pressure paralyzes the sympathetic nerves of the body. These drugs also lower the blood pressure, but they have undesirable side effects such as blacking out, fainting, eye problems and urinary problems, and cannot be used by all high blood pressure patients. They must be used with great caution under the direct supervision of the physician.

Possibly the best drugs in use today for the treatment of hypertension have been those which act to free the body of excess water and salt. Technically known as chlorothiazide and similar compounds, they have enjoyed long and continued success in controlling high blood pressure with a minimum of undesirable side effects. Since the best treatment of high blood pressure today seems to be the lessening of salt content within the body, the ideal drug therapy proceeds along the same line. These drugs are effective in "wringing out" salt from the body of the high blood pressure patient.

Surgery for High Blood Pressure

Several operations called sympathectomy have been devised for the treatment of high blood pressure and were widely performed several years ago, before the advent of our modern drugs of today. The operation of sympathectomy has been discarded as a routine treatment, and is reserved now only for the rarest of high blood pressure patients.

Chest Pains

When pain strikes in the chest, one question leaps to the fore-ground—is the pain coming from the heart or from somewhere else? It is the same for all people, young or old, including doctors them-selves, who as a group seem particulaly singled out for heart difficulties.

Figure 91: Chest pain strikes fear of heart trouble and possible sudden death. Most pain in this region is not from the heart, however, but from several other distinct causes. It is important not to disregard this pain which may be a warning of more serious possibilities ahead.

A well-rounded idea of chest pain is most important to us, more than the much publicized danger points of cancer, because heart disease is the greatest killer in the United States today.

Although knowledge of chest pain is of great importance, it must coincide with the opinion of your physician who is skilled in interpreting pain and associated findings into an exact diagnosis. In studying chest pain possibilities, we know that a slight pain for one of us might be decribed as unbearable by someone else. Also, we must realize that the severity of chest pain does not always reflect exactly the seriousness of the underlying disease. Chest pain should never be taken lightly, for all too often genuine heart pain is disregarded completely. The story is frequently heard after it is too late—"He thought it was only a little indigestion."

What can we know of chest pain for our own benefit? First of all, we should know that most chest pains are not caused by the heart but are caused more by:

1. The breathing mechanism.
2. The muscle, ligament and bone of the chest.
3. Inflammation or tumor growth.
4. The swallowing tube (esophagus).
5. Pain originating from the abdomen.
6. Nerves (often called effort syndrome or neuro-circulatory asthenia).

Pain from the heart can be understood best after other sources of chest pain have been studied first.

1. Let us first examine pain caused by the breathing mechanism. Breathing pain is pleurisy pain, and it is the most common type of pain felt when the lungs or inside of the chest walls are diseased. If pain is definitely *related to the movement of breathing in and out*, and ceases when breathing is stopped, it is nearly always the pain of pleurisy.

What causes pleurisy pain? The lungs are coved by a smooth, wet envelope called the pleura which normally slides over a similar wet surface on the inside of the chest wall with each breathing motion. If either of these smooth surfaces is irritated, inflamed or roughened in any way, the smooth gliding movement between the lung and chest wall causes friction during the breathing motion and brings about pleurisy pain. Pleurisy can be caused by lung disease such as pneumonia, tuberculosis, lung abscess or a blood clot in the lungs (infarction). The smooth chest wall can also cause pleurisy pain when it is irritated by pus (empyema), fractured ribs or chest wall injuries which penetrate completely through the wall.

Pleurisy pain is easy to understand and to identify because it is produced by the motion of breathing in and out, and we know this is not the kind of pain produced by the heart. It is well to know that pleurisy pain rarely accompanies any kind of heart disease.

2. Let us examine next the chest pain which originates from bone, muscle and ligament of the chest wall (Figure 92). This type of pain is *produced by movements of the chest and body,* such as twisting, bending, rounding the shoulders, throwing out the chest, and coughing or lifting. These pains are most likely of arthritic origin or pressure on nerve roots from the spine. They are common about the neck and chest and usually respond to heat and aspirin. Pain and soreness of ligaments often follows unusual or heavy work like several hours of hard digging in the garden.

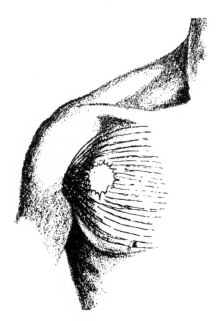

Figure 92: Muscle Pain. Pains, aches and soreness of muscles are made worse if the sore muscles are worked. Usually a come and go story, muscle pain is related to cold, damp weather, and may be relieved by aspirin and heat application. If—as a test—pain is produced when the involved muscle is pressed, it cannot be coming from the heart.

Pain and soreness of these muscles and ligaments also seems *related to damp or cold weather* and is often called myalgia, neuralgia, fibrositis, myositis and other names. Pain that comes about from a change in the weather seldom makes a person worry that his pain may be originating in the heart.

Pain occasionally found in the front wall of the chest and often thought to be heart pain can be produced by a soreness of the cartilage rib points which join the end of the rib to the breastbone or sternum. This pain is *produced easily by pressing on the ribs in front of the chest* and can never be mistaken for heart pain, because pressing upon any part of the chest wall never elicits heart pain (Figure 93).

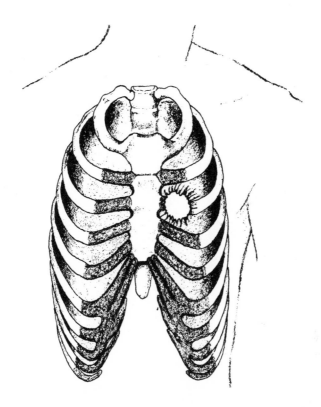

Figure 93: Chest Wall Pain. Pain of the front chest wall—referred to as Tietze's Syndrome—is fairly common. Like any other joint, the cartilage joining the rib to the breast bone may become very painful; unlike other joints, it cannot be rested unless breathing is stopped. There is a definite sore spot (usually over the heart) and pressing on it causes great pain. This eliminates the possibility of heart pain which cannot be produced by pressing anywhere on the chest wall.

3. Chest pain due to breast irritation or tumor growth is also fairly easy to recognize. Breast pain, of course, is more common in women; but is occasionally seen in men. The pain and soreness of breast pain tends to be steady with a possible increase of pain just before the menstrual period. Breast tenderness, soreness and other sensations usually are identified as coming from the breast tissue itself, and they bring about more concern about cancer than about heart disease. It is comforting to know that painful breasts are rarely any idication of cancer, and even less often any indication of heart disease.

One particular form of pain in the male breast is caused by administration of hormones for the treatment of cancer of the prostate, or bone difficulties elsewhere in the body. A knowledge of the foregoing hormonal treatment usually clears up the issue for the patient and the doctor, so that he may know the pain is not

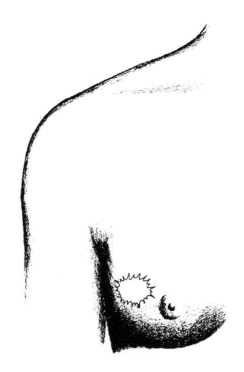

Figure 94: Breast Pain. Caused by several different disease possibilities, pain in the breast probably will afflict almost all women at some time or other. By comparison the undeveloped male breast is only seldom the seat of any trouble. Most people are surprised to learn that breast pain hardly ever means cancer, but that pain usually means a benign (non-malignant) condition, like "cystic disease of the breast." Breast pain never means heart disease.

originating from the heart. See Figure 94 for possible area of breast pain.

Shingles (Herpes Zoster) is a *burning, aching pain usually on one side of the chest wall often accompanied by a skin eruption*. We know the source of the pain as soon as we recognize shingles, for the skin eruption usually shows up over the course of the pain in a few days to a week. Also in shingles, pain is produced by pressing the finger between the ribs where the nerve lies—and we know now that any pain produced by pressing against the chest wall is never recognized as heart pain. See Figure 95 for usual areas of shingles pain.

Chest pain due to tumor growth of the chest wall itself is extremely rare. We will only say here that the tumor enlargement will certainly be noticed much before any chest pain. This alone will bring the patient to his physician.

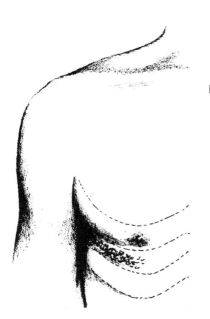

Figure 95: Shingles Pain. Often called Herpes Zoster, the pain of shingles is due to soreness of a nerve itself. The pain typically burns, aches and stabs, and follows the nerve route between the ribs (generally the 4th, 5th and 6th ribs). The usual shingles skin eruption may appear within a few days, itching furiously and inviting constant scratching.

4. Chest pain of great importance may originate from the swallowing tube (esophagus) which runs from the throat to the stomach. This type of pain is very common, and often very severe.

Pain from the esophagus which might be confused with heart pain is nearly always due to heartburn (reflux esophagitis or achalasia), in which acids which belong in the stomach back up into the esophagus to cause intense burning pain. Because the esophagus itself is in the chest, in the heart region, this pain is incorrectly named heartburn.

Heartburn can be very severe, but is separated from the picture of heart pain through its identifying characteristics. First, it comes on soon after eating; second, it is suddenly and miraculously relieved by a drink of soda water or even plain water which simply wash the irritating acids down into the stomach (Figure 96).

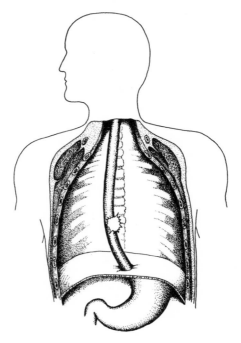

Figure 96: The name heartburn is misleading. The burning pain has nothing to do with the heart, but is felt in the area thought of as the "heart." The source of "heartburn" pain is the swallowing tube (esophagus) which is "burned" by stomach acids washing upward toward the mouth. These stomach acids irritate the esophagus, causing intense pain. The patient may fear a heart attack, but is relieved when the acid is washed down with water, soda or milk.

Heartburn is a very common chest pain that has one real danger to it—when a person who has been accustomed to the pain of heartburn, actually does have some real heart difficulty, he is likely to confuse the two and to regard the real heart pain also as "indigestion."

5. Pain in the chest may have its cause in the abdomen. It is relatively uncommon, and is usually identified by the fact that it occurs at the same time after meals or after certain types of food. The stomach, gallbladder, pancreas and some difficulties of the colon (discussed in another section) occasionally can cause chest pain. It may take a careful physical examination by the physician to reveal the real source of the pain, which will eventually be found to be outside of the chest itself.

6. Chest pain may be more imagined than real. This situation can occur in people who only think that they have heart trouble. Often explanations of this type of "heart trouble" finally boil down to a lazy person's excuse for his unwillingness to work, or to explain his failure at a certain work. Most of these people with imagined chest pain, who complain so bitterly of heart disease for many long years, have had several good doctors tell them there is nothing wrong with them. However, they fear losing their good excuse of "heart disease" above anything else, and it may take a physician skilled in psychiatry to uncover their real underlying problems.

Heart Pain

The cause of genuine heart pain is directly due to too small a supply of blood to the muscle of the heart itself. Even though all of the blood in the body goes through the heart to be pumped, the heart muscle itself is actually receiving an undersupply of this blood. See Figure 97 for a typical pain pattern.

Small ateries called the coronary arteries (heart arteries) must carry all the blood to work the heart muscle itself. But if these arteries for any reason cannot carry the supply of blood required by the heart muscle, the blood-hungry heart cries out in the only way that it can—with pain. This makes heart pain understandable.

Heart pain is nearly always felt just in back of the breastbone, but it can travel down toward the abdomen, up into the neck, and out through either shoulder. The most common path of pain from the heart seems to be from the breastbone up and into the left arm.

The production of heart pain is always due to a lack of blood for the heart muscle, but the mechanics which produce the lowered supply of blood may differ and so we must recognize three different kinds of heart disease attended by chest pain.

1. Heart attack—sometimes called "coronary thrombosis," "myocardial infarction," or "a coronary."

2. Arteriosclerosis—sometimes called "coronary insufficiency."
3. Angina pectoris—known as "temporary ischemia."

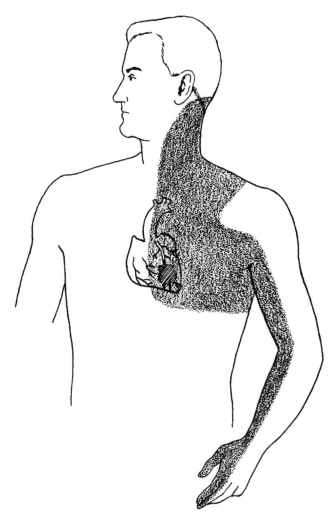

Figure 97: Heart pain varies greatly in intensity and duration. Its location, however, follows a fairly typical pattern involving the left chest, neck and inner surface of the left arm.

Heart Attack Pain

We know now that all heart pain is due to a lack of blood supply to the heart muscle (Figure 98). In a coronary, a blood clot has blocked one of the heart arteries, thus reducing the heart muscle's blood supply. If the blocking in the heart artery is out near its end,

Figure 98: Pain of Heart Attack. Pain is felt in the heart muscle when it is deprived of its blood supply. The supply is reduced or blocked by a clot in the heart (coronary) artery. "Coronary thrombosis" —or "coronary" for short—means a heart artery is blocked by a blood clot. Almost invariably, pain is felt behind the breast bone. From there it may appear to travel into the arms or neck. Heart attack also has other symptoms, such as difficulty in getting the breath (dyspnea), a feeling of pressure on the chest (orthopnea), and perhaps nausea and vomiting.

then most of the heart artery branches will still be functioning well and only a small portion of heart muscle will be deprived of its blood supply. The pain, in this instance, will not be severe. A new pathway of small arteries, called a collateral circulation, will usually build up around this area in about six weeks to two months. Thus, a mild coronary goes on to recovery. We may remember a national figure or personal friend who has gone through such an experience.

The other side of the picture in heart attack is more foreboding. If one of the major heart arteries is blocked with a blood clot near its beginning, a large portion of the heart muscle will be deprived of blood. In this case, a major portion of the heart muscle cannot go on, and the patient will die. In such cases, the frequent story is that "he dropped dead on the spot."

Typical heart attack pain slowly spreads across the chest, toward the neck and left shoulder. A feeling of pressure on the chest wall begins and the victim feels a shortness of breath. Usually a wave of nausea comes on along with extreme weakness and perspiration. If the pain grows severe the patient may faint or collapse.

Heart pain is obviously felt, of course, only while the patient is still conscious, but in heart attack victims who recover, severe pain in the chest may last for many days and be accompanied by other symptoms as well.

Modern medicine can do a lot to save the heart attack patient, but obviously very little when his future is measured in minutes. Probably the best thing that the patient with a severe heart attack can have is a clear conscience as he is about to meet the master physician very shortly.

Arterioclerotic Heart Disease Pain

Arteriosclerosis is our second kind of heart disease accompanied by chest pain (Figure 99). In this disease the heart artery, along

Figure 99: Pain of Arteriosclerosis. Pain is felt in the heart muscle because the blood supply is greatly reduced by the diseased and narrowed heart artery. The disease is termed arteriosclerosis (artery-sclerosis), and gradually closes and narrows the artery until it can't carry enough blood. The undersupply of blood to the heart (ischemia) results in pain of possibly severe degree.

with other arteries of the body, has a much thickened and roughened wall which greatly reduces the size of the artery. This narrowed coronary artery allows a flow of blood through it which is insufficient to keep the heart in a satisfactory, well-nourished state. Thus the name "coronary insufficiency" is sometimes used instead of arteriosclerotic heart disease.

Arteriosclerosis causes a good deal of narrowing in the heart arteries of some people but very little in others. Since the insufficiency of blood to the heart will therefore vary, the pain produced will also vary. With just a little arteriosclerosis, heart pain may not be noticed at all until great exertion or hard work is undertaken. Then pain will develop. In arteriosclerosis, therefore, we are allowed to work our hearts only in proportion to the size of our "coronaries" and their ability to carry blood, because with further exertion, pain will definitely be felt. A few people have such severe arteriosclerosis that their narrowed heart arteries cannot deliver sufficient blood to the heart even while they are at rest. When rest itself is too much of an effort for the heart, "rest pain" in the chest results. Immediate medical care is necessary, for these hearts which are barely "hanging on."

Angina Pectoris Pain

Angina pectoris is a well-known heart pain which like all heart pain is due to heart arteries that do not bring enough blood to the

Figure 100: Pain of Angina Pectoris. Pain is felt in the heart muscle because its blood supply is reduced by a heart artery which is clamped down or in "spasm.""Spasm," which narrows or closes the artery, is related to work (e.g., walking uphill), tobacco and emotional upset. Often a little alcohol helps to relax the condition. Tobacco is restricted in nearly all cases.

heart muscle (Figure 100). But, in addition, anginal pain is felt when the heart is working hard and demanding more blood than it can get. The heart works hard when we walk uphill, walk or run too fast, and during severe emotional upsets.

The heart artery in angina pectoris is narrow because of a temporary spasm in the artery itself which distinguishes angina from the permanently narrowed artery of arteriosclerosis. Relaxing this constricted artery and allowing it to dilate allows more blood to be delivered to the heart muscle again and the pain of angina pectoris is relieved.

Ordinarily, patients with angina pectoris have a so-called emotional nature with intensified spasms in their arteries. Because of this, these patients are usually advised against activities which will bring about spasms of the arteries. Smoking is one of these activities, and many doctors forbid their patients any tobacco after the first symptoms of angina pectoris. With this restriction alone, heart pain may be completely relieved.

Sometimes angina pectoris patients are advised to use alcohol as a medicine. In the form of whiskey, alcohol is noted for its ability to relax the arteries of the heart and often to help dispel the pain of angina pectoris.

Heart pain probably is most often caused not just by one, but rather by a combination of these diseases. Actually, some authorities believe angina pectoris pain rarely occurs without the presence of some arteriosclerosis, and many doctors believe that real heart attacks never occur without the presence of at least some arteriosclerosis. Thus, the easy separation of chest pains on paper is not quite so clearly defined within the chest wall. We may study types of heart pain and learn to distinguish them from pains which are not coming from the heart. It is felt, moreover, that such a study will prompt one to visit his physician regularly, even before any heart pain makes itself known.

Heart diseases are most difficult to deal with. If this were not so, we should not have so great a number of physicians dying of heart diseases each year. It takes the best of medical brains with the help of laboratory tests to deal adequately with genuine heart disease. While things for the individual to do and not to do in his routine way may be very important, total evaluation of the heart patient and his activities must finally be dictated by his physician.

Section

4

THE ABDOMEN

The abdomen is the factory of the body and the seat of most of our bodily ills. Since the abdomen takes care of itself and the rest of our body as well, its diseases immediately influence our entire system. Any organ or area of the abdomen can have difficulties, but each organ's function and diseases are very vague for most people. A study of the abdomen is very enlightening and may be especially rewarding when disease strikes in our own home.

Examination of the Abdomen

Examine the bare abdomen in a well lighted room before a full-length mirror in both standing and reclining positions.

1. Observe the abdominal skin for a yellow discoloration called jaundice. It could be congenital (born with) disease in young people, or gallbladder and liver disease in adults.
2. The ear held flat against the abdomen can normally detect a soft gurgling or swishing sound. If absolute silence accompanies definite abdominal pain, peritonitis or serious disease is present. This is true at any age.
3. In the painful abdomen, press gently but steadily for a minute. Let up suddenly, and if pronounced pain is registered, seek the physician immediately for serious abdominal disease.
4. Observe the hair growth over the chest and abdomen. An abundance of hair popularly indicates manliness in the male, but masculine hair distribution on the female may mean ovarian or adrenal gland difficulty.

179

5. When lying down flat on our backs, we normally can see our toes. If the abdomen rises to block this view, it is abnormally enlarged. If a "spare tire" can easily be lifted, it is possible that we are overweight.

6. Examine the skin of the abdomen for visible blood vessels. A few fine veins and skin blemishes are usually present at any age, but more so in later years. Large vivid veins on the abdomen may signal cirrhosis of the liver or a serious blood vessel blockade deep within the body.

7. Feel the abdomen—the skin should have a doughy firmness. A tight shiny shin and a ballooned up abdomen usually means excessive fluid or tumor growth inside of it. If a finger "pit" remains after firmly pressing into the skin, abnormal swelling is present, possibly indicating heart or kidney disease.

8. While lying down, feel the abdomen above the navel. The normal abdomen slopes downward from the ribs, both sides are alike, and no tenderness is present. Tender enlargements on the right side may signal liver, gallbladder or right kidney disease. Enlargements on the left side could indicate disease of the stomach, left kidney or spleen. It is difficult to feel these organs separately or accurately.

9. Feel the abdomen in the navel region. A mass of any size in this region is distinctly abnormal. It could be a tumor growth of the intestines, the colon or even the major blood vessels themselves. Enlargement of the naval which appears when standing or straining, but which disappears when lying down, is likely to be an umbilical hernia (rupture).

10. Feel the abdomen below the umbilicus or navel. It is normally not tender or painful in any way. A definite soreness suggests the possibility of appendicitis, bowel difficulties or ovarian difficulty in the female. A movable ball-like mass in the lower abdomen of the female could mean growth of the ovaries or uterus.

11. In the standing position, observe any visible enlargement in the lower abdomen. Strain purposely and note any protrusion which appears just to the side of the public bone. This is likely to be a hernia or rupture, which is usually not painful and often falls back into the abdomen on lying down.

Abdominal Diseases

Peptic Ulcer (Stomach Ulcer, Duodenal Ulcer)

A peptic ulcer is a painful sore in the stomach, usually at its outlet. It is much like a canker sore of the mouth, with a moon crater appearance varying in size from a match head to an inch or more in diameter. We have these ulcers because the stomach, unlike any other organ in the body, is continually secreting acids that retard and prevent the healing of ulcerations. In this manner, an ulcer is formed.

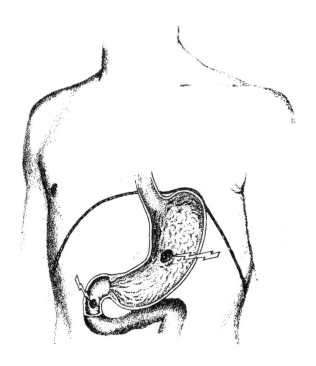

Figure 101: The stomach brings joy to all people at all ages, but it is a victim of modern "push." Ulcers are believed to be a result of too much stress and "hepped-up" living in a world with an uncertain future. The usual active ulcer appears as an enlarged cold sore or small "volcano."

Pain of an ulcer is easy to identify. It is a burning sensation in the upper abdomen that goes away when food, especially milk or alkali is put into the stomach to absorb the acid. The pain returns when the stomach is empty and the ulcer again becomes a clear target for the stomach acids to attack.

Peptic ulcer is a disease of adult life, that bothers men four times more than women. It occurs and recurs most often in the springtime and fall, a fact which has never been well explained.

Although pain is the best known of all ulcer difficulties, there are three other problems of more serious nature that plague the ulcer patient. They are:

1. Serious bleeding of a peptic ulcer, recognized by vomited blood or black, tarry stools.

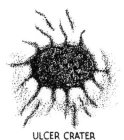

ULCER CRATER

A. Peptic ulcer is known personally by millions of people. Occurring mostly in men, its burning pain characteristically is relieved by drinking milk, soda, or other alkalies.

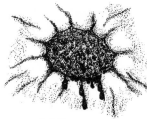

BLEEDING ULCER

B. Bleeding of some degree eventually occurs in nearly all peptic ulcers, mostly when the base is being eaten away by stomach acids.

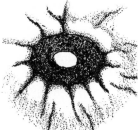

PERFORATED ULCER

C. Perforation of the peptic ulcer is caused by severe erosion—digestion of the ulcer base by stomach acids in unusually great amounts. The hole leads into the free abdominal cavity.

Figure 102: Various stages of peptic ulcers.

2. Blowout (perforation) of the ulcer producing immediate, severe abdominal pain and a grave medical situation.
3. Obstruction to passage of any food, caused by ulcer scarring and stricture, recognized by persistent vomiting.

See Figure 102 for various stages of peptic ulcer.

Neglect of a peptic ulcer often leads to these serious consequences. A competent physician can accurately diagnose an ulcer by examining the patient and x-raying his stomach.

Ulcer care includes adequate diet, medication and possible surgery. The ulcer diet excludes ulcer-provoking foods, such as spicy, greasy, rough, popcorn-like foods. Medications used in ulcer care are mainly acid neutralizers and drugs designed to slow down the overactivity of the stomach. At least five out of every six peptic ulcers are treated successfully with diet and medication while the person goes about his daily work routine. About one ulcer out of ten becomes so severe that a surgical operation becomes necessary. See Figure 103 for guidance to foods for ulcer sufferers.

The physician's advice for ulcer problems is most important even after the ulcer is cured. The patient must be informed accurately concerning an ulcer diet; he must be advised against using tobacco and alcohol and all other items which have an influence on peptic ulcer disease. Occasionally, an ulcer patient is afraid to see a physician because he fears the cure might be worse than the disease. However, most successful ulcer patients have just one regret —that they did not seek expert medical treatment for their ulcer earlier than they did.

Cancer of the Stomach

Cancer of the stomach is a very serious disease, found among men twice as often as in women. Formerly, it accounted for 75,000 deaths per year in the United States.

In the last few years, the incidence of stomach cancer has been dwindling remarkably in the United States but has been growing rapidly in foreign countries such as Japan.

It is also found more often among the poor than among the wealthy, and heavy drinkers have much more stomach cancer than non-drinkers.

Stomach cancer is a disease of later years. It might appear in a man of 40 or over who has a loss of appetite, indigestion and possibly pain similar to ulcer distress—temporarily relieved by eating food

This diet will act as a reminder of what foods your doctor allows you to have and what foods he wants you to strictly avoid.

Generally, foods that are strong stimulants to stomach acid are eliminated. Spices are limited or eliminated entirely because they may irritate your stomach and duodenum.

	Foods Allowed	Foods to Avoid
Beverages	Milk, milk drinks (malted milk), buttermilk, cocoa, Postum, weak tea, decaffinated coffee and Ovaltine.	Tea, coffee, carbonated beverages and alcoholic drinks
Fruits	All cooked fruits. Fruit juices well diluted with water — orange, apple, apricot nectar. Ripe bananas. Pureed fruits such as applesauce, prunes, pears, peaches and apricots.	All raw fruits. Dried fruits such as figs, dates and raisins.
Vegetables	Baked, boiled or mashed white or sweet potatoes. Shredded lettuce. Pureed or strained vegetables (may be canned, frozen or fresh) such as beets, asparagus tips, peas, spinach, string beans, wax beans, carrots and squash.	All raw vegetables except shredded lettuce. Brussels sprouts, cauliflower, corn, cucumbers, onions, cabbage, radishes, celery, tomatoes, lima beans and broccoli. Dried beans, peas and lentils.
Soups	Vegetable soup without meat stock made from allowed vegetables. Milk soups made with vegetable puree.	Meat stock and thick cream soups. Bean, split pea or lentil soups. Broth and bouillon.

	Foods Allowed	Foods to Avoid
Meats, fish, poultry, eggs and cheese	Broiled, baked or boiled lean, tender beef, ham, veal, lamb, chicken and turkey. Baked or boiled fish except shellfish. Soft-boiled or poached eggs. Cottage and cream cheese.	No tough meats. All mutton and pork except ham. Fatty and fried meats and fish. All cheese not mentioned under foods to eat. Avoid all other meats, fish and fowl not mentioned. Fried and scrambled eggs.
Breads	White bread, toast or roll with butter, plain soda crackers, Saltines, melba toast, Zwieback.	Whole wheat and dark breads. Rye bread with seeds. Seeded rolls All crackers not mentioned.
Cereals and cereal products	Cooked and strained cereals (oatmeal, Cream of Wheat and farina). Prepared refined cereals such as Puffed Rice, Rice Krispies, noodles, refined rice, macaroni, spaghetti, etc.	All whole grain cooked cereals. Dry, ready-cooked cereals.
Desserts	Tapioca, bread, rice or cornstarch pudding without raisins. Ice cream. Plain cakes. Jello. Stewed and strained fruits such as apple-sauce, prunes, pears, peaches, ripe bananas and apricots.	Pies, pastries and excessively sweet desserts.
Miscellaneous	Jams and jellies in moderation. Salt and sugar. Butter, margarine, Jello.	Oils. Highly seasoned foods such as chili, ketchup, mustard, relishes.

Figure 103: Many diets exist for ulcer disease. This one seems sensible.

or liquid. Often there is a vague sickness in the abdomen spoiling any desire for food, and consequently the patient does not eat much. The result usually is a weight loss of great proportions. Unfortunately, the story of stomach cancer is not always the same, and usually early symptoms are ignored.

After the age of 50 years, any kind of stomach upset lasting more than several days should prompt a visit to the physician for an examination, possibly including an x-ray of the stomach to determine if a cancer problem exists. There is not other disease of the body in which early diagnosis is more important in achieving a final cure than cancer of the stomach.

Achlorhydria (No Acid in the Stomach)

The normal stomach regularly secretes hydrochloric acid which aids in digestion of foods. Frequently we find people who have less than the normal amount of acid in their stomachs, and about one person out of ten who possesses little or no hydrochloric acid at all. If they are given hydrochloric acid along with food at meal time, the result often, to their great satisfaction, is an improved appetite and digestion.

The Gallbladder

Gallstones (Cholelithiasis)

Gallstones are found in about seven percent of our adult population and they are known to increase with years—so that at the age of 75, almost one-third of us have stones present. Women have four times as much gallbladder trouble as men, and according to medical history the typical patient with gallstones is "fair, fat and forty."

Gallstones are formed in the gallbladder by the water-absorbing action of the gallbladder wall itself. Just as salt crystals form in the bottom of the pan of evaporating salt water, stones form in bile from which water has been absorbed. From this point, irritation and inflammation by the stones are only steps away. Typical gallstone formations are shown in Figures 104 and 105.

Most people have no trouble with gallstones while others have vague indigestion and are bothered by "gas." Still others have exceptionally severe pain requiring medication, diet restriction or an operation. It is well to know that gallstones can never be dissolved in any manner, regardless of their kind, location or age.

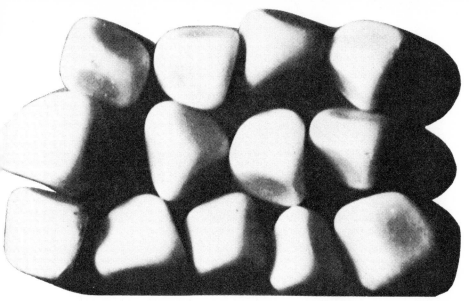

Figure 104: Gallstones come in all shapes, sizes and numbers. About half of them can be seen with the x-ray because of the calcium salts absorbed in their structure. Approximately 7 percent of all mature people are carrying gallstones whether they know it or not. More than 60 percent of people weighing over 300 pounds have gallstones.

Figure 105: Cut section of a gallstone shows its layer formation.

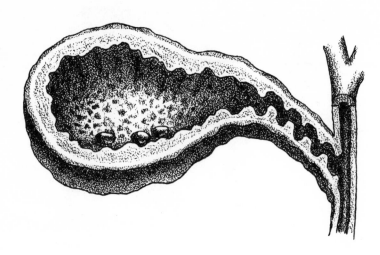

Figure 106: The gall bladder when severely inflamed has a greatly thickened wall and may contain stones and pus. It then has the appearance of a boiled lobster.

Gallbladder Attack (Acute Cholelithiasis)

A gallbladder attack usually arises quickly as a result of gallstones. The irritation progresses rapidly to a highly inflamed stage and the former toy balloon appearance of the gallbladder gives way to that of a boiled lobster, filled with pus and very tender to the touch. There is usually a high fever, sweating, chills, nausea and vomiting, and frequently great pain in the right side of the abdomen just under the ribs. The attacks last about a week and are often accompanied by jaundice. People who have had these acute attacks dread having another.

The inflamed gallbladder requires immediate medical attention.

Chronic, Recurring Infection of the Gallbladder

Once the gallbladder has become acutely inflamed, it is likely that a low degree of irritation will persist indefinitely. In the presence of irritating stones, frequent flare-ups may occur to make the gallbladder's future even more miserable with continuing indigestion, gas, and inability to tolerate fatty, greasy foods.

Some people with gallbladder disease are carried along in fair comfort by their physician on proper diets and medication. The severely diseased and stone-containing gallbladder, however, is not

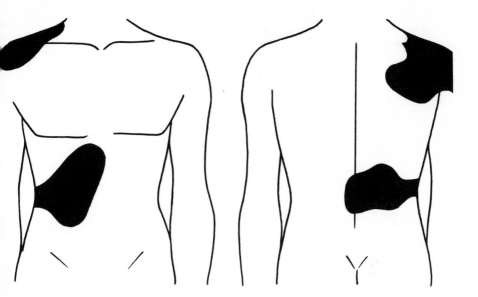

Figure 107: Gallbladder pain is characteristic. It occurs most often in the right side of the abdomen just under the ribs, and also in the right shoulder area at the base of the neck. Shoulder pain is called referred pain.

so easily handled and the doctor may advise surgical removal. This is particularly true in the elderly patient who usually has more difficulty with his gallbladder from year to year.

Cancer of the Gallbladder

Cancer in the gallbladder usually becomes known only after the gallbladder has been removed because of pain, stones or infection. Cancer is found in about one percent of all gallbaldders which are surgically removed, and in this group the outlook is dark indeed.

Gallbladder stones have been blamed for the irritation which is probably responsible for cancer, and for this reason, many doctors recommend removal of the gallbladder whenever stones are found.

The Pancreas

The pancreas is the sweetbread of the body. From it come the digestive juices essential to the digestion of carbohydrates and proteins in the intestinal tract. The pancreas also secretes insulin into the blood stream for the regulation of blood sugars within the blood itself, and absence of this hormone immediately results in diabetes.

Diseases in the pancreas are uncommon and difficult to diagnose when they do occur. Infection, cancers, and wasting away of this gland produce body difficulties such as pain, jaundice and intense prolonged diarrhea.

The physician's investigation alone can bring to light pancreatic difficulties because this organ and its hidden away location cannot be felt, examined or in any way mechanically investigated. Complex laboratory tests must be relied upon to uncover any disease of the pancreas.

Diabetes Mellitus (Sugar Diabetes)

Diabetes is a failure of the pancreas to manufacture the hormone, insulin.

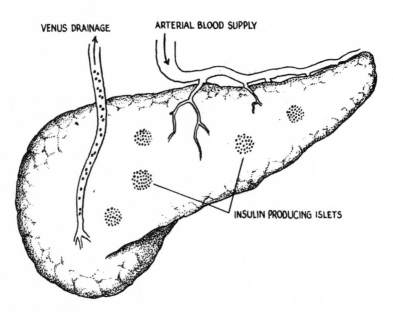

Figure 108:   The pancreas also produces the hormone insulin which is poured into the bloodstream. Absence of insulin means diabetes, unless it is given by hypo as a replacement.

Normally, the sweets and starches we eat are absorbed as sugar and policed in the blood stream by insulin from the pancreas, so that the body can use them. In diabetes, where insulin is lacking, there is a flood of sugar into the body during eating, and it actually spills over into the urine through the kidney. The strength, vigor and repair of the body falls below par and serious complications can arise.

Several difficulties plague the diabetic person. Probably the best known of his difficulties is diabetic coma, for which many diabetics carry identification cards informing strangers what to do for them in case they are found unconscious. Another well-known difficulty of diabetic people is poor blood circulation, especially in the extremities and toes. Unfortunately, in the diabetic of senior years, gangrene of the toes can develop rapidly following the slightest injury or infection, and the most delicate care is necessary to prevent this unfortunate complication.

There are over one million diabetics in the United States today, and many of us do not realize that we may be diabetic ourselves. A study operated by the Board of Health in one of our large cities has discovered that when a middleaged population was actually investigated for diabetes, over five percent were found to have previously unknown diabetes.

Since two-thirds of all diabetics are over the age of 40 years, it is apparent that this disease increases with age. Diabetes starts most often between the ages of 40 and 50 years; it is twice as common in women as in men, and is especially so in married women who have had children. Diabetes seems to be a racial characteristic, heavily afflicting the Jewish race for some unknown reason. Inheritance also is a factor in diabetes, and if one our close relatives is found to have this disease, we ourselves become possible candidates and an examination for diabetes is in order.

The greatest number of diabetics comes from the obese group, and schooled opinion exists that the fat person is continually looking down the gun barrel of diabetes.

Stress also brings about diabetes. Following the stress of a severe burn, high fever, pregnancy or severe emotional upset, an examination often reveals for the first time the presence of previously unknown diabetes.

Control of diabetes means control of sugar within the body. In light diabetes, restriction of sugar in the diet may be sufficient, but in severe diabetes, extra insulin (which should have been manufactured by the pancreas) becomes necessary to effectively control sugar.

Diabetics usually wonder why they cannot take insulin by mouth. The reason is that insulin is also a protein, and it would be simply digested away like other foods. There are now, however, drugs such as Orinase and Diabinese taken orally which do have a pronounced effect on diabetes, and it is eventually probable that complete treatment of diabetes will be entirely by the oral route rather than by the unwelcome hypodermic route. Another similar advance involves the use of a gel disc, containing insulin, which is held in the cheek to allow absroption of insulin through the buccal (cheek) membranes.

Effective treatment of diabetes demands the initial care and continued observation of an able physician. Whether the treatment is by diet restriction, insulin usage or oral drugs, an intelligent approach to the diabetic problem today will allow a normal and active life within very wide boundaries.

The Liver

The liver is the factory and storehouse of the body. Everything we eat is digested and carried to the liver which stores and regulates glucose, manufactures and distributes our blood clotting mechanism, clears the dead blood cells out of the blood stream and detoxifies many of the poisons which would otherwise accumulate in our bodies. The liver has been intensely investigated by medical science, and we know that its many functions are necessary for continued life. We have approximately six times as much liver as is necessary for normal living.

Diseases of the Liver

JAUNDICE

Yellow jaundice is a diseased state in which bile accumulates in the blood stream and stains all the body tissues yellow. It is first noticed in the whites of the eyes, but eventually the jaundice covers the entire body and may even be seen as a yellowish tint in urine.

Bile is manufactured from worn-out red blood cells in the liver, and is then normally drained via the bile passageways into the gallbladder and intestinal tract. When the bile, for any reason, cannot be excreted by the liver into the intestinal tract, it backs up into the blood stream and jaundice begins.

Jaundice is a complex medical problem and is caused by one of three situations:

1. Disease of the spleen and liver.
2. Gallstones or tumor growth blocking the bile duct from the liver into the intestinal tract.
3. Infection of the liver itself called hepatitis.

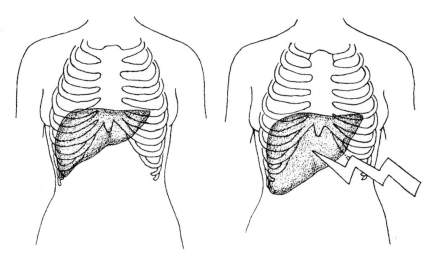

Figure 109: The liver ordinarily is tucked up under the ribs, but in disease may enlarge greatly to occupy nearly half of the abdomen. In such diseases, it becomes quite tender and is occasionally accompanied by jaundice.

Uncovering the exact cause of jaundice may be a very taxing problem even for the most learned physician. The jaundiced patient requires a detailed examination along with numerous laboratory tests to confirm or dispel all disease cause possibilities. We should realize that only the physician is qualified to recognize the extremely serious possibilities of this disease. Though the cause of jaundice may be quite simple, or deeply rooted, the jaundice is often completely relieved through good medical treatment by the pyhsician. Delay in seeking adequate treatment of jaundice may be foolhardy, but attempts at home remedy or drug store cures for jaundice are open invitations to disaster.

HEPATITIS

Jaundice often accompanies hepatitis, a virus-caused disease in which painful swelling in the liver may be felt on the right side of the abdomen. It is a disease which may have a long course to recovery, with an uncertain future, but most patients eventually make a recovery. This disease has a slow onset, and may at times be mild lasting only about a week and accompanied by a fever, a distinct loss of appetite, occasional vomiting and diarrhea. It may also be a severe disease of fulminating character with destruction of the liver followed by death in a few short weeks.

In making the diagnosis of hepatitis, the physician often finds his ability fully taxed. He must distinguish hepatitis from cancer within the bile duct passageways or between gallstones also lodged in these pathways.

The successful treatment of jaundice requires the very best medical care and medical brains working together within a hospital equipped with the best of laboratory facilities.

CIRRHOSIS OF THE LIVER

Although cirrhosis is about the best known of all liver diseases, it is still poorly understood. In this disease, the liver has a roughened, hobnail appearance and was formely thought to be the result of alcoholism. However, since the disease so often occurs in non-drinkers, its cause still remains unclear.

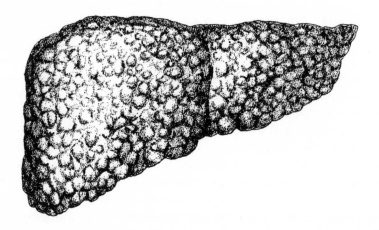

Figure 110: Cirrhosis of the liver creates a hob-nailed appearance and leathery texture. Sometimes connected with chronic alcoholism, the disease means eventual destruction of the liver and death.

A large swelling of the abdomen from an accumulation of watery fluids within it and sudden vomiting of large amounts of blood may be the first indication of cirrhosis. Large veins can be seen on the surface of the abdomen and in the skin covering the chest wall of these unfortunate patients. Cirrhosis usually is diagnosed only after it has existed for a long time and when it is considered incurable. The physician, however, can usually prolong life comfortably with medication, blood transfusions, diet and other measures.

OBSCURE LIVER DISEASE

Other lesser diseases of the liver are commonplace, but they are poorly understood and difficult to recognize even by experienced physicians. Continued study of liver function and disease is being carried on constantly in many medical research programs.

The Colon

The colon, or large intestine, consists of the final five feet of the intestine and its primary function is the condensing of fecal residue (waste material) as it nears the anus for final elimination. Defecation is mostly an automatic mechanism, but this reflex can easily be subdued and controlled by the will.

Very little regard is given to the colon for its contribution to routine living, but there is obvious truth in the saying "Civilization itself was founded upon an intact sphincter of the colon".

Appendicitis

The appendix, attached to the first portion of the colon, has gained notoriety in people of all ages. Usually we thing of appendicitis as a disease of childhood and young adults, and this thinking is correct. People under 40 years of age have four out of every five cases of appendicitis, but less than one in a hundred at this age will die. Only one out of every five cases of appendicitis is found in people over 40 years of age, but in this age group we find three-fourths of all the deaths from appendicitis.

It is a fact that nearly 2,500 United States citizens die each year from appendicitis, and most of these deaths occur between the ages of 64 and 74.

Why is appendicitis more serious in later years even though it is more common in youth? The reasons are:

1. The aged appendix has a much weaker defense mechanism than it has in youth, and the infection develops much faster and more seriously.
2. The appendix is not difficult to recognize in youth, but it is "atypical" in later life, and the usual symptoms of appendicitis in the elderly are much harder to recognize.

3. We grow accustomed to aches and pains here and there as we get a little older. Many of these difficulties are well tolerated with a little patience, but a serious attack of appendicitis often hides among these everyday irritations until irreparable damage is done and treatment is futile.

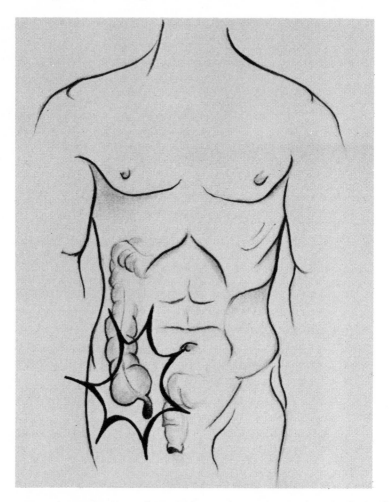

Figure 111: Appendicitis produces pain in the same area as several other diseases. It is most dangerous in later years of life, when it is easy to miss and allowed to continue on its life-threatening course until it is too late. More people die of appendicitis at age 64 than at any other age.

The usual history of appendicitis begins with vague nausea which progresses gradually to one or two episodes of vomiting. At first, moderate pain is felt all over the abdomen, but gradually it localizes low in the right side. A definite soreness in the appendiceal region, along with fever and possibly bloating, helps, to complete the picture. The whole process may begin and grow to obvious proportions within six to 24 hours.

In contrast to the usual story of appendicitis is the atypical course of the disease in later years. The elderly patient with a severe attack of appendicitis may appear to be only slightly ill for the first few days. Nausea, if present at all, frequently does not progress to vomiting. The pain in the abdomen might be only a slight discomfort and might not localize in the right lower side of the abdomen. Temperature usually is not elevated in proportion to the seriousness of the disease.

To add to these difficulties, the picture of appendicitis, in later years, can easily be complicated by other chronic disease symptoms, such as constipation, gallbladder disease or arteriosclerosis.

Appendicitis may be most difficult to diagnose even for the expert physician, and for this reason, no one should attempt to make this diagnosis on himself—not even a doctor. However, everyone, especially parents, should know something about appendicitis and have in mind this typical picture of appendicitis, because over 2,000 deaths a year in the United States might be prevented if only the possibility of appendicitis were considered in time.

The treatment of appendicitis, of course, is surgical. This operation is a simple procedure in the early course of the disease, but it can become a hazardous operation if the disease is allowed to progress until complications occur.

The knowledge that appedicitis is still a dangerous disease tells us that abdominal pain in senior members of our family should not be "taken like a man," but handled more wisely by calling the family physician.

Colitis

This very common disease, also called irritable colon and ulcerative colitis, is accociated closely with the nervous system.

The main characteristics of colitis are frequent and painful cramping of the colon along with periods of diarrhea and constipation. In severe cases, the painful, bloody diarrhea brings about a great loss of health and forces great changes in one's way of life.

There is no definite single cause of colitis, but its beginning seems to involve emotions and tensions concerned with disappointments in life greater than one can stand. A person with colitis is said to be "speaking with his colon," when he cannot translate his troubles into words.

Relief from colitis is best accomplished by consulting a physician schooled in the ways of psychological lessening of fears and tension. For the severe ulcerative colitis case, where the life of the patient itself is in danger, surgery must sometimes be the treatment. This includes possible removal of the entire colon with the formation of a new bowel opening, an "ileostomy," on the abdomen.

Occasionally, a difficulty thought to be colitis is found to be caused by allergies of unsuspected sources. Fortunately, these cases are completely cured with simple dietary restrictions of foods or avoidance of particular drugs.

Diverticulitis

This disease of the later age group is often called left-handed appendicitis. It is an inflammation of the many appendix-like out-pockets of the colon found in five percent of all people at the age of 40 and in 40 percent of all people at the age of 80. Like an appendix, these outpockets can become inflamed and be a source of great pain and bleeding. Usually it is the constipated and older person who has most difficulty with the disease, because the number of diverticulae increases with age.

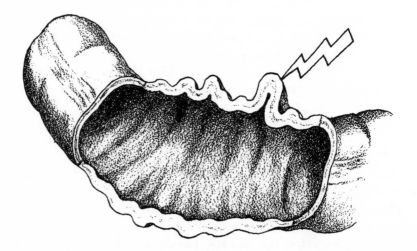

Figure 112: Diverticulitis is caused by inflamed outpockets which become sore and resemble appendicitis. It is found in 1 out if 20 adults and frequently causes bleeding found in the bowel movement.

The irritation of colon diverticulae is thought by physicians to result from seeds or other small particles in the fecal material. A desirable diet eliminates seeds, bones, nuts and other sharp articles which can lodge in these outpockets to start trouble. In severe cases of diverticulitis, surgery may become necessary to remove the segments of colon with inflamed diverticulae.

Diverticulitis frequently is suspected to be a cancer of the colon and necessitates a close investigation by a physician to make the correct diagnosis.

Constipation

This is a frequent complaint with increasing years. Constipation is either a prolonged time between bowel movements, or great difficulty in bowel evacuation itself.

Wide confusion exists concerning just what is normal for bowel regularity and function. In youth, we move about quickly and the bowel, being constantly shaken up, is of little concern. In later life, however, fast-moving activity is just a memory and bowels become a matter of great concern.

To most people, a bowel movement is desirable or necessary every day, and anything less than a daily movement, in people with time enough to notice, immediately establishes the complaint of constipation. Bowel activity for most people is one movement per day, but a daily movement is not the infallible index of good health.

Another function of the colon is to absorb water out of the fecal waste. If the waste moves through the colon rapidly as in active people, water absorption cannot be completed, and a soft bowel movement results. If the bowel movement, however, moves very slowly through the colon, is it does in inactive or bedridden people, nearly all its water moisture becomes absorbed, and a hard, granular marble-like stool is produced.

For relief of ordinary constipation, attention is necessary to only two factors of diet: first, sufficient fiber type foods to absorb water and form a moist stool, and secondly, a healthy food stimulant for the bowel, as obtained from prunes, grapes and other fruits.

The regular activity of body exercise is the normal colon stimulant to promote daily bowel function.

Physics, Laxatives and Enemas. The soaring sales of bowel stimulants and constipation cures is widespread today because we invite constipation, especially in mature years, by our trend toward a sedentary rather than an active leisure time. Television, with its hour-after-hour sitting inactivity, is an outstanding contributor to this situation.

How do physics and laxatives work?

Strong physics such as castor oil directly irritate the intestinal tract, and stimulate in it great waves of propelling activity. This forces the intestinal stream to gush through the colon and anus, producing its well-known clearing out effect. Other physics, such as Epsom Salts and well-advertised bulk laxatives, have a great blotter-like action, and draw large quantities of water into the intestinal tract to make the bowel movement bulky, soft and even watery.

Probably the simplest way of putting in water to clear the colon is with an enema. Though it is much overdone, an enema is essentially harmless, is quite simple to do, and is often used in hospitals.

There are times when physics, lavatives and enemas are of great value, but most of the time their effect can be obtained by drinking more water, including a little more fibre in our diet, and getting some regular exercise. Remedies for constipation however will probably crowd our drug store counters for many years to come, as our population ages and our sedentary lives create more drug store dependents among us.

Cancer of the Colon

Cancer of the colon and rectum is a common disease, usually in the older age group. It is a serious disease but its chances for cure

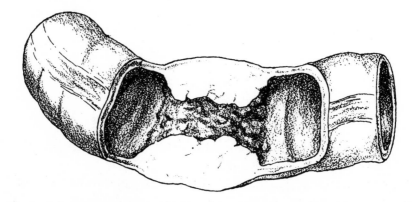

Figure 113: Cancer of the colon is announced nearly half the time by rectal bleeding. It is a disease of senior years and can be treated satisfactorily when discovered early.

are better than 50 percent. The important concern in colon cancer, as in cancer everywhere, is the question of spread of the disease into the neighboring or distant parts of the body. Since the possibility of spread (metastasis) increases with each passing day, about the best hope in colon cancer is that it be found early.

Discovery of cancer in the colon requires a physician for exact diagnosis, but we can help him and ourselves by watching for the symptoms which so often accompany this disease. These symptoms are:

1. Bleeding from the rectum—often the first indication of any trouble in the colon. Bleeding is more often caused by hemorrhoids than by cancer, but it is always a sign that something is definitely wrong and the physician should be consulted at once.
2. A change in bowel habit—a difference in the usual manner of bowel movement (increasing constipation or diarrhea), especially when persistent, may signal definite colon trouble. An examination is in order.
3. Pain from the colon has several identifying marks. An aching pain in the rectum with a feeling of fullness and a sensation of incomplete or continuing bowel movement, sometimes arises from a colon growth and should not be ignored.
4. Cramping or griping originating in the colon is felt in the abdomen below the umbilicus when the colon attempts to move a tumor growth along. Cramping is a message to the physician.

An x-ray of the colon and an examination through the rectum with a tube-like instrument (sigmoidoscope) are part of the physician's routine in this examination.

Treatment of colon cancer is strictly a surgical procedure, consisting essentially of removing the segment of colon containing the cancer. The operation is complex and must be done by an experienced surgeon. The prospects of complete recovery from colon cancer are very good when the cancer is discovered early and removed before it has a chance to spread into other regions of the body.

Hernia (Rupture)

Hernias are noted in all ages as inguinal, femoral and diaphragma-

Figure 114: Side view shows continuity of the abdomen and a hernia. Abdominal contents fall into the hernia sac.

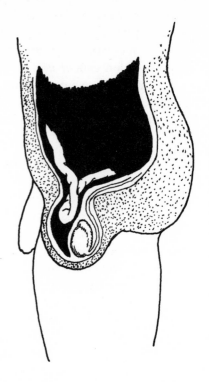

tic hernias. Our abdominal wall is built of layers of strong muscles and fascia, which normally hold the abdominal contents snugly inside the abdomen. A hole anywhere in this wall will allow the inner contents of the abdomen to protrude through abnormally. Such a hole is called a hernia.

Hernias often remain very small and unnoticeable until adult life when they are noticed for the first time. Though present since birth, and very small at first, the hernia eventually can become very large. It is legally popular today to disregard the real beginning of a hernia and to blame it on accidents or strain occurring at work. An injury at work constitutes legal grounds for compensation—the so-called greenback poultice.

Hernias are found much more often in men than in women, and are noticed usually as a bulge, slightly to one side, under the public hair (Figure 115). This is the inguinal region, the site for most hernias. The reason for this is that the abdomen which was built for use in a horizontal position is used by mankind in an upright manner.

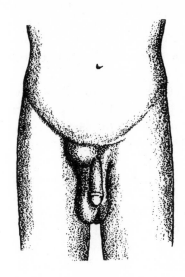

Figure 115: Hernia in the male is most often in the lower abdomen, called the inguinal region. Usually found on the right side, it is treated best by surgical operation. A truss also is found satisfactory in some people.

The most serious thing about hernias is the tendency to strangulate any abdominal contents pushing out through the neck of the hernia and imprison them so tightly they cannot return (Figure 116).

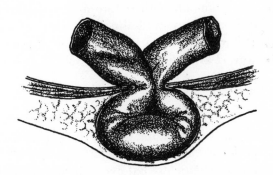

Figure 116: Rupture (hernia) may entrap and strangulate a portion of intestine at any time; immediate operation then becomes necessary to save life. It is best to have hernia operation performed before serious trouble arrives—not afterward.

When the blood supply becomes choked off in this manner, immediate surgery becomes necessary to save the patient's life. The possibility of this danger is an important reason for the surgical repair of most hernias before troubles begin.

The diaphragmatic hernia is an internal type where the hernia or rupture hole is in the muscle of the diaphragm and allows contents from the abdomen to push up into the chest. This hernia has popularly been termed "upsidedown stomach," because a portion of the stomach organ itself is within the chest rather than in the abdomen.

Diaphragmatic hernia is common in senior years and is noticed as heartburn after eating. Often the hernia is slight and therefore the symptoms are slight, but occasionally the pain becomes unbearable, almost constant, and prevents a person from doing his daily work.

The treatment for diaphragmatic hernia is the simple closure of the enlargement in the diaphragm and a rebuilding of the correct alignment of the esophagus to the stomach. This operation however is very technical and must be done by an experienced surgeon.

The Uterus

The uterus or womb is an organ located in the lowest part of the abdomen and is a major part of the female sexual system. It is normally the size of a hen's egg, and difficult to feel within the abdomen unless it is quite enlarged. In adult life, enlargements of the uterus are very common both before and after the menopause and can be felt in the low mid-abdomen. One of these tumor enlargements, the fibroid, is the most common of all tumors and may become very large. Large fibroid tumors often cause low back pain.

The Ovaries

The two ovaries, the fundamental part of the female sexual system, are located in the lower abdomen, one on each side of the uterus. They are the origin of the menstrual cycle during the child-bearing age.

Normal ovaries are too small to feel, but when enlarged, they can range from apple-size up to watermelon-size and often tax the physician heavily for correct identification.

Because of the serious possibilities of these ovarian growths, the physician must advise their operative removal. (See Diseases of the Female Genital Region.)

Figure 117 shows the location of the uterus and ovaries.

Figure 117: The uterus and ovaries are the machinery of the female reproductive system. In them, minor or major diseases can arise that sometimes require hospital care.

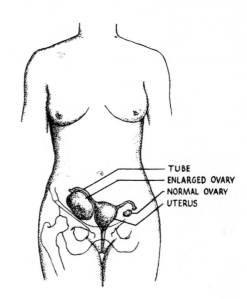

TUBE
ENLARGED OVARY
NORMAL OVARY
UTERUS

Pain in the Abdomen

Pain in the abdomen nearly always means that something is definitely wrong inside. It is nature's warning signal to us and though it is not welcome, it is rarely present without a good reason. To be brave about abdominal pain may mean strong character, but certainly not long life. Unfortunately serious disease in the abdomen is often allowed to progress to death's door and beyond, simply because the pain was thought to be nothing serious.

When an organ with the abdomen is the source of pain, the problem is deciding what organ is involved, and what kind of pain could be serious.

How can we recognize a serious pain? Of the many pains and discomforts so common in the abdomen, some are serious and others are of little importance. Fortunately, pain itself usually gives many clues, and frequently identifies its own source.

A serious possibility is present in the abdomen:

1. If the pain has begun very recently (not months ago), and is very severe.
2. If the pain is accompanied by nausea and vomiting.

3. If the pain is associated with distension (blowing up) of the abdomen.
4. If the abdomen feels hard or rigid, and if pressing upon it causes more pain.
5. If the pain is also accompained by bloody or tarry bowel movements.

Any one of these characteristics lends importance to abdominal pain, whereas absence of all of them would probably mean pain of lesser importance. Some of these less important pains might be stomach ache due to "green apples," minor food poisoning or mild constipation. Most of us have had a few abdominal disturbances along with some mild pain, but when there is any doubt at all about the significance of the pain in the abdomen, the physician should be consulted to rule out any serious possibility.

To study abdominal pain, let us examine each area of the abdomen separately to see which organs can produce pain in each area. Then we can study each organ individually and learn to identify its pain pattern.

Upper Abdominal Pain

Abdominal pain above the umbilicus is most likely to be caused by the stomach, liver, gallbladder or pancreas (Figure 118).

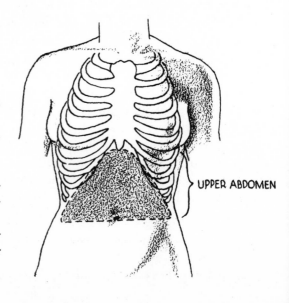

Figure 118: The upper abdomen is above the umbilicus and below the chest. Difficulties in this region include stomach, gallbladder, pancreas and liver-spleen diseases.

UPPER ABDOMEN

STOMACH PAIN

Pain from the stomach is felt in the upper abdomen. It is usually felt in the midline, but occasionally it goes through to the back. It is caused mainly by ulcers, gastritis and cancer.

Peptic Ulcer and Gastritis

Peptic ulcer and gastritis produces a burning or gnawing pain in the upper abdomen close to the midline, and has one characteristic identifying mark. This pain is relieved by food or alkali, and returns when the stomach is empty again.

Cancer Pain

Cancer pain is about the same as ulcer pain although not as severe; there is often additional "stretch" pain just as food is put into the stomach. The pain from enlarged, far-advanced cancer of the stomach is often felt in the back, neck and elsewhere, depending upon the spread of the disease. Stomach cancer is hard to identify with certainty by the pain it produces. This is a job for the physician.

Gallbladder Pain

Pain from the gallbladder is usually felt on the right side of the abdomen just below the ribs. It starts as a dull ache but increases steadily to a peak in about an hour and is called a gallbladder colic because of its come-and-go nature. This pain may also go through to the back and be felt just under the right shoulder blade. As inflamation of the gallbladder develops, the severity of pain also develops, and the upper abdomen becomes very tense and painful when touched.

Liver Pain

Pain of liver origin is usually not very severe. It is more often a dull ache or soreness in the upper abdomen, more to the right side and sometimes felt in the right shoulder as well. The area just below the ribs on the right side is painful when tapped and when a deep breath is taken. Liver pain is frequently found in late stages of heart disease, generalized cancer and hepatitis.

Pancreas Pain

Pancreas pain is usually severe and in the middle of the upper abdomen, drilling straight through into the back. It is difficult to pin down pancreas pain without the aid of laboratory tests and x-ray which are usually necessary to make certain of the pain's origin. This pain often increases to an agonizing state and remains so for several days. It is made worse by eating; sitting up straight or leaning forwards affords a small measure of relief, but real relief from pancreas pain demands a hypo from the physician.

Pain in the Side of the Abdomen

The side of the abdomen is the site for pain caused by the kidneys and the ureter leading down into the urinary bladder. Pain origi-

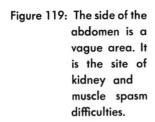

Figure 119: The side of the abdomen is a vague area. It is the site of kidney and muscle spasm difficulties.

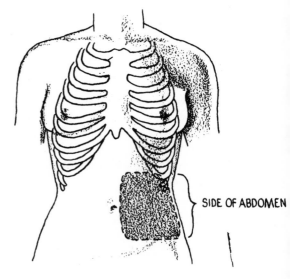

SIDE OF ABDOMEN

nating from the musculature or nerves of the abdominal wall is also most noticed in this location (Figure 119).

Kidney Pain

Kidney pain comes in two distinct types—dull aching pain and colicky cramping pain. The dull ache of kidney infection is felt in the back, just under the ribs and somewhat off to one side. Pushing or punching of this area is usually very painful. Our second kidney pain, the colicky cramping type, is felt not only in the back, but also running around the side to the front of the abdomen and down into the groin region. This is called kidney colic; it can be excruciating and means that a kidney stone possibly is being milked along the ureter to the urinary bladder. Such severe pain is never forgotten.

Pain of the Abdominal Wall (Shingles)

As in the chest, shingles may suddenly appear in the abdominal wall. The pain is typically burning and sometimes is thought to be appendicitis or some other internal disease. The appearance of the rash along the painfully involved nerve route makes identity of the shingles pain very obvious.

Lower Abdominal Pain

Abdominal pain below the umbilicus is usually due to the colon, appendix, ovary, uterus, bladder or a hernia (Figure 120). Pain and discomfort due to the cyclic changes of the menstrual cycle are, of course, confined to the female and not present after the change of life.

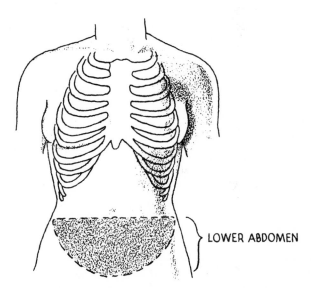

Figure 120: The lower abdomen is below the umbilicus down to the groin. Difficulties here include hernia, appendicitis, colon disease and troubles with the urinary tract.

LOWER ABDOMEN

Pain of the Colon and Intestinal Tract

Pain from the large and small intestine is identified by the "cramp," a pain felt every few minutes in come-and-go fashion— the typical pain of intestinal origin. It is often called gas pains, and ranges from slight discomfort to severe anguish, with a short period of relief in between cramps. Intestinal pain colic is felt usually below the umbilicus and above the groin. It will be readily identified as pain originating from the intestinal tract when the characteristic cramping is remembered.

Appendicitis

Appendicitis at first produces discomfort more than real pain. It is most often felt about the umbilicus and is nearly always accompanied by nausea and vomiting. After a short time (eight to twelve hours) the pain moves to the right side, and lower in the abdomen; eventually, a soreness of the right lower abdomen will predominate. If the abdomen is pressed inward, even lightly, considerable pain will be felt directly over the inflamed appendix. In younger years, when appendicitis is so common, parental knowledge and fears of this disease keep it uppermost in mind and the disease is seldom missed. The typical pain of appendicitis is seen in childhood with the sick child, the sore abdomen, the nausea and vomiting, and the worried parents. In later years, appendicitis is similar but more difficult to identify—usually because of conflicting pains within the abdomen.

Pain of the Female Organs

The variable pain from diseases of the uterus is felt in the lower abdomen, down the inner surface of the leg and, at times, in the lower back.

The beginning of female genital tract pain usually occurs during the maturing state—roughly, from 11 to 13 years. During this time, the stuttering ovary, under the influence of the pituitary gland hormone, is enlarging and exerting its own influence upon the uterus. This growing influence can at times be quite painful with small cysts occurring and subsiding on the ovary itself, and sometimes the 11- or 12-year-old abdomen becomes very sore. The time of life, the elimination of other disease possibilities, the personality changes and the location of the pain deep in the side of the abdomen usually make the diagnosis. For any degree of certainty, of course, this diagnosis must be made by the physician. Much is heard of menstrual pain. Although some women seem to have no pain associated with the menstrual cycle, others will have slight to excruciating pain just preceding and during the menstrual period.

Just why one person should have so much pain and another have none at all is difficult to understand, but it is probably related to each person's ability to feel pain.

A close examination of the pelvis is in order in cases of severe cyclic pain in order to exclude any significant possibility of ovarian or uterine disease at this time. (See diseases of the female genital tract.)

The difficulties of the menstrual period, for some reason, seem to taper off after pregnancy and the painful premenstrual periods are somewhat lessened. Other pain of the adult female genital tract, besides menstrual pain, is distinctly non-abdominal, but rather a "bearing down" or "falling out" type of pain.

The ovary in post-menopausal years may be the site of severe disease, but the pain is not very great and can be interpreted correctly only by the physician.

Urinary Bladder Pain

Bladder pain is felt first when the bladder is overstretched with urine and secondly, when the bladder is completely emptied and its walls collapse against each other.

The first pain begins as a distressful fullness and grows to extreme pain when the bladder cannot be emptied. Pressure or tapping over the bladder region (low in the abdomen) is very painful, and welcome relief is obtained only when the bladder is finally emptied.

The second bladder pain is experienced when the inside of the wall of the bladder is irritated and inflamed (cystitis). When the irritated bladder empties itself completely, the painfully irritated walls touch and rub against each other momentarily, causing a knife-like pain at the end of urination. This pain is characteristic and cannot be mistaken for other abdominal pain.

Hernia Pain

Hernia or rupture is often hard to see in overweight people and may be unknown to many others. Long-standing hernias usually produce a dull aching, more noticeable when standing than when lying down.

In adults, hernias produce their worst pain when they are just beginning or getting larger. Usually the long-standing hernia is practically painless in itself, and any pain produced is likely to be due to entrapped intestinal tract or other abdominal content caught in the hernia.

The pain of hernia is distinguished by its location at the side of pubis and is much more frequent in the male than in the female.

General "Entire" Abdominal Pain

Pain of the entire abdomen often reflects infection or disease all over the abdomen. These disease possibilities include peritonitis, obstruction of the intestinal tract or free bleeding within the abdominal cavity (Figure 121).

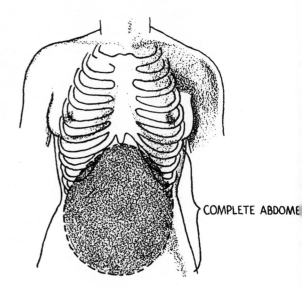

Figure 121: The entire abdomen may be involved in spreading diseases like peritonitis, internal bleeding or gaseous distention.

COMPLETE ABDOME

Pain of Peritonitis

Peritonitis is the name applied to an inflammation of the abdomen or peritoneal cavity. In overwhelming disease such as a perforated ulcer, or following severe trauma, the whole peritoneal cavity is inflamed and pain is felt everywhere. When the peritonitis is localized or confined to one area, the pain also is localized to that area.

Obstruction of the Intestinal Tract

Similar to a kink in our garden hose, an obstruction blocks the passage of the intestine. Pain is felt first as a cramp at the site of the obstruction, but soon the blocked intestine balloons up and pain may be felt everywhere. If the obstruction is not relieved quickly, the intestinal tract becomes diseased, its contents escape into the peritoneal cavity and generalized peritonitis develops.

Free Bleeding Within the Peritoneal Cavity

Blood is often found free within the peritoneal cavity following severe trauma such as automobile accidents in which abdominal organs are injured or torn apart. This happens when the liver is torn, the spleen is ripped, or the large blood vessels within the abdomen are torn free. Another source of free bleeding within the abdominal cavity is the ovary, which occasionally bleeds with the ovulatory period. This is the middle of the month or "middle schmertz" time when the ovary throws out its ovum to begin the menstrual cycle. While ordinary ovulatory bleeding consists of only one or two drops of blood, this type of bleeding can reach major proportions and fill the entire abdomen painfully with blood. Surgery, of course, is indicated for this severe problem.

The Kidney

The kidney, in the back of the abdomen, is the main part of our urinary system. It excretes many poisonous wastes along with water, salt, acids and other body chemicals. The structure of the kidney is shown in Figure 122.

During good health, the kidneys work silently and call no attention to their important and unceasing function. But disease causes them to cry out in the language of pain, fever and bloody urine.

Pain of kidney origin is usually felt in the back, just under the lowest ribs, possibly extending around to the front of the abdomen and down into the testicles. Kidney pain varies from the mild ache of a slight infection to the knife-like horror of a colic that comes with the passage of a kidney stone.

Fever of a severe kidney infection often reaches 103 degrees with severe chills, whereas a long-standing, smouldering infection may produce only a half-degree of fever in the afternoons. When fever is due to kidney infection, there are usually other kidney symptoms also present to help identify it.

Blood in the urine is not visable in minute amounts, but in slightly larger quantities it begins to appear as a smoky, rust color, and with greater quantities the urine darkens to assume finally the color of blood itself. Finding blood in the urine might be only an isolated instance and perhaps entirely painless, but it is always of great significance and should be thoroughly and quickly investigated.

The kidney structure embraces a tremendous number of small blood vessels, and any disease of the blood vessels therefore also involves the kidneys. This is particularly true of high blood pressure, hardening of the arteries and diabetes.

Diseases of the Kidney

CYSTIC DISEASE OF THE KIDNEY

This disease is congenital (found at birth) and affects the kidney

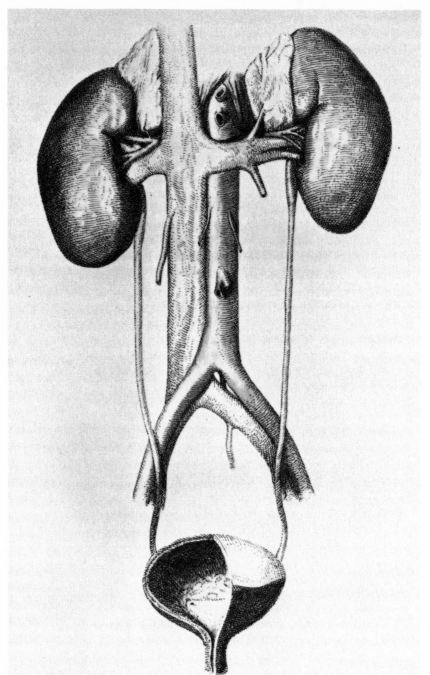

Figure 122: The kidney has a tremendous amount of blood flowing through it and the urine it manufactures flows through the long tubes, called the ureters, into the urinary bladder. When we urinate, it is a bladder function; the kidneys are working constantly.

by the presence of countless cysts in the kidney instead of normal kidney tissue.

When milder cystic disease of the kidney is not discovered at birth, the disease grows with the years until the 20's or 30's, when its symptoms become pronounced. Since there is no cure for this disease, many who would otherwise succumb have been given treatment with the artificial kidney, and more recently have undergone the widely publicized kidney transplant operation.

The difficulties encountered in the newer treatments of kidney transplant and artificial kidney are so great, and the expense is so large, that considerable research must still be done before these treatments become practical.

AGENESIS (ABSENCE OF ONE KIDNEY)

An uncommon finding is the total absence of one kidney, as a developmental defect. Ordinarily, this does not cause any great discomfort or disease, but it does create one hazard of importance. The hazard is faced when trauma, disease or surgery might indicate removal of a kidney. If it is not known that the other kidney is totally absent, removal of the patient's sole kidney would mean death. A diseased or damaged kidney is better than no kidney at all.

NEPHRITIS

Infection of the kidney tissue itself is disease termed nephritis or Bright's disease.

This disease involves the tiny blood vessels, tubes and renal tissue of the kidney itself. It is an infection usually of the streptococcus bacteria, and can range from a mild infection to one which is overwhelming and possibly fatal. Often, nephritis starts in youthful years, when infections may go unnoticed and their serious possibilities unrecognized, and it is not until later years that the kidney is suddenly found completely worn out by years of continuing infection.

Infections of the kidney in the nephritis group invite diseases of the heart and blood vessels—especially high blood pressure. Sometimes pain is absent, but often it is felt in the back just under the ribs on the side of the affected kidney. Blood is usually present as a cloudy appearing urine, and fever is often a prominent symptom.

The treatment of kidney infection cannot be successful through the use of advertised mineral waters or kidney pills, which claim to flush out the kidneys. The successful treatment of kidney disease calls for expert and rigid therapy from a physician well versed in kidney diseases.

PYELITIS

Infection of the kidney's urinary tract, called pyelitis, involves the "end" of the kidney—after the urine has been formed. It is usually not found alone, but is more often associated with infection of the entire kidney organ, and it is often noticed by the sufferer himself who may find pus or blood in the urine and have considerable burning pain during urination. Pain of the kidney is often felt in the back and sides, and to many people this location of pain identifies kidney pain.

KIDNEY STONES

Kidney stones are very common and frequently found in the senior years of life. These stones are caused by faulty body metabolism of minerals like calcium, by bone diseases, by parathyroid disease and possibly by kidney infections themselves.

Pain of the kidney stone is characteristic. It is a severe cramp-like pain starting in the back, traveling around to the front of the abdomen and down into the scrotum in the male, or the sides of the vagina in the female (Figure 123). This location of pain practically diagnoses itself as kidney-urinary tract pain.

Often a stone in the urinary tract can be seen with the x-ray. Soon after he feels the pain the patient may pass a gravel-like stone in his urine. If the stone is so large it cannot pass down the urinary tract, it may be necessary to remove it surgically.

It is difficult to prevent kidney stones, but people who have had renal colic pain may find relief by eliminating certain foods and including others in the diet. The physician must be consulted for treatment of stones for there is the risk of possible rapid deterioration of the kidney.

UREMIA

Uremia is a well-known disease caused by failure of kidney function to clear from the blood the waste substances which tend to pile up in the blood and eventually produce unconsciousness and death. The disease is produced if the kidneys are suddenly lost through an accident, but more often it grows over a long period of time from diseases which slowly deteriorate the kidney. Uremia

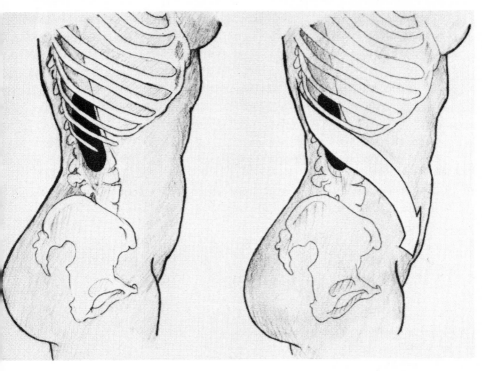

Figure 123: The kidney is located in the back, under the ribs, alongside the vertebral column. Pain from the kidney, however, radiates from the kidney region, around the side from the abdomen and down into the groin. Kidney pain has a colic or cramp to it; it is sometimes light, but more often severe. It is one of the most significant of all human pains.

begins when kidney function falls to less than 30 percent of its original ability.

Uremia is a difficult disease. In its beginning, the typical uremic patient might appear sleepy, lethargic and slightly mentally unbalanced. These symptoms increase and, in the very latest stages of the disease, there may appear the characteristic uremic frost, a fine powdery snow or frost on the skin. This frost represents an effort of the skin to assume the role of the kidney through the process of perspiration rather than urination. Long before the stage of uremic frost however, the patient has usually lapsed into an unconscious state. To diagnose uremia accurately requires delicate laboratory tests which indicate the presence and extent of kidney failure. It is interesting that uremia has become well-established, general knowledge in the minds of so many people.

As medical science continues its rapid strides, the treatment of uremia looks with interest to the new advances in kidney transplantation and to the use of the artificial kidney as well. These avenues of treatment, unknown just a few years ago, hold out new promise to an otherwise doomed victim of kidney disease.

The Urine

Throughout all history, the urine has always been regarded as an index of the body's state of health. Its variations, amount, color, odor and clarity have meant many things to many men, but the urine as a laboratory testing substance has taken on new importance.

There are now laboratory tests of many kinds, each designed to wrest from the urine a fact or two which indicate certain forms of disorder to the investigating physician. These laboratory tests are a study in themselves, but the person unschooled in medical ways can also know several important facts about his health with only an elementary study of urine. A few chemical crystals found in urine are shown in Figure 124.

Under normal circumstances, the volume of daily urine of the average adult is about one and one-half quarts, depending upon habits of fluid intake. This is easily measured by the simple use of a quart bottle and recording of the urine's daily volume. Some days there will be a large increase in a day's urine volume from over-drinking or perhaps from fleeting diseases. However, a constant, daily urine output, far exceeding one and one-half quarts, may indicate the possibility of certain diseases. Some of these disease possibilities are uremia, hyperthyroidism, diabetes or simply nervous people drinking too much water.

Normal urine secretion from the kidney is about four times as great in the daytime as during sleep. This is natural, because we are awake three-fourths of the day and asleep only eight hours and we drink fluids only when awake.

It is abnormal to pass great amounts of urine during sleeping hours. It happens where poor kidney function exists, or if there is beginning heart failure, where body fluid within the body is held away from the kidney until a lying-down position is assumed. In disease states, nighttime urination (nocturia) often amounts to three or four routine awakenings.

It is not abnormal to find that after heavy eating or drinking, we must arise at night to urinate.

URIC ACID   CALCIUM OXALATE

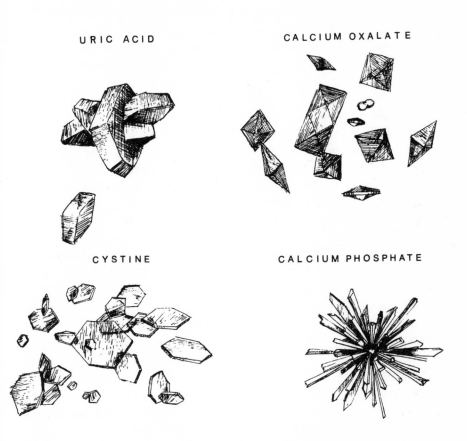

CYSTINE   CALCIUM PHOSPHATE

Figure 124: The urine has many chemicals in it thrown off by the body when they reach too high a level. All of the parts and findings of the urine would fill volumes. A few of the chemicals found in the urine occur as crystals when examined under the microscope, as shown here.

Color Significance of Urine

Normal urine is clear. When a haziness or sediment can be seen floating on the urine or settling to the bottom we must suspect the presence of blood, pus, crystals or bacteria themselves.

Normal urine is straw colored, but it can change to nearly any color.

What do the colors of the urine mean? A red color is usually due to blood coming from the kidney, bladder, prostate gland or the testicles. This is a serious finding, but we must remember that medications and some foods also color the urine and give rise to false alarms.

A deep yellow or brown color frequently means bile in the urine. Bile enters the urine whenever jaundice appears, because bile intended for excretion into bowel matter is forced into the urinary stream. If the foam in the urine also has a yellowish tint, it is again probable that bile is in the urine. This finding has great significance.

Brown urine which turns black on standing contains the body pigment melanin and may mean a tumor growth in the body.

When the urine is clear at first, but turns black on standing or after drying, there arises the possibility of the rare disease ochronosis, which characteristically produces bluish-black pigment in the whites of the eyes and about the ears and nose.

A blue color, an occasional reddish tint and even a yellowish green fluorescence seen in the dark, may occur from eating chemicals often used in laxatives and vitamins.

The normal urine produces a slight white foam when gently shaken. If a large amount of soapy foam forms, there is probably protein in the urine, a certain indication of disease.

Odors and Taste of Urine

The odor of urine is well-known and after several hours, normally changes to an ammonia ordor. The odor of sweet fruit most often means diabetes. A foul ordor to the urine almost always means an infection in the urinary tract.

The simplest test for sugar in the urine is its taste. A drop of urine on the finger tip may reveal the taste of sugar, which means diabetes.

Acidity and Alkalinity Indicators

What about the urine's acidity or alkalinity? In normal health, the urine's acidity is exactly as in the blood stream; checking on this is a routine in laboratory urine analysis. When the body is forced through punishing episodes, such as pneumonia or diabetes, the body leans to the acid side and the urine responds quickly by excreting a highly acid urine, thus bringing the acid content back into balance. In ulcer patients, the body may become more alkaline than is usual, because these patients have been taking so much alkaline medication to counter their ulcer problems. Here the urine becomes distinctly alkaline as the kidney again attempts to help the body regain its balance.

Personal home testing of urine for acidity, alkalinity or sugar is now done by using inexpensive commercially prepared test paper which will indicate these changes in the urine with an easy-to-read cover scale. Most drug stores carry this urine testing paper.

Personal observations of the urine may uncover abnormalities, but of course they do not make a complete or definite diagnosis of any certain disease. Yet obvious abnormalities in the urine as described above should never be overlooked through sheer carelessness; these urine findings are clear warnings that something is wrong in the body, and that it is time for the schooled study and opinion of the physician.

Section
5

THE GENITAL REGION

The Subject of Sex

Life's main reason for sex and the genital region is the proud moment of birth—the regeneration of life. The reproducing process, as it binds man and woman in the closest of physical bonds, also creates the building block of all society—the family.

To be learned, we must understand sex as a natural function, as necessary to man's life as breathing itself.

Sex has many legitimate meanings. To the infant, sex is the gentle and enduring security of his mother's arms, and the massive protecting strength of his father.

Up to the age of nine or ten years, youngsters see mother as the all-understanding, loving and forgiving figure, while father becomes the symbol of authority, leadership, and perhaps discipline. In the pre-puberty child, mother is the first sweetheart and father the great all-around champion. And with puberty, when boys and girls discover each other, the quiet status of childhood starts growing into the dynamic force of everyday adult living.

For the adult, sexual activity also includes many roles. They include playmate, helpmate, sweetheart, wife, husband, mother and father.

The most intense sexual activity, of course, is in sexual intercourse, which, unfortunately, is a source of great misunderstanding, disappointment and difficulty for many people. The reasons for this are very apparent in other people but difficult to see in ourselves.

The biggest difficulty arises in misunderstandings. Today's widespread and colorful advertising tells us that sex is the final goal of happiness and full satisfaction, and that all difficulties will melt away before it.

How wrong can we be? Sex is not an isolated island of life, where everything else is set aside. Sexual relations actually involve the full man—his desire to serve or his need to dominate—his spirit of generosity or his habit of "me first."

Consider the typical young man during his courtship and honeymoon days. With his best foot always forward, he tries only to please. He is well-dressed, generous and entertaining; he promises the world and he states that his intended is the most important of all worldly treasures.

How does he follow through a few years afterwards?

Often he isn't even interested in where his best foot is placed; his attempts to please have given way to dull routines. Is he still well-dressed and clean-shaven, or does he appear more often in his undershirt with a stubbly beard as a member of the great unwashed? Is he still the dashing Lothario of courtship days—and how generous is he now with the whole world he once promised?

Will the dream-like vision of happiness spring from sexual relations, when one's spouse has just been told how ignorant, fat and unsuccessful he is? And what married partner is "in heaven" with a spouse she knows is creating other heavens with several other partners.

A married person's sexual relations reflect not just an anatomical fact, but his entire personality and background as well.

The Male Genital Region

Sexual development in the male has always had great psychological significance. As proof of virility, men feel they must have standard development, and under-development of the penile-scrotal region or the loss of a testicle is a catastrophe. Since on-coming years usually mellow this opinion and to a great extent wither this ability, time itself is probably the greatest soother of jangled nerves in the male over-absorbed in his sexual prowess.

Examination of the Male Genital Region

Examination of the external genital system in the male requires only some privacy, and a well lighted room which can be darkened. The use of a small flashlight is also required.

1. Examine the scrotum between the thumb and forefiner and determine the presence of two testicles. Note any filling tendency of the scrotum on one side which seems to disappear when the patient lies down. This may mean the presence of a hernia (rupture).

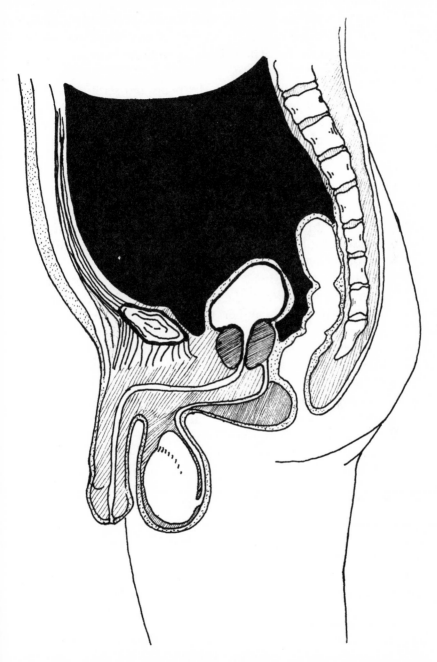

Figure 125: The male genital system is combined with the urinary tract. The testicle is placed outside in the scrotum because it must have a cooler temperature than the inside of the body.

2. Examine the head of the penis for any reddened irritation or pus after the prepuce skin is pulled back. Also, observe any discharge of pus from the urethra when the penis is gently squeezed. These findings indicate internal infection of the penis or prostate.

3. Examine the entire skin of the penis and scrotum. Note the presence of any open sore, and whether or not such sore is painful. This skin finding includes the possibility of the chancre of syphilis, the Ducrey bacillus chancroid, early cancer of the penis, boil-like infections or large sebaceous cysts (blackheads).

4. In a darkened room, examine the scrotal sac which holds the testicles. Stretch the scrotum over the lens of a flashlight and examine it for any painless enlargements through which light passes readily. Light transparent enlargements within the scrotum may mean hydrocele or water cysts.

5. Examine the testicles within the scrotum. One testicle is normally higher than the other, but both should be painless. Note any pain in either testicle with gentle palpation or squeezing. Note also any apparent shrinkage or firm enlargement in either testicle. Such findings may indicate the presence of testicular tumors, atrophy or infection.

7. Observe the urinating stream. Determine if there is a lengthened period of time required before urinating begins and compare the force of the urinary stream with earlier years. Note also any burning during or just after the act of urination. Hesitant urination and weakened or burning urinary stream may mean prostatic or infection difficulties.

Diseases of the Male Genital Region

The male genitals are beset with a definite group of difficulties, as noted in the following paragraphs. Some of them are common at both younger and older ages; they may arise from infection, developmental problems, malignant and non-malignant growth, erection difficulties or urinary problems due to prostatic disease.

Developmental Problems

OPEN URETHRA

This is a developmental defect noticed at birth, which sometimes has mild significance. When the urinary tract along the penis is open, the urine stream may be deviated or difficult to control. This difficulty may be very inconvenient but it is not serious.

UNDERDEVELOPMENT OF THE MALE GENITAL REGION

Under-development of the male genital region is a finding often associated with pituitary gland disease. The under-developed state may be associated with an apparent partial development of a female sexual system in the same person. This is called hermaphroditism (bi-sexualism) and it can give rise to many embarrassments, including the question of exactly what sex a person truly is.

Treatment of an under-developed genital system in the male includes hormonal therapy and perhaps surgery. Results, however, may be discouraging and psychotherapy is often very helpful.

INFECTION OF THE PENIS

Infection of the end of the penis often occurs because the foreskin cannot be retracted to expose the head of the penis for cleaning. This contracted and narrowed foreskin is called phimosis; it keeps the head of the penis wet, contaminated and an ideal breeding ground for infection.

Infection of the penile skin can be due to bacterial infection like skin anywhere on the body. It may also be due to infection and scratching from fungus or louse disease. The dark, moist skin of the penis and groin invite not only the common infections of ordinary skin, but also the fungus infections which seek damp, dark skin areas in which to breed.

A widely know infection inside the penis is gonorrhea, sometimes called clap. This infection can be acquired at any age, but it is almost always acquired from sexual relations with an infected person. The disease begins by producing large amounts of pus draining out of the urethra, starting about a day after sexual intercourse. The pus discharge and the accompanying burning urination last about a week, but the disease will respond rapidly to the physician's administration of the proper antibiotics. When gonorrhea is allowed to go untreated, the possibility of prostatic infection will arise, often accounting for arthritis, kidney infections and other difficulties in later life.

CHANCRE OF SYPHILIS

Syphilis, a serious veneral disease, has been known down through the ages. It is heralded by the chancre, a shallow, ulcerated and painless sore on the penis, which lasts about two weeks. The chancre develops on the head of the penis after sexual intercourse with an infected person, as a small pimple which soon breaks down into the characteristic shallow painless ulcer. Syphilis is a systemic disease, with the causative spirochete circulating within the blood stream, in the salivary secretion, and in other parts of the body. A blood test will show a positive serology to definitely establish the diagnosis. An illustration of a penile sore is shown in Figure 126.

Figure 126: A penile sore usually brings up the question of venereal disease. However, the penis may be afflicted with skin diseases found anywhere on the body. It is only logical to wash hands before, as well as after, touching this organ.

Drugs are now available for the cure of this disease, and when properly administered by a physician, they are extremely effective, but repeated checks are still desirable to determine the effectiveness of treatment.

CHANCROID-DUCREY INFECTION

Chancre-like sores on the penis and other parts of the body, often thought to be syphilitic in nature, are sometimes caused by nonvenereal types of bacteria and organisms such as the Ducrey bacillus. Other penile sores are the result of simple chronic irritation.

CANCER OF THE PENIS

Cancerous growths of the penis are not common, but occasionally, after the age of 50, they will appear on the end of the penis. They are thought to be caused by chronic irritation from a contracted foreskin. Cancers can be mistaken for syphilis or some simple infection, but they differ in one respect—they do not heal. They are also painful, and have a tendency to bleed and to enlarge rapidly.

Cancer of the penis differs from other cancers in one important distinction. It travels extremely fast and can spread throughout the body at a very early stage. Therefore, any sore on the penis should be seen by the physician as soon as possible.

CYSTS, HYDROCELE, SPERMATOCELE

Hydrocele and spermatocele, often called water cysts, occur frequently in the male genital tract. They can be felt on either side of the scrotum as a smooth, balloon-like enlargement, which slowly enlarges to the size of a lemon or an orange. Although these cysts are painless and not serious, they frequently become a nuisance because of their size and location about the testicles.

Water cysts in the scrotum can be identified easily in a dark room with a flashlight placed against the back of the scrotum so that its rays shine through the scrotum. The cysts will illuminate readily, whereas the solid testicles appear as dark, nonilluminated masses.

A needle is often used to drain the enclosed fluid of the cyst for temporary relief, but the fluid nearly always comes back again. These cysts are best removed by a simple surgical operation.

TESTICLE DISEASES—ABSENCE, PAIN, TUMOR

Many men with just one external testicle have fathered several children and have noticed no lack of virility through the absence of one testicle. It is important, however, that undescended testicles in adult life be removed because of the high rate of cancer in the undescended testicle.

The atrophic or smaller sized testicle, often noticed in adult men, is usually the result of virus infection in childhood—especially mumps. The smaller sized testicle remains the same throughout life, but has no male hormone or sexual ability. When both testicles are involved in this manner, it usually renders a man sterile.

Pain in the testicle is common, because it is a very sensitive organ and pressures cause immediate and severe pain. But the sudden onset of severe pain of the testicle often heralds an infection within the testicle or its tract, especially if accompanied by a bloody discharge. The severe pain forces the patient to drop his work and seek treatment. The physician may prescribe antibiotics, ice bag coverage, or occasionally, incision and drainage in a surgical manner.

Tumor growths of the testicles are usually found in early youth and adolescence, but there is no guarantee against a growth of the testicle in later years. Most growths of the testicles are cancerous in nature and should command an early visit to the physician for his examination.

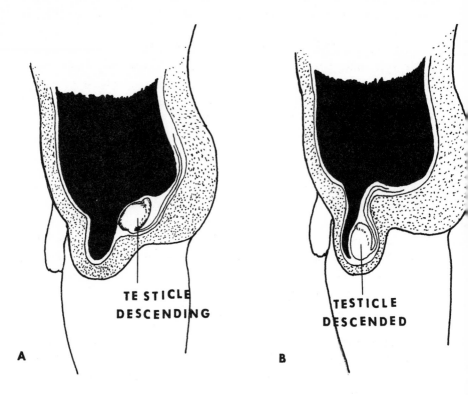

TE STICLE
DESCENDING

TESTICLE
DESCENDED

A   B

Figure 127A: The testicle descends from the abdomen into the scrotum usually before birth. Often, it will descend afterward. When it does not descend, surgery is indicated since this testicle is prone to many diseases including cancer.

Figure 127B: As the testicle descends into the scrotum, it creates a channel within the abdomen itself. Unless it grows together as normally expected, this channel remains as a hernia.

SCROTAL HERNIA (RUPTURE INTO THE SCROTUM)

Large hernias frequently descend into the scrotum and create enlargement of the scrotal sac. On standing or straining the mass appears to fall from the abdomen, under the skin and into the scrotum which balloons up to the size of an orange or even more. Usually these enlargements will return to the abdomen when the patient lies down, or when pressure is placed on the enlargement in the scrotum.

Hernia has been treated many ways. The simplest thing to do is wear a truss which puts constant pressure on the hernia to hold it in the abdomen. But since trusses must be tightly worn to be effective, they are cumbersome, often painful and limit physical ability.

A truss will not heal a hernia, but we often find men who have worn a truss for 20 years in the belief that the truss will soon fix their rupture, who finally realize that the hernia has been slowly enlarging all along. Only a few people who wear a truss for their hernia are really satisfied.

Besides trusses, other treatments for hernia have existed for years, but a surgical operation for hernia is our most satisfactory treatment today and is usually followed by complete healing, complete comfort and a strengthened body wall. It is thought that within six months of the surgical hernia repair, the repaired region will be stronger than the same region in the average person.

Surgical repair of hernias is not completely fool-proof, since a recurrence after operation follows in nearly one out of 12 cases. But it is still by far the most satisfactory treatment available for hernia at present.

ERECTION DIFFICULTIES

Sexual activity in the male has been designated by Mother Nature primarily as a function of youth. After adult years, varying with the individual, erection of the penis and sexual activity are not as frequent as in earlier years. Inherited tendencies, accidents and psychological environment also affect this function. In this manner, nature decrees that only the youthful male will become a father, able to work in the years ahead necessary to raise his child into adulthood. It would be unfair in many ways for children born into the world to have parents who are 60 and 70 years of age, because fatherhood calls for much greater and much longer ability than fleeting sexual activity.

As a result of trauma, scar tissue can form on the penis and a painful erection called Peyronie's Disease may occur. The scar tissue along one side of the penis will not stretch and creates a curve in the penis with so great an angle that intercourse is difficult or impossible. Considerable surgical and medical skill is necessary for any kind of satisfactory treatment.

An erection that is normal, except that it is painful and unrelated to sexual function, is known as priapism. This difficulty is in the later years of life, and is due to disease affecting the nervous system, the blood or the penis itself. It calls for a complete physical examination to determine, if possible, the responsible bodily disease.

Prostate Difficulties

Infection in the Prostate

Most prostate infections are incurred during youth in the active sexual years and are caused by gonorrhea or similar infections, while in later years these infections more often come from infection of the teeth or tonsils. When an infection is harbored for many years by the prostate gland, the infection tends to spread into the urinary tract and the rest of the body as well.

Prostate infection can be very stubborn and difficult to eradicate completely. It is often a suspected underlying cause of arthritis and other troubles, and complete cure of this infection becomes very important.

An infected prostate cannot be cleared by drinking large amounts of water, flushing the kidney or other simple remedies as advertised in newspapers. The complete cure of this infection is often most difficult and time-consuming even for the experienced physician who must direct the patient through many weeks of scheduled treatment before effective cure is certain.

Growth of the Prostate Gland

Prostatic growth in younger ages is almost unknown but it is one of the most common and troublesome difficulties for males in adult years, and creates urinating difficulties known the world over. These troubles begin by slowing the stream of urine. Gradually, the stream becomes weakened and eventually even becomes dribbling. There might develop a full minute or more of waiting before urination commences, and finally the weak urinary stream is only a faint shadow of the forceful stream of urination known in youth. The enlarging prostate not only obstructs the urinary flow, but also makes complete emptying of the bladder impossible. Then like a half-emptied glass of water, the bladder is quickly refilled and makes frequent urination necessary, especially at night when sleep is interrupted possibly five to ten times. Figure 128 indicates a prostate situation.

An increase in the problem may eventually find a person unable to urinate at all, and a state of emergency arises. The urine is completely blocked; the urinary bladder is overstretched; a mechanical drainage of urine from the bladder becomes necessary

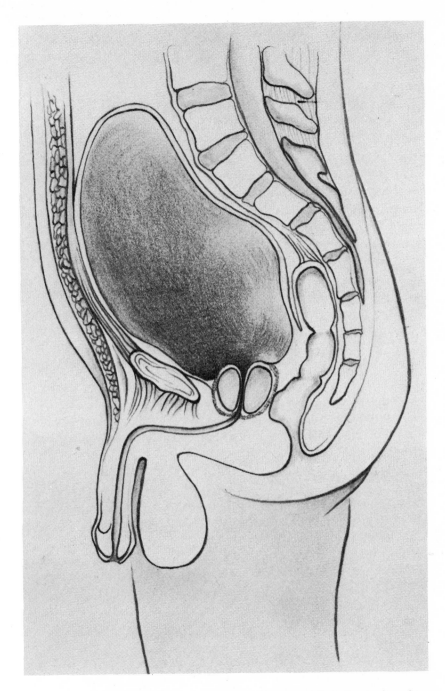

Figure 128: The bladder that cannot empty because of a diseased and enlarged prostate often reaches great proportions. The obstructing
prostate gland must be removed for normal bladder function.

immediately. This is done by catheterization, the introducing of a small tube through the urethra of the penis into the urinary bladder to provide an opening for the escape of the entrapped urine.

Several aids of doubtful value in common practice today, which attempt to encourage urinating ability, include the psychological benefit of running water from a faucet or sitting in a tub of warm water.

The only lasting cure of prostatic growth is the mechanical removal of the prostate tissue responsible for obstructing the urinary channel. This operation, called prostatectomy, allows the urine flow to return to a youthful free flow as indicated in Figure 129.

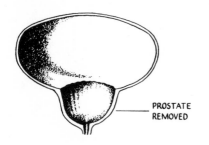

PROSTATE
REMOVED

Figure 129: Once the prostate gland is removed, the urinary stream again becomes forceful.

The operation does not interfere with sexual relations, so far as erection of the penis is concerned, but it does usually render a male sterile.

Cancer of the Prostate Gland

The cancerous prostate gland behaves exactly like benign (noncancerous) enlargement of this gland and is treated in the same manner—removal of the gland itself.

Unfortunately, this disease can also spread to other sections of the body just like any other cancer, and so in addition to its removal the treatment includes the use of hormones which are very effective in slowing down prostatic cancerous growth.

The Female Genital Region

The female pelvis and genital region, and diseases of this region, are the field of gynecology. Diseases of women is a vast specialty, and an understanding of the normal female reproductive system is necessary before we can recognize abnormalities or diseases of the genital region.

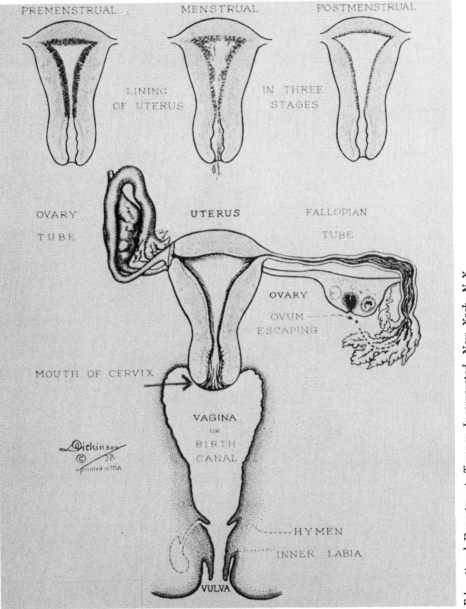

PREMENSTRUAL   MENSTRUAL   POSTMENSTRUAL

LINING
OF UTERUS

IN THREE
STAGES

OVARY

TUBE

UTERUS

FALLOPIAN

TUBE

OVARY

OVUM
ESCAPING

MOUTH OF CERVIX

VAGINA
OR
BIRTH
CANAL

Dickinson
©   J.P.
printed in USA

------HYMEN

-----INNER LABIA

VULVA

Educational Department, Tampax Incorporated, New York, N. Y.

Figure 130: The uterus is the center of the female genital system. It is located at the top of the vagina or birth canal and is attached on either side to the ovary. Its periodic cycle involves three stages—the premenstrual stage, the menstrual stage, and the post-menstrual stage. Ordinarily, menstruation stops during pregnancy, but on rare occaions it continues uninterruptedly.

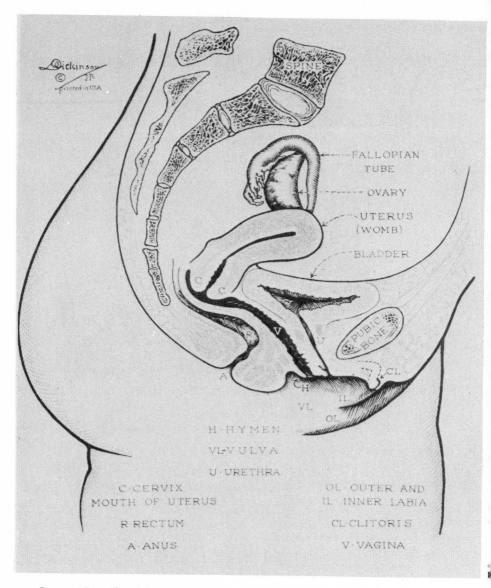

Figure 131: The side view of the uterus and pelvis shows the uterus in a completely protected position. It is at the top of the birth canal and has but one function—the function of childbirth.

Especially in the female, it is true that sex is not simply a mechanical fact of anatomy. Unlike her male partner in life, a woman must undergo great physical changes frequently. Beginning in youth, she experiences regular monthly changes often associated with disturbing irregularities; during her adult life, she is involved in the enormous process of child bearing and birth; and in her later years, she is faced with another significant change in the menopause. Since these changes are all attended with great periods of tension, anxiety and misunderstandings frequently arise.

Examination of the Female Genital Region

A self-examination is best carried out lying on the back with the knees well bent and held widely apart. With good light and a large mirror, the external vagina and its component parts can be easily seen.

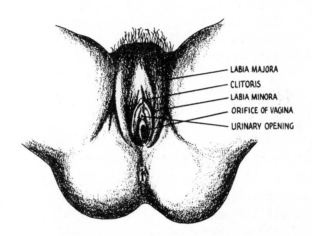

Figure 132: External female genitalia include only the unimportant skin folds about the vaginal entrance. The urinary tract exit is visible recessed into this region. Most diseases of the external genitals are not serious.

1. Carefully examine the skin of the vulva, the labia majora and minora surrounding and enfolding the entrance of the vaginal vault. Note any fecal material in or coming from the vagina itself. Abnormalities indicate possible malformation in the size or the development of the external genitalia and rectal region.
2. Note any areas of drying, leathery whitening or skin cracking about the vulva. Note any irritation, redness, ulceration or sore on these skin structures. These possibilities may mean leukoplakia, infection or cancer of the vulva.
3. Feel the labia themselves and note any one-sided ball-like enlargement under the skin, creating a painful bulge. Such enlargement may be a Bartholin cyst.

4. Look closely at the urinary exist, the dimpled-like opening just at the entrance into the deeper vagina. Observe any reddended or bleeding polyp-like growth about it or extending out from it. The possibility here is a urethral polyp or caruncle.

5. Examine closely the entrance of the true or deep vagina. Note any membranous closure blocking the entrance into the deeper vagina. Such a blocking membrane, whether complete or partial, is an imperforate or virginal hymen. Note an irritated, reddened skin, with a coating of pus over it. This is the appearance of vaginitis.

6. With a hand separating the labia on each side, strain with great effort as in childbirth or at stool, and note any balloon-like structure from the vagina coming into view. Such an apparent structure may be a fallen bladder (cystocele), a fallen uterus (prolapsed uterus), or a fallen rectum (rectocele).

Diseases of the Female Genital Region

Female genital tract disease through the adult and post-menopausal period includes several disease characteristic of the menopausal period, and some genital diseases which persist from birth through life. Most diseases of this region occur in mid-adult years, but age is no barrier or preventer of disease.

IMPERFORATE HYMEN

Examination of the vagina may show a completely closed surface where the vaginal canal should be. Most often this means an imperforate hymen, a vaginal orifice closed by a membranous tissue which, of course, is the normal virginal state.

THE MENSTRUAL PERIOD AND ITS DIFFICULTIES

The age of beginning menstruation (the menarche) is anywhere between the ages of 9 and 14, but usually about 12.

The 10- and 11-year-old girl needs to be told that the oncoming menstrual period is a normal and natural thing, and that it is a sign that she is growing into young womanhood. She should be told that her breasts will enlarge, that hair will begin to grow in the genital region, and that her body will begin to grow and look like other young ladies about her.

In former days misinformation was frequently handed down to

young women in a frightful way. For example, it was often taught that if the menstrual period did not flow freely to the outside, it would certainly flow inwardly and cause tuberculosis. Since many of these wrong ideas are still present and seem to find their way into young women's minds, it becomes all-important for mother-daughter talks to be thorough and correct, as well as friendly and unthreatening. The mechanism of pregnancy and the mechanics of child bearing and childbirth are the rightful knowledge of all young women entering puberty.

The first menstraul period can be attended by abdominal cramping and can last a week or more. It is probable the first few periods will be irregular and of varying amount. Often an examination by the physician is in order if pain is severe and regularity not achieved. It is common for the menstrual period to take a year or two to achieve real regularity.

1. Heavier-than-normal menstrual flow (hyper-menorrhea) is frequent in young women in their teens and early twenties. It is usually due to an imbalance of hormones in the body, between the thyroid, pituitary and ovarian gland. This situation again arises in older women approaching the menopause when hormonal imbalance again becomes frequent and periods may be excessively heavy.

   A heavy menstrual flow in the middle of the child-bearing age usually is caused by disease in the genital region, mostly by growths, including cancers and infectious or inflammatory disease of the pelvic organs. Periodic check-ups, including the smear test on a yearly basis during the child-bearing years, will certainly help to eradicate any serious possibilities.

2. Lighter-than-normal menstrual periods (hypo-menorrhea) often accompany other disease of debilitating character, but are also normally seen with advancing years.

   Tumor growth of certain kinds must be considered here. These conditions, of course, require elaborate medical investigation and perhaps surgery for relief.

3. Painful periods (dysmenorrhea) are a difficult problem to evaluate. The same pain considered mild by one woman, is considered severe and even incapacitating by another. This difference in reaction to pain among women often seems to "go with" the person's personality. The hard-working woman

is a rare complainer of menstrual pain, whereas the non-working woman who seems to tire even while resting, nearly always has severe menstrual pain. About half of all menstruating women will suffer some discomfort during their menstrual periods.

4. Missed periods (amenorrhea) are very common before real regularity has set in and are nearly always due to a disturbance of the endocrine glands and hormones concerned in the menstrual period. It is often difficult to know which gland is at fault, or if more than one gland is responsible. The ovary, the pituitary, the thyroid and the adrenal glands are almost always the seat of the difficulty in missed periods other than those of pregnancy. The physician can test and examine these glands as the need arises.

5. Extra periods (polymenorrhea) are also due to disturbed hormonal function in younger women and in older women approaching the menopause. In the central years of the child-bearing period, tumors, fibroids, polyps and infection of the genital tract are the most likely culprits. The physician's pelvic examination will usually indicate where the fault lies.

6. Continuous spotting (metrorrhagia) is usually indicative of possible serious disease. In the child-bearing age, it may indicate pregnancy, a threatened abortion, or a tubal pregnancy.

In older or non-pregnant women, inter-menstrual bleeding can be an indication of cancer in the cervix of the uterus. Spotting at any time, therefore, becomes significant enough for the physician's early examination and testing.

LEUKOPLAKIA OF THE VULVA

This is a disease of later life, after the menopause, and is primarily a skin disease. The skin surrounding the vagina has a distinctly dry, whitened and thickened appearance, and seems to shrink the vaginal entrance itself. Leukoplakia produces severe itching, inviting scratching and further increase of soreness.

Genital leukoplakia is associated with a decrease of female hormone in the body at the menopause and it will continue its irritating course until properly treated. This disease is definitely considered a pre-cancerous condition, for it does indeed often turn into cancer.

Treatment of leukoplakia in the vulva frequently is a series of female hormone shots which will temporarily reverse the disease course. But the only permanent treatment for leukoplakia is surgical removal, a simple treatment with a lasting cure.

VAGINAL DISCHARGE (LEUKORRHEA)

Vaginal discharge (leukorrhea) is the most common complaint in the adult female genital tract. There is normally a slight secretion in the vagina, but an excessive or pussy discharge is nearly always an infection.

The most common causes of vaginal discharge are the infections of gonorrhea, moniliasis, trichomonas and senile vaginitis.

Since most of these diseases have the common symptom of profuse vaginal discharge, the separation of one from another must be undertaken by the physician to determine the exact identity and treatment to be given. Most often, cleansing, antiseptic applications, douches, and antibiotics are the treatment for these infections.

BARTHOLIN CYST

Rounded, fluid-filled enlargements on one side of the outer vagina usually are enlarged Bartholin glands which have become blocked up because of infection or scaring. When not infected, the enlarged Bartholin gland can grow to the size of an English walnut with little or no pain. But when infected and filled with pus, these cysts become excruciatingly painful and walking or sitting is extremely uncomfortable. Bartholin cysts are not cancerous, but they do cause great cancer fright because they are readily detected in the genital region, and the patient knows she has something painfully wrong.

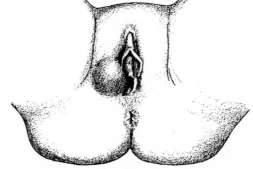

Figure 133: Bartholin cysts are fluid-filled enlarged glands of the vaginal orifice. When infected, they can be exquisitely painful.

Treatment of Bartholin cysts is simple surgical removal.

The common urethral caruncle is blood red, very tender and sometimes infected, and looks like a small polyp growing out of the urinary exit.

Urethral caruncle is non-cancerous and be be easily removed with minor surgery.

VAGINITIS

This generalized irritation of the entire vagina creates a pussy discharge and constant soreness. It is commonly found in the post-menopausal vagina and is usually due to lack of estrogen, the female hormone.

The customary care of vaginitis is the promotion of cleanliness, and small amounts of estrogen hormones.

FALLEN BLADDER (CYSTOCELE)

A downward falling of the urinary bladder is usually a result of childbirth, but it is seen on occasion in childless women. It appears as a bulging at the vaginal opening when straining or standing, and often effects a loss of urine in straining efforts such as laughing, coughing, sneezing or lifting. Cystocele feels like an uncomfortable bearing-down sensation in the vaginal region, and is often noticed for the first time may years after childbirth has been forgotten.

Lying down gives temporary relief from the symptoms of a fallen bladder, but permanent relief is obtained only through surgery. The operation is a simple procedure which replaces the bladder in its normal position.

FALLEN WOMB (PROLAPSE OF THE UTERUS)

A fallen uterus is also a result of child bearing plus the strain of hard physical work. Sometimes, inherited weakness of the tissues aids in bringing about this condition, but it is rarely seen in women who have not borne children.

Childbirth stretches and sometimes tears the pelvic tissues to form a "hole" in place of a tube for the vagina.

Then heavy work and effort push the uterus down and through this defect, and giving the sensations of bearing down, falling out, backache and vaginal pain. During straining, a buldge of smooth, moist tissue can be seen and felt at the outlet of the vagina, and it may grow to an orange-sized mass. Then on lying down, the fallen womb retracts in the vagina and returns to its normal position. The treatment of a fallen womb occasionally is the pessary, a mechanical device inside the vagina designed to hold the womb in place. Permanent cure of the fallen uterus, however, requires that it be removed or sutured back into its normal position in the pelvis.

Prolapse of the uterus is very annoying and sometimes disabling. It is not, however, a serious situation that threatens life. The treatment for each patient must be determined by the physician with experience in this field.

RECTOCELE (HERINIATED RECTUM)

A rectum that bulges forward and out through a weakened vagina, also feels like something falling out of the vagina. Also as a result of childbirth, the weakened vaginal walls allow the rectum to slide into space normally reserved for the vagina itself. In appearance, the back wall of the vagina bulges out through the vaginal entrance.

A rectum out of its ordinary surroundings enlarges and empties only with increased straining, which enlarges the rectocele defect. This condition is also not life-threatening, but it is most uncomfortable. Surgical repair with replacement of the rectum to its normal position will achieve complete relief.

PERINEAL WARTS

Wart-like growths about the external vulva are frequently caused by virus infection. The moist, warm and easily infected region of the vulva makes a choice region for virus growth.

Treatment of perineal warts is simple cautery removal and application of anti-fungicidal-viral lotions.

On rare occasions, a wart of veneral origin associated with syphilis will appear. The treatment of this disease, of course, requires treatment of the systemic disease by the physician.

CANCER OF THE VAGINA AND VULVA

Cancer at the entrance to the vagina (the vulva) is generally a problem in older women. Often looking like a small ulcer, it begins in an area of leukoplakia, an itching skin irritation definitely regarded as a pre-cancerous condition. For this reason continuing itching and soreness at the entrance to the vagina should always be regarded as a warning of possible cancerous disease.

The treatment of cancer in the vulva is surgical removal, or at times, x-ray treatment. At no age should treatment of cancer be postponed, because a very simple treatment today can easily be changed into a nightmare of trouble tomorrow.

CANCER OF THE UTERUS

The uterus is one of the most frequent sites in the human body for the development of cancer. This organ is most often involved in its external portion—the cervix, visible at the uppermost top of the

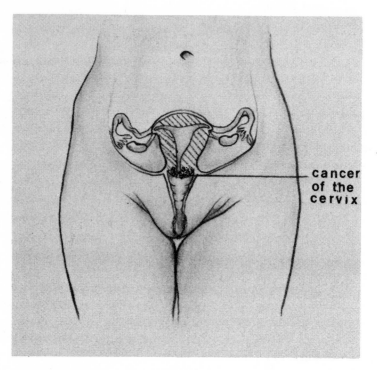

cancer
of the
cervix

Figure 134: The uterus is open to the outside. Its neck, called the cervix, is one of the most common sites of human cancer. It is best detected early through routine and periodic smear test examinations.

vagina. As in all cancer, the cause of uterine cancer remains unknown, but it seems to be related to infection, irritation, and scars. Because of the irritations in childbirth tears and lacerations of the cervix, great suspicion about cancer has been directed toward uterine trauma in childbirth. A study of actual statistics show that 90 percent of uterine cervix cancers are found in women who have had children, regardless of any other physical findings or associations.

Cancer of the uterus is usually painless. Its first warning signal is abnormal vaginal bleeding, such as occurs in spotting (bleeding in between the regular menstrual periods), or bleeding after the menopause (always abnormal). There is one strikingly important feature about cancer of the cervix which is well-known but poorly understood—there is a racial incidence to cancer of the cervix. All races are afflicted with this form of cancer with the exception of the Jewish race, which for some unknown reason apparently escapes this disease.

It is fortunate that the uterus is in a semi-exposed position, where the smallest cancers can be seen, diagnosed and treated early by complete surgical removal or adequate x-ray therapy. The smear test for cancer of the uterus is now available everywhere, allowing women to keep ahead of cancer in the uterus or to discover it in its infancy when its treatment is relatively easy and its cure most certain.

THE MENOPAUSE—THE CHANGE OF LIFE

The menopause is the time of life when function of the ovaries slows down and the menstrual period stops. This normal change follows the reproductive or child-bearing age, and usually takes place in the late forties or early fifties.

Menopausal life introduces a new period, free from the responsibilities of childbirth and its associated tribulations, but it also presents temporary physical discomfort due to the withdrawal of the female hormone to which the body has been accustomed. These discomforts vary considerably from person to person, but they most often include hot flashes, sleeplessness, irritability, unreasonable fears, muscle twitching and extreme nervousness. Irritations and infections also occur later in the genital region.

Most women go through the menopause with very little difficulty, but about 10 to 15 percent will need medical treatment ranging from mild sedation to female hormone replacement. This treatment is very desirable because it relieves disabling symptoms and allows a woman to live her normal day. Contrary to misleading tales, we know that treatment of the menopausal state does not prolong this period or delay its day of reckoning; it simply allows women to pass through a difficult period gracefully. Extreme menopausal discomforts sometimes last several years, a long period of life which would otherwise be completely lost to these women without the simple medical relief available everywhere.

It is true that many difficulties experienced in the menopausal period can also occur at other times of life and, of course, are not caused by the menopause in every instance. For this reason, the change of life is an excellent time for a complete physical examination to discover and treat other difficulties as well as menopause symptoms. Far too often, tragedy is invited into a household as a cancer or similar disease because its warning symptoms were brushed aside and thought just due to the change of life.

Another difficulty at this time is the way "old age" difficulties following the menopause are allowed to progress unncessarily. For instance, it is known that hormone withdrawal begins a thinning-out process of the bone structure, especially about the major joints. This softening of bones then presents joint pains which are often thought to be simple arthritis. The unnecessary result is a slowing down of joint function, along with muscle atrophy, ligament fixation and eventually the restricted, hesitant and guarded movements of the body so often seen in senior years of life.

Adequate treatment during the menopausal state seeks to balance the entire physical condition and to direct treatment wherever it is needed. This may include replacement hormones, minerals and vitamins for the prevention of the more commonly expected diseases and disabilities in the later years of life. Figure 135 is a representation of one facet of change of life problems.

Sexual Activity after the Menopause

Does the menopause mean the end of physical sexual ability? To this important question, the answer is no. The menopause simply means a transition period which ends a woman's child-bearing ability but not her sexual ability. She can continue to experience and engage in sexual relations to the end of her years.

The menopause is also nature's safeguard for the protection of the human race. The bearing of children and the hard task of raising them is allowed only to the young and most physically able; it would be difficult indeed for a woman of 60 or 70 years to begin the ardors of new motherhood, and the menopause guarantees that this will not happen.

The menopause varies in length from one-half year to several years, and technically means a decrease in function of the ovary with a cessation of the menstrual period. During this period, about one-third of all women experience difficulties described as hot flashes, dizziness, irritability and crying spells. Happily, treatment for this difficulty is simple and easily obtained.

Figure 135: There are times during the change of life when problems may seem to be larger and more dangerous than they truly are.

For the male sex, there is no real menopause as women know and experience it. But both sexes experience a gradual diminution of sexual vigor to the extent that other body functions also diminish. Correctly understood, sexual ability, visual ability and other physical abilities are gradually lessened but rarely do they fail completely. People in their sixties do not expect to run the four-minute mile, and they do not ordinarily expect or want their sexual desires and abilities to be as they were at the age of 20, but they can expect them to be present and active according to their outlook on life.

Sexual relations are of great interest to most people, but they are not equally appealing to all. Just as some people play tennis well into old age, some of us will be absorbed with sexual matters until the age of 100, but most of us begin to lose interest somewhere along the line after our youth. Losing interest in sex, however, and developing tastes for other facets of life, such as golf, reading or traveling, does not mean that sexual abilities are lost; they are only set aside.

A normal development after the age of 50 is a replacement of the passionate and demanding physical sexual relations of youth by a deeper and more endearing marital relationship revolving more about family activity, interest in children and grandchildren.

Enduring, satisfying and happy social relations after menopause, as well as before, are built not only upon sex, but far more upon the solid virtures of faithful and unselfish marriage.

Section

6

THE ANAL REGION

In all of history, good bowel function has been a mental image of good health, and just about every human malady has at some period been judged better or worse, depending on the answer to the question, "How are the bowels?"

This picture in our minds that good health and good bowel function are closely associated is actually based on facts reflecting age, activities and physical abilities; probably not even the space age will greatly reshape this idea.

Rarely do we realize that bowel function has a tremendous social aspect to it, and that it has a great impact on modern living. Universal demand has brought about the scientific advantages of modern plumbing, privacy and sanitation as we now know them, and the lack of these advances, more than anything else on earth, would make our urban world of today impossible.

Diseases of the rectum and anus have always been vexing problems, often producing great pain, and always demanding great sympathy. When Louis XIV had his rectal operation in 1686, his many attendants were ordered to wear bottom bandages to show sympathetic respect.

Fortunately, treatment of rectal diseases has risen from its backward state of a generation ago and is today given great respect everywhere.

Examination of the Anus

To view the anus directly, uncover the anal region and assume a squatting position about eight or ten inches directly above a mirror lying on the floor. This will give a clear view of the anal region between the widely separated knees.

The normal anus is a small, puckered and indented opening. It remains closed, of course, because the anus itself cannot open except by having something forced through it. Straining will make the anus stand out slightly and appear a little larger than usual. Its color and hair distribution follow individual body characteristics.

1. Examine the skin surface of the anal opening in the adult without straining. Observe any large skin folds and distended veins, or any sore, irritated-appearing spots. Observe also the existence of any generalized irritation of the entire anal region. These findings can be indications of diseases such as mere skin flaps, external hemorrhoids, fungus infection, or the anal itching of pruritis.

2. Note the contour of the anus and surrounding skin during straining. Observe any mass of tissue protruding from the anus. Note any pus or blood from the anal opening. Note any pimple-like opening near the anal region from which pus or fecal material appears. These findings may indicate internal hemorrhoids or external fistula formation.

3. Observe the skin forming the anus itself. During straining, examine the skin for any raw, split appearance in the fold of the anal skin. Such a skin crack is possibly a fissure.

4. Note the texture of the skin of the anus and the immediate surrounding areas. Look closely for a whitened, thickened, water-soaked appearance of the skin of the anus or its immediate surroundings. Also examine to see if there is any clear, weeping, water-like discharge from this skin. This finding may accompany internal hemorrhoids, drug allergies or the chronic irritation of leukoplakia.

5. With one finger, gently press upon different areas of the skin surrounding the anus. Note any enlarged, painfully reddened, or boil-like sores surrounding the anus. Such a finding in this region is possibly an abscess or fistula in formation.

6. Examine the skin of the exact center line in the fold between the buttocks. Look for any dimple-like indentation of the skin about two inches back of the anus. This is probably a pilonidal cyst and possibly will discharge a drop or two of pus when the surrounding skin is pressed upon.

Diseases of the Anal Region

Figure 136 indicates the structure of the normal anus.

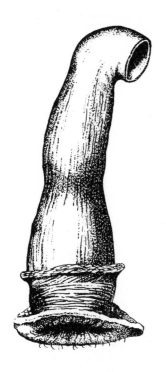 

Figure 136: The normal anus is a sphincter-type closure for the tube-shaped
rectum. There are two sphincters for the anus: one is controlled
automatically and the other is voluntary and controlled by the will.

The anal region does not suffer long in silence, and its many
difficulties are very soon called to our attention by pain, often of
severe degree. Most of us know very little about the anal region,
and the idea of hemorrhoids, fistula, or fissure brings to mind only
a vague picture.

Piles

This term means rectal disease to most people and usually means
any kind of skin trouble about the anus. The most common of these
is the skin tab. It is usually only an extra fold of skin about the
anus which no longer contracts to a smooth skin surface after
it has been over-stretched. It may mean only that this individual
has seen younger years.

Hemorrhoids

Hemorrhoids, sometimes called piles, are really only enlarged blood vessels about the anus, exactly like varicose veins of the legs. Since these veins are usually painless, many people who have hemorrhoids do not even know about it. When the enlarged vein is on the outside of the anus, it is called an external hemorrhoid; when it appears as a mass coming out through the anal opening, it is called an internal hemorrhoid.

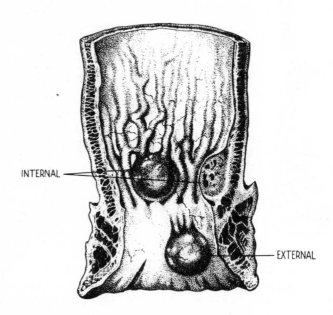

Figure 137: Hemorrhoids are only enlarged blood vessels. Inside the rectum, they are called internal and are painless. On the outside, they are called external and may be very painful.

Many reasons have been brought forward as the cause of hemorrhoids. Some of these reasons have real merit and some do not. They are:

1. The erect position. Standing erect, unlike our four-legged animal friends, probably helps hemorrhoids to occur. However, not all upright people have hemorrhoids.
2. Straining—as in constipation or pregnancy. This possibly enlarges hemorrhoids which are already present, but it is also very true that hemorrhoids are not always present in all constipated people, nor are they always present in all women who have borne children.

3. Inheritance. A tendency towards hemorrhoids may be definitely inherited, but many people with hemorrhoids have children who have no hemorrhoid problems at all.

One also hears many unusual and completely unfounded ideas about the cause of hemorrhoids. They include sitting on the cold ground, eating too much roughage, and even bow-legs. These ideas are not based on any genuine facts and should not be given any serious consideration.

The most likely and reasonable cause of hemorrhoids is infection about the anus. An infection here weakens the wall of the veins and allows them to stretch to form the widely dilated veins which we call hemorrhoids.

Most people know when something is wrong about their anal region, but not what is wrong. A suspicion may exist for many years that the protrusion from the anus during bowel movement is hemorrhoidal trouble, but often these protrusions are simply pushed back up into the rectum. This practice frequently goes on for long periods until painful itching, bleeding or other symptoms become annoying enough to drive the person to his physician, where the difficulty can become exactly diagnosed.

Rectal bleeding, as seen on the toilet paper or in the bowel waste, is most often caused by hemorrhoids. But since it can have other more severe meanings such as cancer, rectal bleeding makes necessary an examination by the physician to be sure no serious disease is present.

Protrusions of the anus noted in straining during bowel movements are often endured for a long time, simply because no pain or bleeding is present. The protrustion is easily tolerated and demands no immediate treatment even though it usually means that internal hemorrhoids are present to a marked degree. When a protrusion appears, it is almost inevitable that the more troublesome difficulty of hemorrhoidal pain and bleeding will soon follow.

Since hemorrhoids are usually not considered a life or death disease, their care is quite variable. Mild hemorrhoids as seen in the mirror may cause no trouble at all, but severe painful hemorrhoids with itching and bleeding may demand immediate care. Pain relief from hemorrhoids is best obtained with ice packs for the first day, followed by warm water soap baths for about 10 days.

The pain of severe and acute hemorrhoidal disease can occur

during pregnancy or at any other time. But regardless of when this inhuman disease occurs, most of us are forced to seek relief and let the world go by until we succeed.

The treatment of hemorrhoidal disease has gone through long evolutions. Once, injection treatment of hemorrhoids was very popular, but now it is rarely used. Injections were often temporarily successful, but they were accompanied by many compliciations and recurrences. Even so, today, injection treatment is still preferable in some bedridden patients who cannot possibly stand even the mild rigors of the operating table because of some severe debilitating disease.

Modern surgical treatment of hemorrhoids is now a very effective operation when done by an experienced surgeon trained in this field. Unfortunately, the field of hemorrhoidal disease has for many years been filled to overflowing with healers who are poorly trained, and who give less than the best of treatment for rectal diseases.

Once again, the qualified family physician has no equal in his ability to give his patients the best advice and treatment for hemorrhoidal disease.

Anal Fissure

An anal fissure, or fissure-in-ano, is a crack in the skin of the anal wall, similar to a crack in the corner of the mouth. The anal fissure is actually draining pus from underlying infected tissues in the wall of the rectum itself.

The difficulties of anal fissures include abscess formations and continual drainage, but from the standpoint of the man who owns one, a fissure's most important feature is pain. Characteristically, fissure pain accompanies and follows a bowel movement. While the smaller fissure might cause only a slight, fleeting pain, a larger fissure often feels like a bowel movement of fire itself. Often this pain continues long after the bowel movement as an aching pain about the anus.

When bleeding accompanies a fissure, it is usually in small amounts, and only on the toilet tissue. Bleeding may worry the fissure patient, but more often it is the great pain that sends him to his doctor.

Constipation is very common when fissures are present. People soon discover that fissure pain is brought on by bowel movement, and to prevent the pain they unconsciously delay the movement.

This, of course, brings about a harder, larger stool which is even more painful when it passes through the painfully fissured anal outlet.

The basic care for anal fissure, as for most anal diseases, begins with proper cleansing about the anus. Soap and water cleaning are probably more indicated—and less used—in the anal region than anywhere else on the body. The severe fissure will need definite medical care by a doctor qualified to treat anal diseases. His most successful treatment is a surgical procedure which completely removes the fissure along with the infected tissue beneath it.

Anal Abscess and Fistula

Because anal abscess creates the anal fistula, they can best be described together. The abscess is simply a boil-like porcess about the anus which finally drains to the outside skin and forms a continuous draining tract called a fistula.

An anal abscess will produce an intense throbbing pain in the supersensitive anal regions. This pain is not related just to bowel movement; it becomes intense under any pressure, even that of just sitting. This abscess is caused when fecal material "leaks" through the wall of the rectum and begins a boil-like infection. As it grows into a reddened, swollen and painful state, it bulges the skin beside the anal opening and may grow so large as to crowd the anus off to one side.

At this stage, the anal abscess is intensely painful, and the sufferer eagerly seeks relief because he is completely disabled for any other activity. Sitting in warm water will give temporary relief, but permanent relief is obtained only by open drainage of the abscess itself. Sometimes this happens spontaneously, by the abscess heading and draining itself, or through an incision and drainage operation by the physician. At this point, the beginning of the fistula may start. After it is drained, the abscess collapses into a string-like channel from the leak site in the rectal wall and out through the skin where the abscess was drained. If fecal material continues to leak into this channel and cause continuous reinfection, there will be continuous formation of pus draining out through the skin opening. Thus is a fistula born.

A fistula looks like a small red pimple in the skin close to the anus. It is usually not very painful. What soreness there is, is due to the irritation of the skin by the fistula's continuous drainage material. If the anal fistula should heal over on the outside, the oncoming pus becomes blocked and forms another abscess which will soon penetrate the skin and re-establish the fistula.

In treating a fistula, localized heat applications such as hot baths will give temporary relief, but the fistula must be surgically removed or it will recur again and again.

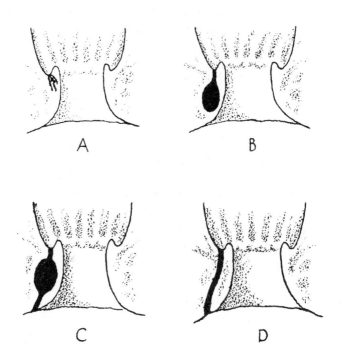

Figure 138: Fistula formation begins with infection perforating the rectal wall. This brings about abscess or boil formation, which in turn heads and ruptures through the outer skin at a distance from the anal opening. Instead of healing, the entire tract thus established continues to act like another anal outlet.

Anal-Rectal Pain

What can pain tell us about the state of the rectum? Rectal difficulties are described in terms of pain, bleeding, or protrusion, but there is always concern that cancer is present or soon will be.

Each rectal disease has a characteristic pain pattern which helps to identify the disease present.

Anal pain of great intensity which starts suddenly and remains constant, which is painful to touch and slightly worse with bowel movement, means that we probably have a hemorrhoid present. The sharp pain is due to the irritation of a blood clot forming within an external hemorrhoid vein. The pain remains intense for about a week or ten days, but happily goes away completely after that time.

This accounts for the success of drugstore remedies for the anus. Since the pain will disappear soon anyway, even the application of fresh strawberries could be "successful."

Severe pain to one side of the anus, which is constant, intense and throbbing, in a hardened enlargement just under the skin, resembles the pain of an anal abscess. This pain does not begin suddenly; it arises over a day or two, and grows to intense proportions. The intensely painful and disabling anal abscess can be relieved only by drainage—by spontaneous heading and rupture, or by a small incision.

The pain of a fistula, frequently following an abscess, is usually not severe. There is a more or less constant drainage of pus and sometimes of tiny food particles from the small opening which is the drainage site of the original abscess. But fistula pain actually constitutes more of soreness than a real pain. It can be very irritating and annoying, but it is not disabling.

Pain about the anus, possibly severe, but present only during and following bowel movement, is the typical pain of an anal fissure. It looks like a crack on the side of the anal opening, but the fissure spreads out into a raw expanse as the anus expands for bowel passage. When the fecal material touches the open fissure, it creates pain which can be slight or as intense as a bowel movement of razor blades. Fistula pain usually subsides after the bowel passage, but may linger as an aching pain for a short time afterward.

Itching pain in a sore macerated skin area about the anus is probably caused by internal hemorrhoids (which are painless by themselves). They hang like grapes on the inside of the rectal wall, and their engorged condition causes them to secrete a sticky mucous material which works out through the anal opening to continually bathe the anal skin. This secretion produces a macerated, itching and excessively sore anus. The hanging grape-like hemorrhoid inside the rectum can also protrude from the anus with straining at the bowel movement.

In short, the various types of anal disease can be recognized by their pain: the sudden but temporary pain of external hemorrhoids;

the intense boil-like pain of anal abscess to one side; the continual skin irritation around a visible fistula; the severe pain at bowel movement with a fissure; and the constantly sticky, macerated and irritated anus of internal hemorrhoids with occasional protrusion.

These pains do not speak for the pain of cancer in the anal-rectal region. Cancer of the rectum has no characteristic pain; it produces only an uncomfortable ache, and possibly the sensation that the rectum is constantly filled. By itself, it never produces sharp or severe pains in the anal region.

We should know that the anal-rectal region can have two or more diseases at the same time. Even though the pain present today might indicate a non-serious type of anal disease, a second non-painful disease could be present only inches away. For this reason, whenever anal or rectal diseases are present and severe enough to cause bleeding, pain, protrusion, or continuous itching, it is well to have the entire anal-rectal region examined by the physician.

The Bowel Movement

Bowel waste matter, called the stool, tells us much about body function. Through its color, form and other characteristics, it announces possible serious disease, and often is the only abnormality present to clue us on approaching troubles. Normally, the average bowel movement occurs about once a day. It is semi-soft, banana-shaped, and about walnut brown in color. It sinks in water; it is usually slow to dissolve; and its odor, always disagreeable, can be especially obnoxious during disease.

What can be learned from the abnormal bowel movement? The question of normal frequency always arises. A direct answer to this question is simple. Normal bowel movement frequency varies from one or two movements a day up to a movement every two or three days. It is not necessary to have a movement every day to maintain good health. In the newborn, bowel movement is frequent and it may seem (at least to mother) almost constant. As we grow older, our lessened activities tend to slow down our bowel action.

The average bowel movement is once a day, and some people seem adjusted like clock work—a result of training and habit, more than a sign of good health. To the doctor, only one question about bowel frequency is important. "Has there been a recent change in the bowel habit?" Thus, constipation for many years has little meaning, but constipation of sudden onset or of rapid development could mean disease in the colon, such as an obstructing growth, and should be investigated by the physician as soon as possible.

The solidity of the bowel movement, at times, approaches the consistency of thin mud in occasional diseases such as diarrhea, food poisoning, flu or colitis in the bowel. A much hardened stool, approaching the consistency of wood, often accompanies the constipation so frequently seen in inactive, bedridden and debilitated people. Sudden constipation, of course, may speak for mechanical obstruction or growth within the colon.

The shape of the bowel movement normally approaches that of a banana, but it may become a thin pencil-shaped stool if any constriction of the colon outlet is present. This may speak for a growth in the colon or more probably, an irritated anal sphincter, often due to a fissure, abscess or other anal disease. With diarrhea, of course, the bowel movement may have very little volume, because only after a period of collecting and packing can the stool assume its usual thickened form.

Color Significance

The color of the bowel movement can have many shades. A clay colored or gray stool indicates a complete lack of bile coming from the liver, from which the normal stool color comes. In this event, jaundice, a yellow tint to the skin, will probably soon be noticed to indicate disease in the liver region.

A black stool can have many meanings. Since iron compounds bring about this color, an inky black stool most often speaks for the ingestion of iron in vitamins, tonics, or other iron-containing foods. However, blood contains iron also and if none of these medications have been taken, the black stool's probable cause is bleeding in the stomach or intestinal tract. Only about three ounces of blood in the stomach is necessary to supply the amount of iron necessary to turn the entire stool pitch black. With less than this amount, only a partly black stool is the result. In this way, the physician can judge how much his patient may be bleeding internally.

Red blood in the stool means bleeding from the lower intestine or colon. If the blood seems mixed with the bowel matter, it is probably coming from a bleeding area in the colon far above the anus itself. If the blood appears only on the outside of the bowel movement as a thin covering, the most likely source of the bleeding is from the anal outlet from difficulties such as hemorrhoids or fissures.

Other Significant Characteristics

Occasionally, a stool will float near the top of the water. This means that it contains more fat content than the normal stool and is possibly due to an occasional meal containing too much fat that has rushed through the intestinal tract, but repeated stools that float may mean a deficiency in digestive juices which should have digested the fat. This, in turn, would point to the pancreas, whose faulty function is not supplying enough digestive juice.

Finally, the odor of the stool must be recognized. The definitely disagreeable odor is derived from chemicals within the stool known as skatol and hydrogen sulfide. These disagreeable odors characteristically and immediately identify their source and act as a safeguard in animals and humans concerned with food preparation.

Human psychology being what it is leads to an amazing fact. We cannot smell any disagreeable odor in our own bowel movement under normal circumstances, although we can rapidly detect it in others. During disease episodes, however, odors arise from other than the usual bowel elements and this change in bowel odor is immediately noted. Each person over the years develops individual circumstances concerning the bowel movement and the stool itself. This is called the bowel habit which becomes medically significant when noticeably and suddenly changed. Daily observation of the bowel movement can often warn us when intestinal tract diseases are in their infancy. They will also be of great value to the physician seeking information concerning our intestinal tract and the rest of the body as well.

Section

7

THE BACK AND EXTREMITIES

The back and the extremities, our orthopedic department, is concerned with bones, joints, muscles and ligaments.

Many of our problems here are congenital (problems present at birth) and often are minor, as in webbed fingers, but also at times major and disabling, as in amyoplasia (a growing together of all joints). We find inherited factors in these problems, but environmental factors are also very important.

Examination of the Back

The adult back is best examined before a full-length mirror, using a double mirror or hand mirror for backward viewing. Examination is made of any deformities, tenderness or limitation of motion. The normal back when viewed from behind forms a straight line, while from the side it presents a graceful wave. Normally, the vertebrae are not tender, and their tips can be felt from the prominent 7th vertebra at the base of the neck down to the sacrum, the center bone of the pelvis. The back's ability to move freely is impressive in infancy and youth, and although its flexibility tends to diminish in later years, the back usually reflects our health, our general physical condition, our age, and often our past diseases. Ordinarily, we can expect a comfortable degree of easy motions in all directions through the average life span.

Deformity

1. View the adult spinal column from directly behind, using a mirror. If one gluteus muscle fold is much larger than the

other, a congenital dislocation of the hip may be present. A curvature of the spine to one side is called scoliosis.

2. View the spinal column from the side. A hunchback deformity called kyphosis may mean deformed ribs and vertebrae or distinct bone disease. A swayback deformity from childhood may be a dislocated hip or faulty bone development such as in dwarfism. Beginning in adult life, it is often spondylolisthesis, the tired horse posture, due to postural strain.

Tenderness

1. Feel each of the vertebral tips, directly in the midline from the lower neck down to the gluteal crease, and thump gently the bony column and the bones of the pelvis. Tenderness or pain in various positions may indicate faulty bone development in youth or arthritis in later years.

2. In the adult, press firmly on the soft muscular attachments to each side of the vertebral column. Tenderness along the soft sides of the back bone can mean strain or sprain.

Limitation of Motion

1. For adults, from a standing position bend well forward, backward, and to each side, in a circling type motion. Back pain suggests either arthritis, ligament strain or intervertebral disc difficulty.

2. Sit firmly erect with arms folded and bend forward, backward and to each side. Soreness in this position probably means arthritic disease in the backbone itself.

3. If the above proceeding motions produce no back pain, repeat forward, backward and sideways bending, now in the standing position. Soreness of the back upon standing, but not on sitting, is probably due to a hip or leg deformity.

4. From a reclining position, raise each leg straight up in the air with the knee straight. Pain in the leg and back in this maneuver may mean slipped intervertebral disc or sciatica difficulties.

5. Pain in the tailbone region during the motion of bending over or sitting down, usually means a painful coccyx (tailbone).

Back Difficulties

Scoliosis Deformity

Curvature of the spine to the side is the most common of all back deformities, as indicated in Figure 139.

Figure 139: Scoliosis or sideways spinal deformity is very common and means very little unless it is pronounced. Nearly 30 percent of us have some scoliosis in our backs.

This condition has usually existed since one's childhood from unrecognized polio, congenital bone disease or more rapid growth on one side of the body than on the other. In severe cases, the deformity continues to worsen until vertebral bone development stops. This developmental age is about 15 for girls and 17 in boys.

Later in life, work habits become involved in spinal curvature. This is because heavy work by right-handed people tends to lower the right shoulder slightly and produce a slight spine curvature to the left. Nearly a third of all people have such a deformity, and are not even aware of it. These minor deviations from the perfect back cannot really be considered as disease deformities until true discomfort results from them.

The treatment of scoliosis depends upon its degree. While mild cases such as those discovered in routine physical examinations may require no treatment at all, the severely deformed back may present serious problems. Since the deformity grows to its greatest proportions during youth, corrective braces, casts, and splints are often used in youngsters in an effort to correct the deformity while bones are still growing.

Kyphosis Deformity

Hunchback deformity is frequently seen in early years when caused by developmental bone diseases such as vertebral epiphysitis where the bone grows improperly. Most often, however, it is due to simple faulty posture. When it is acquired in later life, hunchback is a frequent result of tuberculosis or chronic arthritis of the wearing-out type.

Figure 140: Kyphosis or humpbacked deformity often is the result of bone disease of the spine. It tends to appear in later years as bones soften, though it also can be a result of poor posture habits. Besides a tendency to geater fatigue, kyphosis produces a most unattractive posture which usually worsens with the years.

Treatment of round shoulderedness, hunchback or kyphosis deformity often involves the use of shoulder straps during youth. These are braces designed to correct faulty posture and to keep the spine erect during the formative growth years. This difficulty is very common in later years when our bones grow weaker and actually compress themselves, and gets worse as time goes on. We often see our older folk losing an inch or two of the height they had in youth. This problem is very difficult to correct, and frequently produces chest, abdominal and extremity pains when collapsing vertebrae squeeze down and pinch the nerves between them.

Lordosis Deformity

Swayback or "tired horse" deformity in childhood could be the result of hip joints which do not set normally in their sockets. These hips cannot straighten out properly and they force the back to arch sharply for erect position.

Figure 141: Lordosis or swayback spinal deformity may result from body build or hips which cannot easily straighten out. It often causes no difficulty. But the shearing action of one vertebra upon another may eventually cause them to slip and weight-bearing becomes difficult.

Besides the congenital dislocated hip, lordosis can result from ligaments about the hip joints, shortened by polio, by infection or by accidents which prevent straightening of the otherwise normal hip. The resulting adult "walking horse" posture is regarded by most doctors as a childhood development following through into adult life.

Arrested Development of the Vertebrae (Klippel-Feil Syndrome)

Uncommonly, the vertebrae in the upper portion of the back about the neck will suffer from arrested development, and unfortunately will grow together in one irregular fused mass of bone. The resulting shortened stature makes for disfiguration. The head seems to rest directly on the trunk as though the neck were missing, and of course motion of the head is limited in all directions.

Treatment for this disease, unfortunately, does not exist.

Arthritis of the Spine

Arthritis of the back can begin at an early age, and often prevents young people from engaging in the activities and sports of their friends and schoolmates; it becomes more serious, however, in later years. This world-wide problem is caused mainly by the wearing down of the surfaces of the bones, and by nature's attempt to repair them.

The repair process is inadequate because the wearing down occurs mostly in the center of the joints while the repair process itself is most evident around the edges. Eventually, the spinal joints become calcified with many spicuels and the x-ray then shows not the clean block upon block appearance of youth, but rather the thistle upon thistle appearance of arthritis in its advanced ages.

This spine, dominated by severe arthritis, eventually becomes shrunken, hunched, and at its worst, finally fused into an inflexible "poker" spine. Pinched nerves and irritated surrounding ligaments contribute to the painful stiffness which is often felt as chest and abdominal pain. This condition disables many people who are otherwise in sound health.

The wearing-down process in our backs would not occur if we relieved the spine of weight bearing by walking on all fours, like four-legged animals, but since a change back to this type of walking does not seem likely, we look to other methods of relief for arthritis of the spine.

Hormone therapy is one effective method of treating this difficulty. It is based on the observation that continued sexual function of the testicle and ovary seem to toughen up the bone and prevent spinal wear and tear for some obscure reason. Hormonal and other intelligent medical therapy is usually successful in partially relieving arthritis and should have preference over mysterious and overly enthusiastic fad remedies which must be classified mostly as methods of self-hypnosis.

Many more people would be confined to their wheel chairs today, completely disabled, if it were not for the reliable means of relief now available.

Slipped Disc, Ruptured Disc, Ruptured Nucleus Pulposis, Sciatica

A ruptured or slipped disc between the vertebrae causes pain in the back and possibly down one or both legs. Though it is considered a back difficulty, its chief symptom is sciatica or leg pains more than 75 percent of the time. Figure 142 indicates the position of a slipped disc pinching against the spinal cord.

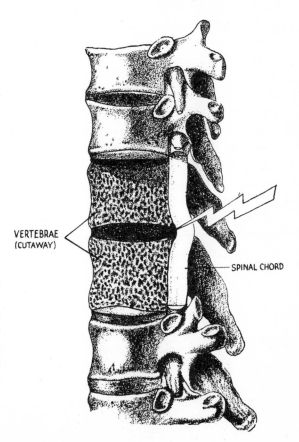

Figure 142: A slipped disc, between the vertebrae, frequently pinches against the spinal cord. Symptoms of back and leg pain frequently are made worse by coughing, sneezing and straining. Removal of protruded portion of disc by operative means usually means complete lasting relief.

VERTEBRAE (CUTAWAY)

SPINAL CHORD

The discs between the vertebrae are made of cartilage which is firm about the periphery, but liquid in the center. When the vertebrae are forced together (as when a chair is pulled out from under a person sitting down), the compressed liquid center of the disc may force its way out through a crack in its rim. The crack is usually directed backward toward the spinal cord, and if the bursting putty-like disc substance comes out far enough to press against the nerve cord, we feel pain in our backs and legs. Then, when we cough, sneeze or exert ourselves, we create more internal pressure which pushes the disc substance harder than ever against the spinal nerve to cause increasing pain in the legs. If this is continued over a long period, the nerve itself becomes sore and sensitive, so that it can no longer stretch as in normal walking. This is now sciatica and its sufferers must find relief by walking on their toes with slightly bent knees. Walking with the legs in this position relaxes the sciatic nerve somewhat, and permits the patient to at least hobble about. In a few people, the protruded disc may create severe back pain without pressure on any leg nerves.

Disc problems are known to occur between vertebrae in any level of the back. They are found in the neck, at the level of the chest, in the mid-back and in the low-back, but since the greatest pressure on the inter-vertebral discs is at the lower levels of the spine, disc troubles also are usually in the lower part of the back. They do not endanger life and will often heal after lengthy horizontal bed rest. But when pain has disabled a person for a long time, complete relief can be obtained only by surgical removal of the ruptured disc. Gratifying results usually follow for those who have this type of surgery.

Strains and Sprains

A back strain is an injury caused by overstretching or overworking the ligaments, the muscles or joints beyond their normal limits. On the other hand, a sprain means actual tearing of muscles or ligaments within the back. Thus, back pain due to bumpy beds, too much gardening or unusual exercise, most often means back strain, a common occurrence often relieved by warm baths. The sprain is obviously a more severe injury. It may follow an automobile accident or a fall down stairs. Actual bleeding within the muscles implies that some tissue most certainly has been torn apart. Thus, a sprain is identified.

Actually, after very severe accidents, we usually have a combination of injuries besides the strain and sprain. Often we find fractures, dislocations, lacerations and frequently considerable bleeding together. These difficulties obviously require hospitalization and the services of the physician immediately.

Fracture

Fractures of any of the vertebrae are difficult problems which may follow trauma such as an automobile accident or serious fall. Not all back fractures are serious, but after any severe trauma, examination of the back with the help of an x-ray will enable the physician to determine whether or not a fracture exists.

Backache

Seventy-five percent of the problems of the back are due to trauma either from an accident or from continuous and severe posture changes often demanded by certain occupations.

The next most common problem of the back is the backache caused by degenerative or the wearing down type of arthritis. This problem, usually found after the age of 45, is made worse by cold, damp weather or unusual activity. It improves with rest, but gives rise to pain and limited back motion after too much activity. Degenerative arthritis is most noticeable in bending forward, backward or sideways in a sitting position, since these actions bring out the ache in the spine itself.

Through our years, the wearing down processes are pitted against the reparative processes of the body as nature constantly strives to rebuild damaged or worn surfaces. In youth, we can absorb lots of wear and tear and expect to recuperate with ease, but in later life, we heal slower and find we cannot take trauma as we did in younger years. In practice, after an accident, backaches are related not only to the severity of the injury, but also to the age of the injured patient. Young people often heal completely after these traumatic episodes, but as we get older a "bad back" or leg is likely to stick with us for the rest of our lives.

Trauma, of course, can be imposed on a spinal column which already has other diseases, thus the mild arthritic begins to have backache after the mildest trauma, especially after 50 years of age when we find trauma of some sort preceding most backaches. It is unfortunate that the back should be so singled out to suffer not only from arthritic disease, but also from mild everyday incidents.

Sometimes back pain radiates down into the back of the leg, and is called sciatic pain. It can be caused by pressure on nerves to the legs from an injury to a disc, or to the vertebra itself. This pain is greatly aggravated by coughing, sneezing or straining, and should be reported to the physician if genuine relief is sought.

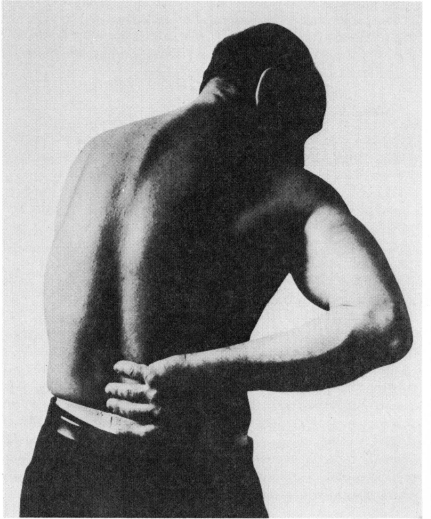

Figure 143: Back pain can be constant or fleeting; it can be severe or slight; it is often disabling and always takes the fun out of life.

Periodic back pain in the same location and under the same circumstances at approximately the same time each day, very likely is caused by mild back deformity which exists in nearly 30 percent of us, even though we are not aware of it. Deformity backache is usually due to too much strain on one set of muscles and not enough on another. For example, a shortness of one leg is often an unnoticed deformity that causes strain in the back region during some types of motions and activities. Back pain from a deformity is most noticeable when standing and attempting to bend forward, backward or sideways.

Considerable skill is necessary to evaluate the deformity and to decide if any treatment is necessary. Although deformity means an incorrect back aligment and causes chronic strain, any resulting backache will vary considerably from person to person.

Poor posture due to ordinary slouching, a poor bed or possibly poor health, forces upon the spinal column a mechanical strain which may eventually result in a backache. Uncomfortable beds are a widespread cause of this difficulty, and many people can recall later that back trouble began when a change was made from one bed to another.

Another very common back strain results from obesity. The spinal column can be greatly strained, supporting an excess of unbalanced weight—a situation easily reversible by losing the excess weight and regaining good posture.

In nearly one-fourth of all backaches, the main cause of the trouble cannot be determined. Some backs may be found to have some arthritis, possibly a mild curvature, and probably the wear and tear to which all of us are subjected. A few ailing backs do not respond to treatment for any of these difficulties, while another back with the same difficulties of even greater degree has no backache at all. It is also true that some of these backaches may have causes which are discovered only after long periods of study.

On rare occasions the abdominal organs, especially the female organs, are thought to be the cause of backaches. At other times mental problems and, occasionally, obscure fevers are at fault. Even diabetes and, at times, sheer nervous tension have been found associated with an occasional backache.

Backache pain from an undetermined cause requires further study. All backaches have a definite cause, but unfortunately, in many cases, time and circumstances do not allow the detailed study necessary to find this cause. We have to understand that the back, like other parts of the body, may be imperfect to begin with, and may also undergo a degenerative process throughout all of life. Its diseases and afflictions are multiple and can occur more than one at a time.

The Extremities

Examination of the Lower Extremities

The lower extremities are examined unclothed, in the horizontal position for the child, and in the standing position for the adult. Examine the entire thigh, knee, leg, ankle and foot in all positions of function, with the aid of enough light and the support of a table.

1. Stand on the leg to be tested and bend the body forward to a horizontal position, putting the other leg straight out behind. Reversing this action, bend backward with the free leg extending straight out forward. Pain and limited motion in the hip indicates probable arthritis within this joint or rheumatism about it.

2. Examine the motion of the knee. In a sitting position, cup both hands over one knee. Then lift and swing the leg and foot back and forth as far as possible. The feeling of a grating sensation indicates arthritis of the knee joint.

3. Examine the ankle motion. Bend the ankle in all directions as far as possible. A swollen ankle with painful motion and soreness about this joint means probable arthritis.

4. Examine the foot's blood circulation. Feel the pulse of the dorsal artery located just beside the highest bone on the top of the foot. A strong pulse in this artery indicates good circulation in the leg; its absence may mean circulatory difficulties.

5. Examine the veins of the leg. Lie down with the feet elevated against a wall or chair for several minutes and observe the disappearance of nearly all veins. Quickly stand erect and see if the veins fill rapidly into large tortuous knots. Varicose veins will fill rapidly in a standing position, but normal veins fill slowly, taking a full minute or more. Examine the skin just above the inner ankle joint for any long-standing sore or ulcer. Such a finding in this location is called a varicose ulcer.

6. Examine the skin sensation of the legs and feet. Run the fingertips lightly over the legs and feet—note any areas of numbness, burning, heat, coldness or pain. Unusual or complete lack of sensation often points to nerve disease in the leg, back or spinal cord.

7. Standing with the feet together and the knees locked, bend over and attempt to touch the floor. Soreness in the back of the thighs extending downward into the calves may mean sciatica. Next, lie flat on the back, lock the knees, and raise the leg straight up if possible. Again, soreness in the back of the thigh or calf usually means some degree of sciatica.

8. Sit on a table with the legs hanging down. With a book edge, tap quickly just below the knee cap, and note the presence or absence of the kicking reflex in the legs. It is absent in some forms of thyroid disease, pernicious anemia and nerve disease. An absent knee jerk almost always has important meaning.

9. Stand before a full-length mirror and compare the size of the thighs as well as the legs. A considerable increase in size of one leg over another may mean milk leg or other circulatory defects.

10. Stand barefoot and completely unclothed on an absolutely flat surface before the full-length mirror and compare the height of both hips. Note any difference in height, bulging or difference in shape between the two hip outlines. Repeat this examination with the back to the mirror, using a hand mirror in front for reverse viewing. Note any difference in height between the right and left gluteal fold, and note the center position of the gluteal crease or its deviation to one side. A consistent difference between one side and the other may mean that one leg is shorter than the other.

11. Examine the feet toward the end of the day. With one finger, exert gentle, constant pressure against the lower leg or ankle bone. If a deep pit remains when the finger is withdrawn, the leg has accumulated some water from the rest of the body. It could mean obesity, heart disease or circulatory disease.

12. Examine the foot and note any growth or thickening enlargement at the toe joints, sides and sole of the foot, and between the toes. These conditions are corns, callouses, bunions and plantar warts.

13. Coat the soles of the feet with a light layer of ink and "finger-print" the footprint onto a clean white sheet, using full body weight. The print can indicate any degree of flat-footedness.

Lower Extremity Difficulties

SNAPPING KNEE

This painless problem of the adult knee is usually caused by a taunt tendon slipping and snapping alongside the moving knee joint. These tendons, the fibrous endings of the thigh muscles, are anchored in and about the knee joint. During sudden or violent change of the knee position, the tendons can snap like rubber bands to create the disturbing sound which so worries the owners of these knees.

Many times the cartilage within the knee joint may be at fault, especially when it can slip suddenly in or out of position during knee bending.

The ordinary snapping knee is not a serious problem; it is usually treated with a simple wrapping bandage or brace.

LOCKING KNEE, FOOTBALL PLAYER'S KNEE, TRICK KNEE, RUPTURED MENISCUS

The normal knee has many ligaments, muscles and tendons to keep it aligned, but it also has a cushion between the bone ends.

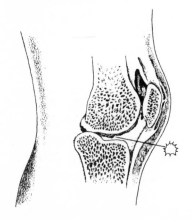

Figure 144: Knee joint difficulties in senior years result from youthful injuries and because the joint actually wears out. Usually, they are not severely painful unless forced to carry the burden of obesity.

This cushion looks like a flattened doughnut into which the rounded bone parts can fit, which makes knee bending a precise and graceful action.

Injury of this pad, called the semi-lunar cartilage or meniscus, is the most frequent knee injury of the athlete. A sudden twisting of the leg with a rupture or tear of the cartilage brings about severe pain and often a locking of the knee joint. If gentle traction is used upon the lower leg, the knee will usually unlock and allow the leg to straighten out with a resultant disappearance of the pain. Following this, however, the young athlete may experience repeated episodes of this kind. He often refers to his "trick knee" and fears that it will lock if he bends his knee too far.

There are several treatments of an injured knee cartilage. If the pain and locking are very mild, a person may elect to cut down on his athletics and forget about the knee. However, if the pain is severe and locking is frequent, removal of the cartilage is usually advised for permanent relief. Though it might seem that the removal of the knee cartilage would affect proper knee function, the many muscles and ligaments still present will easily keep the knee correctly aligned for normal function.

JOINT MICE, LOOSE BODIES IN THE JOINT

Loose floating particles are frequent findings in the knee joint. These particles vary in size form a rice seed to a melon seed or even larger, and sometimes can be seen with the x-ray.

Joint mice are easily felt. In a sitting position, clasp both hands over one knee and lift the leg off the floor. Now bend the knee back and forth several times, and the hands will feel a crunching, grating sensation. Joint mice are crushed particles of the joint itself after years of crunching trauma which simply crumble away the joint surfaces. An example of grinding trauma is that of obesity where the helpless joint is forced to support much greater weight than it was ever intended to bear.

Joint mice can become painful. Ordinarily they are painless, but when a single loose particle is caught between the joint surfaces, a very sharp and intense pain can suddenly be felt along with a locking of the knee joint. With these particles constantly present, physicians wonder why they do not interfere with joint action more often.

The treatment of joint mice or loose bodies within the knee joint is necessary only when they become painful. The surgical opening of the knee joint is a simple procedure and the clearing out of the joint mice carries very little risk. These operative patients are up out of bed and bearing weight painlessly on their new knees the very next day after surgery.

MILK LEG, ILEO-FEMORAL THROMBO-PHLEBITIS

Until recent times, childbirth was frequently attended by a huge swelling of one leg. As the swelling usually began about the time the breast milk came in, it earned the name "milk leg." Actually, the leg swelling is not connected with milk at all; it is due to a phlebitis blockade of blood flowing out of the leg.

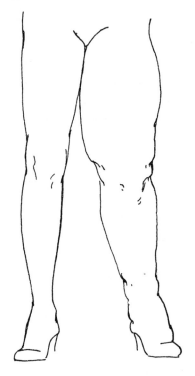

Figure 145: Milk leg, an enlarged leg due to obstructed veins following childbirth, frequently will persist for many years after birth, and at times for the remainder of the patient's life. It is not serious but oftentimes discomforting and frequently embarrassing.

During childbirth, the large vein carrying blood from each leg is temporarily squeezed and traumatized. If the blood vessel was injured, a blood cloth often formed to plug up this vein like a cork. This allowed blood to circulate into the leg, but not out of it. The result was a painful leg, puffed up to twice its normal size, that often lasted for many years with only slight improvement.

Many older women can recall a similar episode of leg swelling during childbirth. Some can demonstrate that they still have the enlarged leg.

The treatment for milk leg is primarily its prevention. Modern obstetrics takes many precautions during childbirth against blood vessel injuries which were so frequent in the "do it yourself" era. The treatment of a milk leg, years after its formation, consists of elastic bandage support, compression type hosiery and definite periods of leg elevation to invite gravity's help in reducing leg swelling. Nighttime elevation of the foot of the bed to a height of six inches often helps to reduce the size of the enlarged legs.

LEGS OF UNEQUAL LENGTH

No two legs are exactly the same length. This will not seem so unusual if one recalls that teeth are different on each side, and one side of the face is usually different from the other.

Often a person with a difference in leg length lives his entire life without even knowing about it. And this is probably fortunate, because most slight differences in leg length have no meaning. Even a significant difference in leg length can exist for years and cause little or no trouble.

But when backache becomes a real problem, or pain in one leg becomes severe, an examination may reveal the fault to be due entirely to legs of unequal length. When this discovery is made, a correction for the short leg is easily made with an elevation built into the heel of the shoe. This very common deformity is very often overlooked in our modern day rush, and many people with chronic backaches could very easily be relieved if only they could take the time to make this simple observation.

WATER ON THE KNEE

Like any joint in the body, the knee can accumulate fluids in its joint capsule for several reasons.

Most often, the water accumulates from a weeping of the membranes surrounding the knee joint itself because of an infection or irritation such as arthritis, rheumatism or severe trauma.

The knee is a very stable joint and can tolerate considerable abuse, as is evident in football players, hockey players and skiers. However, the knee's vulnerable position also allows it to become strained and wrenched during sports, falls and twisting maneuvers. These injuries within the knee joint allow blood or watery fluid to accumulate and produce a painful swelling of the entire knee joint.

Treatment depends upon the cause. Blood and water can be removed from the knee joint with a simple needle operation, but

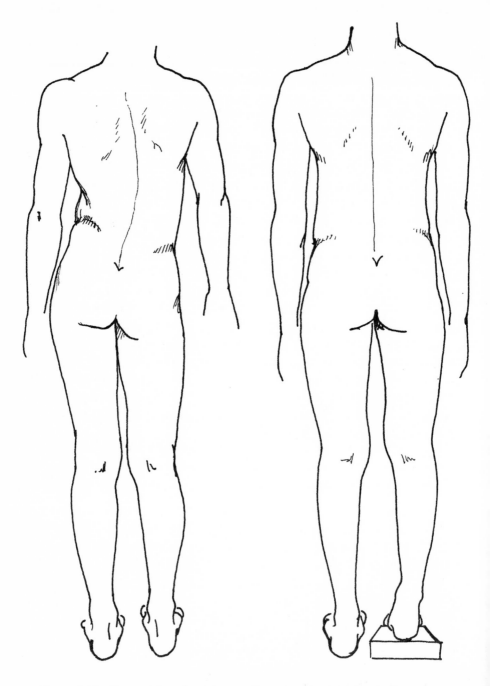

Figure 146: Unequal length of legs will twist and strain the back. It is correctable with a hidden elevation inside one's shoe.

sprains or fractures must be immobilized by splinting or casting to put the knee joint at rest.

The treatment of fluid collection within the knee joint means rest, the application of mild heat and the avoiding of all exertion. After this, the knee becomes a problem for the physician to treat.

BOWLEGS AND KNOCK-KNEES

Bowing of the legs inward or outward is frequently something we have inherited.

During infancy the feet point out, but as time progresses they tend to toe in and eventually end up pointing straight ahead with legs which are also straight. However, feet which remain toeing out often are associated with knock-knee, while feet which toe in are frequently associated with some degree of bowlegs.

Obesity is often a factor in the production of knock-knee, because overstrain upon the knee during formative years will magnify the inward angle normally present at the knee joint.

Occupations will sometimes produce these deformities—as in the cowboy, "born on a horse," walking in his bowlegged stance.

A common cause of bowlegs in childhood is rickets. The bones are soft during the formative years and if they suffer a lack of Vitamin D and calcium, the legs themselves will give way and bend out under the weight of the body. This condition is frequently seen in lands of semi-starvation such as India, where malnutrition and Vitamin D deficiencies abound.

In later life, there is very little that can be done with bowlegs and knock-knees except a surgical correction. This kind of surgery is often unsuccessful and frequently very painful. It is rarely advised.

ARTHRITIS

In youthful years, arthritis in the joints of the legs is likely to be caused by an inflammatory disease such as rheumatoid arthritis, characterized by pain, stiffness and swelling of the joints, along with a redness and increased heat in the overlying skin. Rheumatoid arthritis is usually seen between the ages of 12 and 40, and it affects women three times as often as men. This form of arthritis most often attacks the knee, elbow, ankle and shoulder.

In later years, arthritis or joint pain is nearly always due to a mechanical degeneration of the joint itself. This is a disease of aging; it is not infectious, and most affects the finger joints and weight-bearing joints such as the back, hips, and knees. Degenerative arthritis is a continuous disease, but its pain is usually not intense and it is somewhat relieved by rest. Figures 147 and 148 indicate an arthritic condition of the hands and fingers.

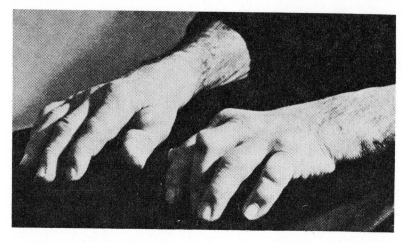

Figure 147: Arthritis in the hands and fingers may produce the gnarled and weakened appearance so typical of long-standing rheumatoid arthritis.

As the years wear on and the joints wear out, particles of the joint structure called joint mice break off and create a crunching sensation during motion. When the joints break down further, a gnarled twisting of the fingers produces the typical arthritic hand of old age.

The effect of damp weather on arthritis is well-known the world over, but exactly what causes increased pain in damp seasons remains unknown. Many arthritics, moreover, have experienced considerable relief after moving to areas of drier climate.

Another unanswered question is why joints wear out in some folks and not in others. Much remains unknown, but the reason seems to be related to the strength and durability of an individual's body tissues. Overweight and exceptionally strenuous activities without doubt help wear out these joints, but there will probably always remain an inequality of suffering among people with arthritic problems.

Reported Arthritis Treatments

The treatment of arthritis has many phases. A physician's ac-

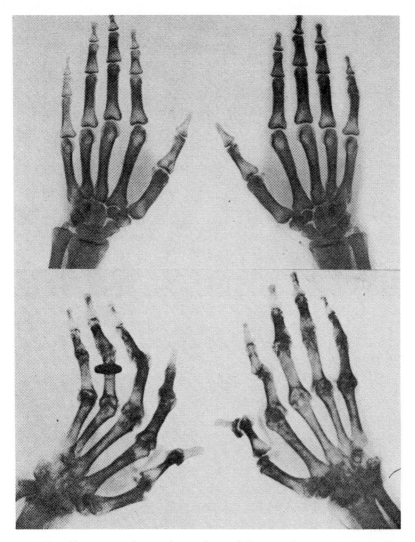

Figure 148: The x-ray shows the striking difference between bones of the normal hand and bones of the hand crippled by arthritis.

curate diagnosis, of course, is all-important. Oftentimes, bone disease, gout, and underlying traumatic episodes are mistaken for arthritis. When the diagnosis of arthritis is definitely established, we must begin thinking of its possible causes—such as working at jobs requiring great joint strain, working in refrigeration plants, or working in areas of high humidity. Next, a focus of infection somewhere in the body, such as an abscessed tooth, must be ruled out, and the possibilities of strain-producing body deformities should be explored. A proper diet as well as proper elimination must be observed. The administration of pain-relieving drugs is then much in order to help the individual with an arthritic problem of unknown cause.

Of great interest are the many cures for arthritis handed down from generation to generation. It is still common to see immigrants coming in from Africa wearing a copper "bracelet" of heavy wire around one ankle to cure their arthritic disease. The source of this widespread practice remains obscure, but somewhere in history, great credence must have been given to copper's arthritic curing powers.

Another well-known cure for arthritis was to descend into old abandoned lead mines where some mysterious influence was said to drive away the arthritic problem.

A more recent "cure" for this disease was the widespread use of honey and vinegar. This treatment reached almost hysterical proportions across the country and even a few doctors thought it was at least worth a try.

There will probably be many fads and cures that will come and go in the future, since the real cause of arthritis is still unknown and its complete cure seems as far distant as ever.

GOUT

This disease is nearly always found in the male sex during the middle or later years and is markedly different from arthritis both in its cause and its appearance. True gout is always the result of too much uric acid in the bloodstream and it nearly always attacks just one joint—usually the great toe. Pain begins suddenly and the joint itself grows very red and swollen for a week to ten days. Then the attack subsides, only to recur again and again if left untreated. Figure 149 shows the appearance of gout on the large toe.

Gout is usually recognized by the physician and definitely confirmed by a simple blood uric acid test, which should always be done in a joint problem even though it is thought to be simple arthritis.

Gout can be prevented with a diet which eliminates foods classed as purines. Examples of purine foods are wines, certain fish, meats prepared from lamb, and whole grain cereals. The physician's identification of these offending foods, and their elimination from the diet, gives most satisfactory relief from further gout difficulties. A list of these high purine foods should always be hanging in the kitchen of the gout patient so that his diets can avoid them, for he must remain on a low purine diet indefinitely.

Figure 149: Gout is a disease of men, usually in their senior years. Caused by an excessively high level of uric acid in the bloodstream, it generally affects the joint of the great toe. It is readily prevented through diet and certain medications.

RHEUMATISM

Rheumatism is also known as lumbago, myositis, and myalgia. Unlike arthritis, it does not affect the joints but concerns itself primarily with the muscles and ligaments. It can occur anywhere in the body except the joints, and is commonly found in the neck, back, shoulders, arms and legs. It is often thought to be a "cold" in the muscles.

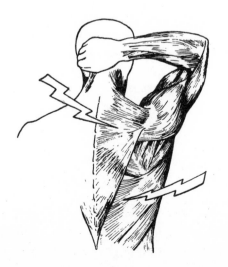

Figure 150: Rheumatism concerns the muscles and ligaments, not the joints. Often called a cold in the muscle, it possibly is caused by infection and is influenced by weather conditions.

The exact cause of rheumatism is not clear; however, overwork and muscular strain are often associated with it, and it is well-known that chilling, wet weather, and body infections can also initiate rheumatism attacks.

The diagnosis of rheumatism is often hard for the physician to make when other diseases are present, and for this reason a complete examination becomes very important. An investigation for a possible infection in the body must be made, along with a search for any physical fault which might create muscular irritation or strain. Avoiding extreme dampness or coldness is also necessary during any kind of rheumatic episode. Attention to many of these details will often stamp out or prevent the widespread difficulties of rheumatism.

SCIATICA

Figure 151 shows the course of sciatic pain from the back into the leg.

This is a soreness of the sciatic nerve, with characteristically sharp, shooting pain along the nerve's distribution from the hip down the back of the thigh and into the calf of the leg. Usually the pains of sciatica are not constant, but are produced in a come and go manner by movements which stretch the nerve itself. These movements include straightening the knee, flexing the hip, or bending up at the ankle joint.

Because sciatic pain often begins by compressing the nerve fibers within the spine, actions which suddenly increase this pressure on the nerve also produce the leg pain. Coughing, sneezing, straining at bowel movements and lifting heavy objects will often bring down the lash of sciatic pain.

In diagnosing sciatic pain and its causes, the physician must always consider the possibility of a slipped disc injury between the vertebrae, a common cause of sciatica along with arthritis of the spinal column. Figure 152 indicates the straight-leg raising test.

After a diagnosis of sciatica has been made by the physician, the correct treatment must be considered. A proper trial treatment is simple traction. The sciatica patient lies down with the foot of his bed elevated slightly, and a belt (like a woman's garter belt) above the hips is attached to a traction rope which constantly pulls with 10 pounds of force. This stretches the spine slightly, and is

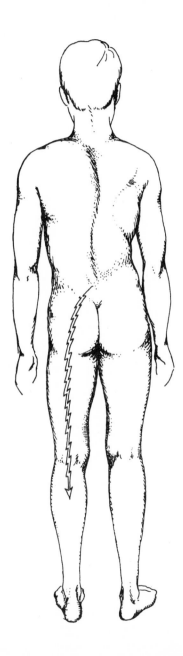

Figure 151: Sciatic pain shoots down from the back into the leg. At first it is fleeting, but eventually it grows constant if not treated.

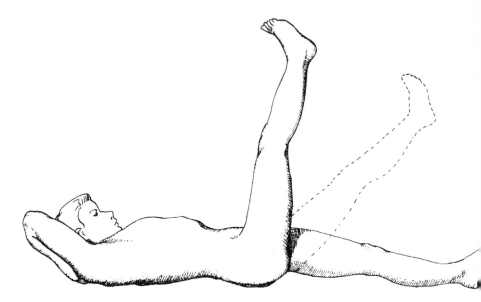

Figure 152: The straight-leg raising test: Normally the leg can easily be raised straight up, but in sciatica, pain begins before the leg is raised even half way.

often enough to completely relieve the sciatica problem. If traction is not successful, the surgical removal of an injured disc in the spine, correction of spinal deformity, or perhaps correction of a leg deformity may be indicated. When sciatica is accompanied by arthritis or injury of the sciatic nerve itself, treatment may also be necessary for these problems at the same time.

ABSENT KNEE JERK REFLEXES

The normal leg has a positive knee jerk reflex. To demonstrate this reflex, simply sit on a table, allow the legs to hang down and lightly tap the tendon just below the knee cap with a book edge. This will cause the leg to kick forward a little because the tendon tap slightly but suddenly stretches the thigh muscle which automatically responds with a quick contraction. Figure 153 indicates the manner of producing the reflex.

The knee jerk reflex is normally present under all circumstances. Its absence may point to disease of the body such as pernicious anemia, thyroid disease, or even disease of the spinal cord or brain itself. Only on rare occasions are knee jerks absolutely absent in healthy, disease-free individuals.

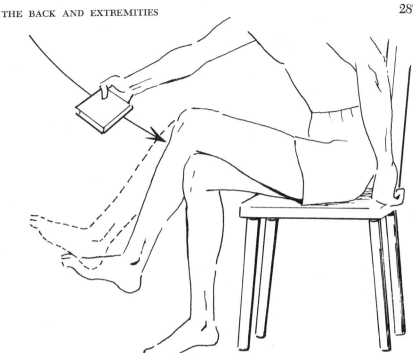

Figure 153: Striking the bended knee just below the knee cap brings about the knee jerk reflex. When this reflex is absent, possibility of neurological disease exists.

CIRCULATORY DIFFICULTIES OF THE LEG (INTERMITTENT CLAUDICATION)

Diminished blood circulation through the lower extremities, often the result of arteriosclerosis, causes several painful leg problems which become increasingly widespread after the age of 40. Comparable to a rusting obstruction in a metal pipe, the arteriosclerotic arteries to the legs become obstructed and are then unable to carry enough blood for all the lower extremities' activities.

In the arteriosclerotic leg, the muscles can do light work effectively even on a poor blood supply, but they will cry out with pain when they are forced to do heavy or continuous work if they are not supplied with enough blood. The pain characteristically felt in the calf muscle is named intermittent claudication and is nature's signal that the leg muscles are being forced to work without sufficient blood supply.

This leg pain can also be intensified by spasm of the leg arteries brought about by drugs such as tobacco, which causes blood vessel constriction. Smoking should always be withheld in this disease.

Gangrene of the lower extremity is an unfortunate but frequent result of severe arteriosclerotic blockade of the arteries to the legs. Gangrene usually results only after many years of circulatory difficulties, but on rare occasions the leg artery can become suddenly and completely blocked by a traveling blood clot (embolism); in these cases, gangrene of the foot and leg will develop rapidly.

The first place that gangrene usually appears is in the toe. This, of course, is incurable and the toe must be removed. Most often, however, removal of the toe is not enough, and complete cure will demand an amputation of the leg high enough to reach an adequate blood supply. Failure to amputate the leg for any reason usually means severe infection, overwhelming toxemia, and eventual death for the patient.

Diabetics in their later years are greatly burdened with the prospect of gangrene of the toe and foot. Diabetes not only fans the fires of arteriosclerosis to reduce circulation, but it also invites infection of the toes and feet. It is a well-known medical fact that poor circulation plus added infection will greatly magnify the possibility of gangrene for the diabetic.

The treatment of circulatory problems of the lower extremities is very rigid. It demands the regulation or cure of systemic disease such as diabetes, and the elimination of blood vessel-irritating factors such as tobacco. Preventive care demands that these people avoid even the slightest accidents or infections in the feet, and extremes in heat or cold. They must also give close attention to gentle, thorough cleanliness as the first line of defense against possible gangrene of the legs.

VARICOSE VEINS

Abnormally dilated and distorted veins of the lower extremities, called varicose veins, are the penalties put on the human race for standing upright. In some people, leg veins can't even be seen, but others less fortunate have varicose veins in the legs and thighs that look like massive, grape-like knots which will bleed heavily if cut or torn.

Varicose veins are usually the result of inherited tendencies, but sometimes they are caused by occupations which demand long standing, and at other times even from pregnancy. The final cause is the weight-force of the blood forcing weaker vein walls to stretch and expand.

Normal veins have valves in them which permit the blood to move only toward the heart, but in varicose veins, the over-stretched

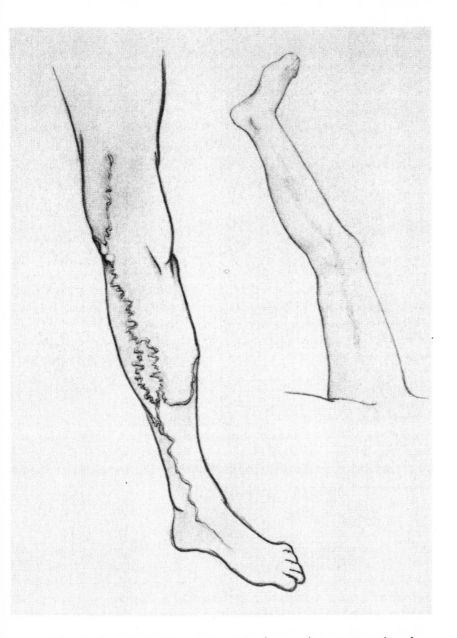

Figure 154: Varicose veins are prominent in the standing position, but they will completely disappear when the leg is elevated. Effect of gravity makes varicose veins worse.

valves will not work and blood actually flows backwards down toward the feet. We can make these veins disappear temporarily by lying down and holding the legs upwards, so that gravity drains blood out of the veins. (Figure 154).

The treatment of varicose veins involves closing up these dilated blood channels. This is done by removing the veins in a surgical operation, or injecting them with irritating chemicals which cause them to grow solidly together. These treatments are very successful when done by a physician who has had experience in the treatment of varicose veins.

An unwelcome complication of varicose veins is the varicose ulcer caused by poor blood circulation in the skin just above the inner ankle. All the body tissues need a constant supply of fresh blood in them to remain healthy, and the skin of the leg and foot is no exception. In varicose veins, however, the backward flow of blood holds back the circulation of fresh blood in the skin about the ankle, and the result is a brown pigmented, tight and shiny skin which finally breaks down and forms the typical varicose ulcer. These ulcers, of course, exist only while the varicose veins exist (Figure 155).

CORNS

A thickened, hardened, growth of skin over a bony projection submitted to continually repeated pressures is called a corn. The most common sites for corns are the toe joints, because of pressure from shoes. If the pressure is removed, the corn cannot long exist and here lies the cure for corns—the discarding of shoes which are too tight or ill-fitting.

The sacrifice of the feet for the style of the moment should be abolished by law.

CALLUSES

A thickening and hardening of the skin over a broad non-pointed structure such as the ball of the foot is a callus. It differs from its cousin, the corn, by lacking a sharp bony projection, like a joint underneath it. Pressure causing the callus is more distribtued to form a wider area of thickened and hardened skin. It often looks like a widely spread-out corn.

The relief of calluses, the same as in corns, demands relief of

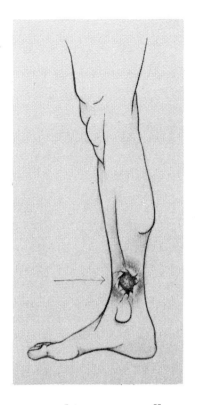

Figure 155: The varicose ulcer is a direct result of varicose veins. This open, draining, and usually infected ulcer occurs on the medial side of the leg just above the ankle. It can be cured, but it must be treated properly or it will continue indefinitely.

pressure against the callused area. Removing this pressure allows the callus to soften and fall away.

BUNIONS

Continual off and on pressure about the feet stimulates not only a thickening of skin, but also a growth of underlying bone. Such a bony growth is most often seen on the side of the foot at the base of the great toe—the ball of the foot. As the bony deformity becomes enlarged, it becomes more exposed and there is even greater pressure and trauma on the bone which, of course, stimulates still greater growth and discomfort. Bunions sometimes grow to outlandish sizes.

Treatment of the average bunion demands removal of the pressure that caused the bunion. This will stop the pain and allow relief for the callus overlying the bunion, but only surgical removal of the underlying bone growth at the ball of the foot can permanently cure the bunion problem.

Temporary relief of bunions, calluses and corns can be found in the wonderfully soothing warm water foot bath, but of course this gives no permanent results.

The biggest cause of most of our annoying foot problems is still ill-fitting shoes, and most of our foot troubles would disappear if only we gave our feet the benefit of properly fitting shoes.

INGROWN TOENAIL

This widespread, very painful toe problem is seen at all ages. And it bothers those people most who give their feet the most care. This is because the ingrown toenail can only occur in the over-trimmed nail.

The ingrown process occurs only after the nail has been trimmed back too far, and then attempts to grow forward against the skin in front of it. The nail grows into this skin, much as a needle would, and the penetration of the skin in a contaminated region like the toe often results in a painful infection accompanied by pus formation and bleeding.

Ingrown toenails can always be prevented by allowing the end of the toenail to grow beyond the end of the toe. If a toenail has already been cut too short and starts growing into the skin in front of it, this nail must be removed or mechanically elevated from the underlying skin. Since these treatments are in an infected area, they should be done by a physician or a foot specialist.

HIP FRACTURE

One of the unfortunate calamities of later years is a fracture of the hip, usually through an accidental fall. The hip can break at any age, but it is more likely to fracture during later years when the bones become weaker. Youthful bones are tough and strong; they bend slightly and are hard to break. But in age, the bones acquire a glass-like brittleness and shatter easily. The hip joint's position makes it a target for punishment in falls, and therefore a likely spot for fracture. A broken bone at this site, of course, means the entire leg is useless, since its sole body support must come through the hip joint itself (Figure 156).

Some hip fractures can be almost painless if the broken bones are rammed together and held impacted in position. But the usual broken hip renders the patient entirely helpless because the separated bones cause severe pain with the slightest motion.

Treatment of a fractured hip, as in any fracture, requires that the broken bones be put together and held in place. There are several ways of doing this, but the best method today is nailing the bone fragments together. A specially shaped nail is driven inside the bone, completely across the line of fracture and into the other bone fragment to lock the bone fragments together. Hip nailing allows relief of pain with early leg motion and quick return to normal activity. It must, of course, be undertaken by a physician with experience in fractures.

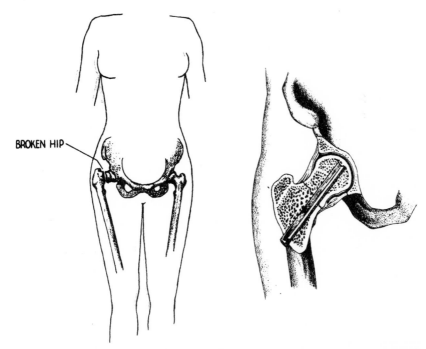

BROKEN HIP

Figure 156A: The broken hip is the most feared fracture of later years. This is because of the brittleness of the bone and the fact that most falls are onto the hip area.

Figure 156B: Surgical repair of a broken hip is effective with the use of a "nail" pinning the bone together across the fracture line. This is a most satisfactory treatment in an otherwise very difficult fracture.

FLAT FOOT

A flat foot is a foot without an arch (Figure 157). Just as the arch of a bow is maintained by its bowstring, the arch in the foot is maintained by a strong ligament on the bottom of the foot. When this ligament weakens, the arch collapses and the foot is flat. With its cushioning arch gone, the spring is lost in the step and the foot must suffer the painful fatigue of typical flat feet. This discouraging foot problem often accompanies obesity, poor posture and bone disease and any therapy for flat foot must also reckon with these problems as well. Arch supports and corrective shoes have long been the aids for the flat foot.

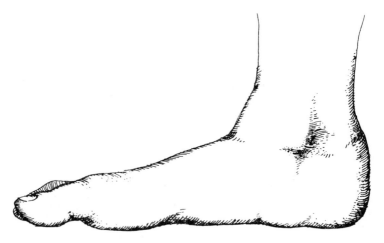

Figure 157: Flat foot is a most uncomfortable foot. The arch in the foot is ordinarily a cushion to walk on; its absence means weary aching and tired feet.

HAMMER TOE

Hammer toe (Figure 158) almost always involves the second toe

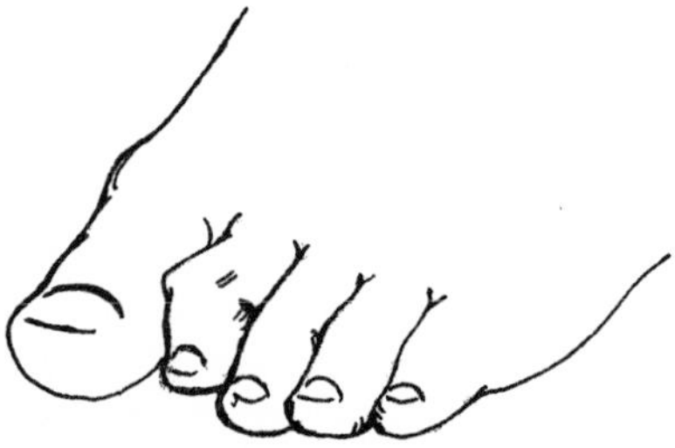

Figure 158: Hammer toe usually involves the second toe of the foot. The distal digit of the toe is in an up and down position instead of a horizontal position. This gives a hammer appearance to the toe which, at times, is very painful. It is not serious unless tight shoes become involved.

with the distal digit held in an up and down hammer-like position. Many physicians believe the defect is due to a squeezed-in position from a deformed metatarsal arch and ill-fitting shoes, but often hammer toe appears in childhood without any apparent reason. Surgery can correct this defect by section of the flexor tendon or removal of the bothersome digit.

ATHLETES FOOT (See Skin Diseases)

GROWTHS AND TUMORS OF THE FOOT AND LEG

Growths of the lower extremities are not as common as in other parts of the body, but bone, muscle and skin frequently develop benign or malignant growths (Figure 159). These extremity tumors have very serious importance. They are most often the sarcoma type of tumor, which is usually found in youthful years. Unfortunately, the extremity must be sacrificed to preserve life for the rest of the body.

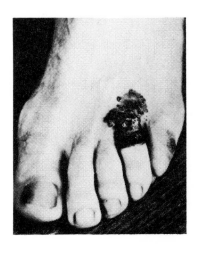

Figure 159: Malignancy can occur on the extremities as well as inside the body. This black growth is a serious cancerous growth called a melanoma.

As with most skin problems, especially cancer, the exposed skin of the foot suffers more than other more covered areas of the body.

PITTING EDEMA

When the feet, ankles and legs are swollen with fluid they can be "pitted" with mild pressure. A finger pressed against the leg leaves a dent and tight stockings also will leave deeply indented bands (Figure 160). A swelling of this nature is usually not a leg disease by itself. It is more often a systemic disease in which fluid from the entire body settles into the lowest places gravity can find—the legs.

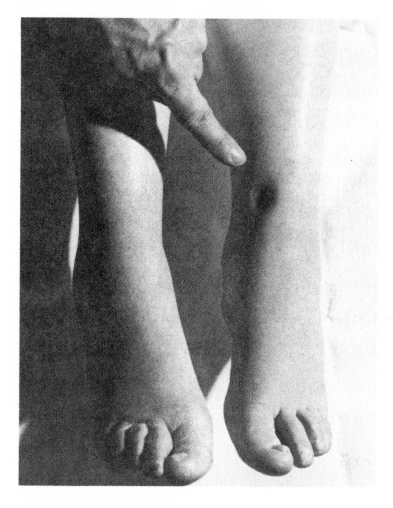

Figure 160: Pitting edema of the lower extremities often means a failing heart. At times it is a sign of malnutrition, kidney disease or liver failure.

Ordinarily, this means heart trouble. If the heart cannot push circulating blood forcefully enough, water begins to settle out to blood and swelling ankles begin. We find the enlarged ankles and feet are most pronounced in the evening after being upright all day, but the swelling will usually disappear after a night's sleep when the body has been horizontal for several hours.

Swollen lower extremities occasionally can have other causes such as kidney impairment or liver disease. It always means that a serious medical problem exists and the physician must be consulted immediately.

The Upper Extremities

Examination of the Upper Extremities

Examination of the shoulders, arms, forearms and hands requires that the upper extremities and chest be unclothed before a stationary mirror and with an adequate light.

1. Examine the shoulder's movement ability. In a standing position, slowly raise the straightened arm outward from the side to a horizontal position. Swing the arms forward to join in front and then backwards as far as possible. Note any pain in the shoulder joints during this action as a probable finding of arthritis or bursitis.

2. Examine the motion of the elbow. Note any painful inability to straighten the elbows completely, or to completely twist the wrist. Such inabilities again, point to possibilities of arthritis.

3. Examine the movements of the hands and fingers. Note any joints with soreness or limited motion in flexing and extending the finger joints and wrist joints. Observe also any swelling or deformity about the finger joints, frequently indicating degenerative arthritis.

4. Note the degree of steadiness of the hands. Note especially, any tremor of the fingers held in a relaxed position and also, in a stiffened, spread out position. Tremors of the hands and fingers may mean thyroid over-activity or neurological diseases such as Parkinsonism.

5. Examine the reflexes of the hands and arms. Place each hand in cold running water for a few minutes, then withdraw it and observe any severe blanching of the skin, with a long delay in return of color. Severe blanching may indicate Raynaud's Disease. Now determine the strength of the grip of each hand by squeezing the opposite wrist in turn. A great difference of strength between the right and left grip could be a first indication of neurological disease.

6. Examine the hand for infection possibilities. Squeeze the

palm and back of the hands to check for painful swelling
or redness of the skin in this region, or in the web of the
thumb. These are the sites for serious hand-palm infections.

7. Examine the fingernails and their beds for infection. Observe any infected boil-like areas alongside the fingernail
with any redness, swelling or pain in the fingers. Infection
in the fingertips and about the nails are felons or nail
infections.

8. Examine the skin for any long unhealed, ulcerated or raw
lump-like sores on the skin, especially on the back of the
hands. This may indicate skin cancer or the common wart,
both of which are very common on the constantly exposed
skin of the hand.

9. Turn the palm upward and stretch out the fingers as much
as possible. Note any cord-like elevation of the skin extending toward the wrist from the ring finger, or from any
other finger. Note the inability to completely stretch out
the finger due to this cord development. This is known as
a Dupuytren's contracture.

Difficulties of the Upper Extremities

ARTHRITIS

Arthritis in the upper extremity is very common, even in youthful years. In the joint swelling and redness of the wrist and shoulder
in young adults suffering from rheumatic fever, there is a great
out-pouring of fluid into the joint's surrounding tissues. This very
painful condition will possibly one day turn out to be a form of
infectious arthritis.

Rheumatoid arthritis, with its gnarled deformity of the fingers,
often extends into later years to produce painful, deformed and
weakened hands. A wearing out of the joints, however, termed
degenerative arthritis, is much more common in later years. Often
the degenerative type of arthritis and the more painful rheumatoid
arthritis can exist together and combine to produce a very debilitating disease.

Arthritis of the elbow, beginning in younger years and concerned
with the revolving motion of the forearm, is known as "tennis
elbow." In later years, it remains as an inability to twist the
wrist completely without pain in the elbow joint. It is neither as
painful nor as disabling as arthritis in other joints.

Shoulder joint arthritis often results from infection in the body, such as rheumatic fever. Trouble in this joint is fairly common, not only because of the general wear and tear of the years, but also because nature has provided the shoulder joint with a loose-fitting, easily dislocated joint. This makes for frequent injury, scar formations and calcium deposits within the joint capsule and eventually arthritic disease of the all-important shoulder joint.

Because joints of the upper extremities are not weight bearing, relief from arthritis is much easier to find through simple means, such as rest, than it is in the lower extremities. As in arthritis of other areas such as the legs and spine, a complete cure of degenerative arthritic disease of the hands, wrists and elbows in later years is impossible. But the latest drugs, administered by the physician, can be expected to relieve three out of four severe arthritic disabilities.

BURSITIS

Bursitis means a painful irritation of the bursa overlying the shoulder joint. This bursa overlies the joint like a deflated balloon and allows free skin motion over the joint structure. Irritation within this bursa is often seen after injury to the shoulder area followed by formation of calcium deposits which prolong the irritation (Figure 161). These deposits invite the frequent return of pain in the shoulder joint during periods of high humidity or even after the mildest forms of exercise.

There are also bursae locations in other sections of the body, such as the elbow and the knee, but bursitis is best known for its shoulder region location where 90 percent of bursitis difficulties occur.

Bursitis can occur at almost any age; the football player's shoulder and the tennis player's elbow are difficulties of young people, but most of the time bursitis is a difficulty of later years. It is only many years after an injury to the shoulder that calcium deposits and scars within the bursae have formed and acquire the ability to cause recurrent stiffness, soreness and disability of the shoulder joint.

For many years, bursitis has been treated by heat, rest and pain-relieving medications, but now calcium-dissolving and anti-inflammatory drugs can be injected directly within the bursa itself. Cortisone preparations have become a very effective treatment for bursitis, along with x-ray therapy which reveals the calcium deposits in the bursa and also has an anti-inflammatory affect. Relief can be expected for the majority of bursitis patients with present day care.

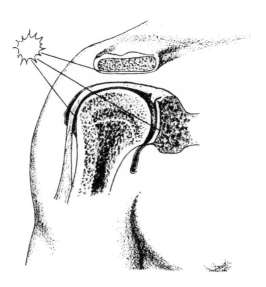

Figure 161: Shoulder joint pain includes arthritis, bursitis, calcification and injuries of joints. A most purposeful joint, disease here can be very disabling. Correct examination and diagnosis are effective in pointing out effective treatment for most cases.

TREMORS OF THE HANDS AND FINGERS

Tremors in the fingers and hands are signs of definite disease. When the thyroid is overactive, the resulting tremor is very fine and often difficult to see with the eye alone; feeling these fingers, however, reveals a fine vibratory tremor.

In later years, the most common hand and finger tremor is Parkinsonism or paralysis agitans, sometimes called "pill rolling disease." This difficulty is a neurological disease thought to be caused by arteriosclerosis within the brain and spinal cord. The difficulty may progress for 10 or 20 years in an entirely painless manner. It disappears in sleep only to return on awakening, and it becomes more pronounced during periods of effort.

Fortunately, today there are new drugs available which have a remarkable effect on the tremors of Parkinsonism. People who once stayed in their rooms in an attempt to hide their problem are now able to step out and do a useful day's work. These drugs are very safe, very inexpensive and now in widespread use.

Several surgical procedures formerly were done upon the brain for relief of Parkinsonism, but with the advent of today's newer drug therapy, these operations are now being done very rarely.

RAYNAUD'S DISEASE

This disease is brought about by a nerve reflex which suddenly reduces blood circulation in the hands which blanch completely white and become extremely painful. The condition is brought on by exposure to cold, such as cold water or cold weather.

Raynaud's Disease is found more often in women in their 20's and 30's, but it often extends as a recurrent problem into older age groups. Probably the most feared result of Raynaud's Disease is the possibility of gangrene of the fingertips. During any of these painful seizures, blood circulation through the hand is very slight, and the fingertips become especially vulnerable to a gangrene as though involved in a severe frost-bite.

Treatment of Raynaud's Disease includes meticulous care and cleanliness to avoid infection problems in the fingers. Above all, this problem calls for the complete elimination of any cold contact to the hands. Very few winter sports enthusiasts are found among sufferers of Raynaud's Disease.

The medical treatment of Raynaud's Disease has improved greatly with the discovery of recent drugs which allay the nerve reflexes responsible for the sudden reduction of blood circulation in the hands. For the most extreme and severe cases, including already gangrenous fingers, a surgical procedure called sympathectomy cuts the involved nerve and permanently stops its reflexes.

PALM-HAND INFECTION

Infections deep within the palm or under the thumb are very serious. They are usually started by perforating injuries from needles, pins and other sharp objects. About a day after the perforating injury, the palm becomes thickened, hot and painful. Red streaks can be seen ascending the arm as a danger signal that infected is spreading.

These deep palm infections are extremely serious, and must be treated without delay. The physician usually starts immediate antibiotic therapy, hot wet dressings, and recommends an immediate incision and drainage of the abscess area deep within the palm.

FINGER AND NAIL INFECTION

Infection around the nail border (Figure 162), called paronychia,

Figure 162: Finger infections about the nail, or deep in the finger portion, may ascend into the hand and arm. They should always be attended to early to afford relief from pain as well as to prevent spread of infection.

often develops from a hangnail or a small cut on the fingertips. It looks like a boil along one side of the nail, or occasionally all around the nail, which is undermined with pus.

Prevention of nail infections means reasonable hand protection, the prevention of biting or pulling at hangnails and the intelligent cleaning and covering of small unimportant cuts on the fingertips. Once a paronychia has started, the physician usually recommends warm water soaking and protection of the infected site from all trauma. With the appearance of a boil-like head, and with obvious pus underneath, an incision and drainage is indicated, but the possibility of spreading this kind of infection in the finger demands that only the physician perform this operation. The pain usually present is severe enough to force the patient to his physician anyway.

Infection in the pad of the fingertips, looking like a deep-seated boil, is caused by pin sticks and other perforating injuries to the ends of the fingers. This infection is called a felon; it produces an extremely serious and excruciating painful finger which is totally disabling.

A felon in its beginning stages occasionally responds to warm soaking and antibiotic treatment. A full-fledged felon, however, demands an immediate surgical incision and drainage of the pus from its deeply enclosed casing within the fingertip. Neglect of such an infection, or crude attempts of a do-it-yourself operation, often result in serious lifelong damage to the finger and hand.

DUPUYTREN'S CONTRACTURE

This painless disease of the hand looks like a cord under the skin of the palm, running from the ring finger back to the wrist (Figure 163). This cord may be very small in its beginning stage or look like a tendon in the hand pulling the ring finger into a flexed position.

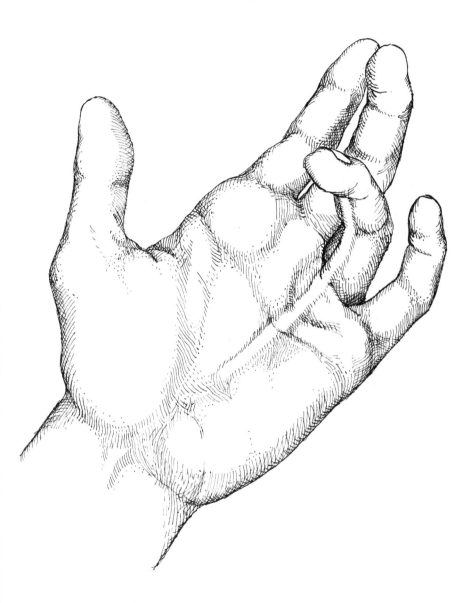

Figure 163: Dupuytrens Contracture. Dupuytrens contracture appears as a cord in the palm. In severe cases it extends to the ring finger which contracts permanently and interferes with hand function.

Dupuytren's contracture is thought by some medical authorities to be an inherited disease, while others insist that rough work with the hands, such as running an air hammer, produces this deformity.

The treatment of Dupuytren's contracture is a complex surgical operation of the palmar fascia which must be removed or cut to prevent further contracture deformity.

SKIN DISEASES OF THE HAND

The hand is in a constantly exposed position where the influence of sunlight, heat, cold and injury to the skin is open and direct.

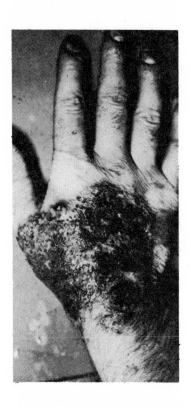

Figure 164: The hand is a target for many eczema-type skin diseases. Often in touch with a variety of chemicals and materials, the eczema on the hand will weep, bleed, and often go away for a time, only to return. It is often associated with an allergy or sensitivity to some particular substance.

The hands are contaminated daily with chemicals, dirt and possible allergic substances which never touch other regions of the body. For these reasons, many skin diseases occur on the hand that do not occur in other regions of the body. They include eczema, wart formation, keratosis, infection, ulcerations and skin cancer. (See Skin Diseases.)

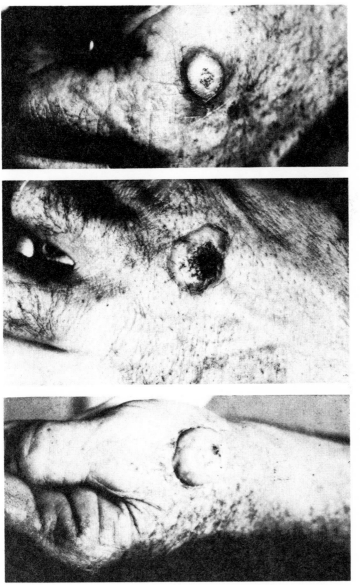

Figure 165: Cancers in the skin of the hands are very common. The constantly exposed hand comes in contact with many irritants such as sunlight, chemicals, et cetera. The cause of cancer is unknown but it is more frequent in areas that are often irritated.

INDEX